M|4

ENERGY
IN CRISIS

Brandts

ENERGY IN CRISIS

a guide to world oil supply and demand and alternative resources

by PETER HILL & ROGER VIELVOYE
of The Times

with a foreword by **Lord Aldington**

Robert Yeatman Limited 1974

First published in 1974 by Robert Yeatman Ltd.
401 Grand Buildings, Trafalgar Square,
London WC2N 5HD

Designed by Melvyn Gill Design Associates
Charts by Celia Stothard
Typesetting by Amos Typesetters
Printed and bound in Great Britain by W. & J. Mackay Ltd

Acknowledgements

We are grateful to many individuals and organisations for their help, in a variety of forms, in the writing of this book. While it would be invidious to list them by name, we would like to thank especially Leo Cavendish and Oliver Case; Paul Slater of Brandts for his enthusiastic encouragement; and Margaret Rumball (and her colleagues) for their assistance.

Finally we would like to acknowledge the value of the tables and charts published by Brandts, BP, H. Clarkson & Co. Ltd., Clarkson's Marine Insurance Group, A. P. Drewry, Fairplay, Fearnley & Egers Chartering, Galbraith Wrightson, E. A. Gibson (Shipbrokers) Ltd., Lloyd's Register of Shipping, Mullion Tankers (Shipbroking) Ltd., OECD, Oil and Gas Journal, Petroleum Economist, The Salvage Association, Seatrade, Shell, and The U.K. Chamber of Shipping, among many whose excellent statistical material we have found invaluable.

Peter Hill
Roger Vielvoye
April 1974

Contents

List of Charts and Tables

Foreword
by Lord Aldington

This book will focus the attention of its readers on the things that matter, both now and for the future, in the business of energy. Whether it be the amount of oil available, the price of oil, transportation of oil, alternative sources of energy or whatever, the facts and the arguments are set out in an interesting and stimulating way.

The co-authors, Peter Hill and Roger Vielvoye, together command a considerable knowledge of shipping and energy. They set out to compile for the first time in one volume a formidable collection of facts and statistics which would only otherwise be available with painstaking research. They do not set out to provide all the answers to all the questions which all the readers might ask. They have had a free hand with their material, and the opinions they have expressed are theirs and do not necessarily coincide with mine. But if I reserve my opinion on what they have written, I give my unqualified support to them for having written it; and my thinks for the hard work which they have put into the book.

Brandts, who commissioned the book, have a history of involvement in the shipping industry stretching back to the early days of the nineteenth century. In recent years our activities have been extended to include many aspects of oil exploration and production, as well as its transportation. Other financial institutions will share with us a desire that our customers and friends shall have access to a full study of the energy situation, and we are proud to make this study available to a much wider readership all over the world.

Chairman
Brandts Ltd
36 Fenchurch Street
London EC3

Chapter One
The End of an Era

In the sumptuous surroundings of the Niavaran Palace in Teheran, two days before Christmas 1973, the Shah of Iran announced new oil price scales which were to undermine the delicately-balanced economies of almost every nation outside the Communist bloc. The Iranian monarch, acting as the spokesman for all the oil producing nations in the Persian Gulf, informed his audience of newspaper and television correspondents from all over the world that for the second time within three months, the price of crude oil was to be doubled nine days later. The full significance of the Shah's statement was obscured, since Government and industry throughout the Christian world had adjourned for the Christmas break. It was only when they returned that the repercussions of raising the posted price for Persian Gulf oil to more than $11.00 a barrel began to be realised. The Organisation for Economic Co-operation and Development (OECD) had assessed the first doubling of posted prices on October 16 and hurriedly revised its estimates to take account of the Christmas crude oil price increase. The Paris-based organisation told its 24 members that in a full year the increase would add $40,000m to their fuel bills with the biggest impact being felt by Europe, where the nine members of the European Economic Community could expect to pay an extra $33,000m for their crude oil imports.

The significance of the Shah's appointment to act as the official spokesman for the Organisation of Petroleum Exporting Countries (OPEC) was not lost on his audience. Two years earlier many of the journalists had been in the Iranian capital when the Persian Gulf members of OPEC challenged the hegemony of the international oil companies and won higher crude oil prices. The producer countries learned a valuable lesson from the first round of price talks in Teheran. Although export prices were controlled under a five year pact that provided annual rises in costs and was designed to compensate for the effects of inflation, it had become obvious during the negotiations that there was little the international oil companies could do in the face of concerted pressure from the countries that were the source of over 90 per cent of the world export trade in crude oil. While the companies transported and marketed almost all the oil consumed in the large industrial nations outside North America, they were given no tangible support in the negotiations by their Governments. OPEC members were surprised at their initial success and continued to demand new concessions, each of which was conceded with very little resistance by the companies. The 1971 Teheran price agreement was twice revised to compensate the producers for revenues lost through two devaluations of the dollar. In addition, the companies were forced to accept the host nations as partners in the operation of their valuable oil producing concessions.

The new situation faced by the oil industry after the first doubling of posted prices was aptly summarised by Mr J. K. Jamieson, chairman and chief executive of Exxon Corporation, the world's largest oil company. In a speech in late November 1973 he said: "All things considered it is a challenging outlook. There has never been a time when the future of our business was harder to predict—even though the demand for our principal products has never been more assured. Energy supply is an increasingly sensitive political and social issue and governments are involving themselves more and more deeply in our business. This is certain to produce growing pressures and demands for further controls on the petroleum industry. Private energy companies will be challanged to justify their existence, in a sense, by demonstrating that their role is essential."

The Exxon chairman was speaking at a time when his and other oil corporations were dealing with problems imposed by the 25 per cent reduction in oil output by the Arab nations. The Arab nations had introduced the "oil weapon" to support the Arab offensive against Israel launched on Yom Kippur, the Jewish Day of Atonement, on October 6, 1973. But as Iraq, the only Arab country to maintain output, explained, the oil weapon could not discriminate between friend and enemy. As a result of the overall cutback in output, the nations friendly to the Arab cause suffered from oil shortages, although these were not on the scale of the nations like

Holland and the United States where Arab oil deliveries were subject to a total embargo. Soon after the outbreak of the Holy war—on October 16—the oil producers in the Persian Gulf had announced the first doubling of crude oil prices and the following day had imposed the production cutbacks and named the countries that would be subject to the embargo. But the bulk of the oil available in the Middle East was produced and transported by the multi-national oil companies and subject to the new prices announced on October 16. The reduced amount of oil available, automatically put pressure on the price for the small quantities of crude controlled by the Governments through the participation agreements. These lots were put up for auction and, in the case of Iranian oil, realised more than $17 a barrel. In the light of these inflated auction prices, the cost of crude on long-term contracts appeared relatively cheap even though these charges had just been doubled. Iran, as the only non-Arab producer in the Gulf, maintained full production throughout the war and the peace talks, and sought to persuade her Arab neighbours to increase the price of the oil available to the companies to just below the auction levels. However, opposition, notably from Saudi Arabia resulted in a compromise being reached of slightly more than $11.6 a barrel. In his surprise announcement the Shah, confirming the doubts expressed by Mr Jamieson a month earlier, said the new crude prices would correspond to the minimum price that the industrialised nations would have to pay to extract oil from shale rock or produce crude oil or synthetic natural gas from coal. He said the industrialised countries could no longer expect Middle Eastern oil production to be expanded to meet growing energy demands; they would be forced to develop an alternative to oil.

His message was painfully clear. The producers realised that a continuation of this policy would virtually exhaust their reserves by the end of the century. Instead, oil would be conserved while higher prices for the amounts that were produced would ensure that producer Governments would not suffer any loss of revenues. The Shah, somewhat lyrically, described oil as a product "too noble to burn". The industrialised nations were "careless" to use oil for heating houses or even generating electricity when this could so easily be done by coal. He warned industrialised countries that they would have to tighten their belts.

"Some people say this will create chaos in the industrial world and create a burden for the poor countries. This is true. But the industrial world will have to realise that the era of the terrific progress and even more terrific income and wealth based on cheap oil is finished. They must find alternative sources of energy. All we want to do is to determine the real value of this precious oil which will be depleted in thirty years. And would like to see alternative energy sources developed so that the oil can be preserved as the feedstock for the petro-chemical industry. If I am not mistaken, about 10,000 products can be made from crude oil when it is used in the petro-chemical industry. Why should we finish this noble product in thirty years time when thousands of billions of tons of coal remain in the ground?" he said.

The termination of the era of cheap energy has struck at the heart of the industrialised society. Until the beginning of the 1970s, ample supplies of cheap fuel to heat and light homes, drive transport and provide the power for industry, were all taken for granted. It had been assumed that society could advance to even higher living standards using the benefits of continued cheap fuel. Indeed, the development of industrial societies and improvements in living standards have coincided with increases in the per capita consumption of energy. Unfortunately, the greater the affluence, the greater the waste of energy resources: the United States, with its high living standards is undoubtedly the most profligate nation in the world in the use of power. Statistically, the average American with his high earning capacity—over $4,000 pa—uses the equivalent of 8 tons of oil each year while in the underdeveloped nations, where the average income is a few hundred dollars per capita, use of energy barely reaches the equivalent of a quarter of a ton of oil a year. In many homes items that at one time were considered luxuries are now thought of as essentials. Dishwashers, air conditioning and gadgets galore all need power. Agriculture in the developed countries is mechanised to the point where fuel shortages could have disastrous effects on harvests, and, daily, industry becomes more automated and dependent upon electricity rather than manpower for routine tasks. The motor car has brought individual mobility at the expense of public transport and is one of the most wasteful forms of fuel consumption. Conservationists and ecologists had warned the industrialised societies that the expansion of living standards at the expense of the world's finite resources of energy and minerals could not be sustained. The validity of their argument was recognised, but governments and industry generally have failed to take steps to conserve resources. The current supply crisis has given Government planners a foresight of a world where raw material resources have been seriously depleted. Specialised Government agencies throughout the world are now looking at ways in which energy demand can be trimmed.

While the supply crisis has been politically inspired and is potentially short term in its effect, the Arab oil producers have proved that they can turn the oil taps on and off at will. No matter what peace settlement is arrived at eventually, the Middle East—which holds almost 55 per cent of the world's proven oil reserves—will remain an area of considerable political instability. This must cast doubt over the wisdom of even maintaining the dominant position of the Middle East suppliers in the world energy market. These doubts constitute a considerable incentive to develop alternative energy, but in the short term the real impetus will be provided by the soaring costs of importing crude oil. The additional $40,000m, that the OECD nations will have to find to pay the oil producers' accounts, will place an intolerable burden on the balance of payments of many countries, particularly those like Britain, whose trade balance has been consistently in deficit, and even Japan and Germany, whose economies are accustomed to substantial surpluses.

Perhaps the most disabling effect will be on the emerging countries, where governments may actually be forced to make substantial reductions in the amount of oil imported, at a time when energy is vitally needed in the development of their economies. These countries also face a reduction in foreign aid programmes from the hard-pressed industrialised countries and a decline in tourist traffic, which over the past few years has brought large amounts of valuable foreign exchange to many Third World countries. The Shah of Iran, however, indicated that the plight of the developing nations of the world might be ameliorated by the oil producers themselves taking over part of the traditional role of the industrialised nations in the provision of aid.

The supply crisis occurred at a critical time for the industrialised nations. Nearly all the major economies experienced a considerable upswing during 1972 and the first six months of 1973, but economists were beginning to forecast the beginning of a decline in world Gross National Product and trade during 1974 continuing into 1975. Restrictions on imports of oil and allocations of deliveries to industrial consumers have upset industry's schedules for meeting long standing orders and could produce serious unemployment. Even disregarding the exceptional circumstances of Britain, general confidence in industry throughout the world has been shaken and, as a result, the down turn in demand could materialise sooner than expected. Japan and the United States of America both forecast zero or negative economic growth for the first half of 1974.

The importance of oil in sustaining the rate of economic growth throughout the world cannot be underestimated. In 1960 total energy demand was 3058m tons of oil equivalent, out of which oil supplied 33.2 per cent of requirements and coal 50.7 per cent. At that stage oil had already begun a rapid displacement of coal as the major source of energy. The price competitiveness combined with its favourable handling characteristics ensured that new industrial installations and power stations made oil their first choice. In 1950 oil was estimated to have been 25 per cent more expensive than coal per unit of energy output. The opening up of the Middle East on a large scale throughout the 1950s completely reversed this position by the end of the decade when oil was between 20 and 30 per cent cheaper than coal. The competitiveness of oil improved throughout the 1960s, and prior to the October 16 price increases, had increased by only 80 per cent since 1962 compared with a 110 per cent rise in coal and coke prices during the same period. By 1970 energy demand had reached 4916m tons of oil equivalent, and oil commanded 43.9 per cent of this increased market while coal production had remained almost static and its share of the market had declined to 34.6 per cent. According to the OECD, by 1980 almost 8500m tons of oil equivalent will be needed unless substantial improvements are made in the efficiency with which fuel is consumed. In mid-1973 the OECD's Oil Committee estimated that oil's share of this massive market would be 47.8 per cent with natural gas taking a further 20 per cent. Coal's share would be down to almost 25 per cent. The dependence of various countries on imported oil varies greatly. The United States, the largest producer in the world is now forced to import 15 per cent of its requirements to make good the shortfall between indigenous supply and domestic demand. Western Europe imports about 70 per cent of its

Chart 1/1 World's primary energy requirements

Million tons of oil equivalent

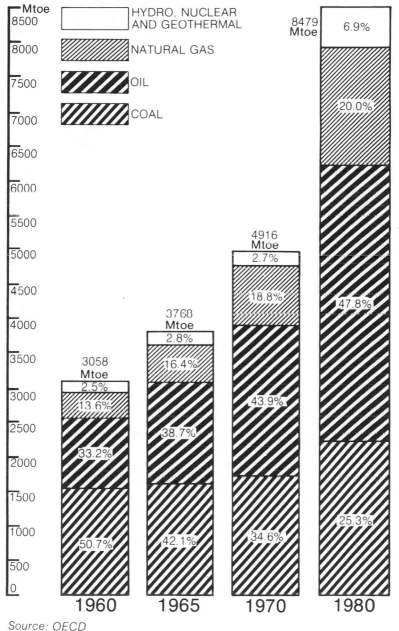

Source: OECD

Table 1/1: World Oil Reserves and Production 1973

Country	Reserves 1.1.74 Oil 1,000 bbl	Gas 1,000 m cu ft	Oil Production Estimated 1973 1,000 b/d	% change from 1972
Asia/Pacific				
Australia	2,300,000	37,700	420.0	23.3
Brunei-				
Malaysia	1,600,000	20,000	325.0	17.7
Indonesia	10,500,000	15,000	1,300.0	22.6
Others	1,235,000	41,000	200.2	
Total	15,635,000	114,200	2,245.2	20.0
Europe				
West Germany	544,000	12,308	133.0	—3.4
Norway	4,000,000	23,000	37.5	13.6
Netherlands	251,000	92,000	28.6	—8.6
Spain	60,000	500	22.2	788.0
Britain	10,000,000	50,000	1.5	—11.7
Others	1,135,000	15,989	172.7	
Total	15,990,500	193,797	395.5	5.9
Middle East				
Abu Dhabi	21,500,000	12,500	1,285.5	22.5
Dubai	2,500,000	1,000	223.0	45.8
Iran	60,000,000	270,000	6,000.0	19.5
Iraq	31,500,000	22,000	1,888.2	30.5
Israel	2,500	25	100.0†	—7.0
Kuwait	64,000,000	32,500	2,890.2	—3.6
Neutral Zone	17,500,000	8,000	507.5	—11.2
Oman	5,250,000	2,000	271.9	—3.5
Qatar	6,500,000	8,000	555.5	15.2
Saudi Arabia	132,000,000	50,000	7,417.9	29.4
Syria	7,100,000	7,000	105.7	—12.1
Others	2,310,000	5,700	128.7	
Total	350,162,000	413,325	21,374.1	18.1

† includes Egypt's Sinai Fields.

Table 1/1 continued

	Reserves 1.1.74		Oil Production	
			Estimated	%
		Gas	1973	change
	Oil	1,000 m	1,000	from
Country	1,000 bbl	cu ft	b/d	1972
Africa				
Algeria	7,640,000	105,945	1,035.4	—2.6
Cabinda	1,500,000	1,500	160.0	14.7
Congo				
Brazzaville	4,888,000	1,000	39.0	490.9
Egypt	5,125,000	4,200	180.0	—15.0
Gabon	1,500,000	6,500	145.0	15.4
Libya	25,500,000	27,000	2,116.6	—4.5
Nigeria	20,000,000	40,000	2,000.0	10.0
Others	1,150,000	1,575	87.9	
Total	67,303,000	187,720	5,763.9	1.8
Western Hemisphere				
Agentina	2,500,000	8,000	442.0	2.0
Columbia	1,432,000	2,500	186.0	—5.8
Ecuador	5,675,000	5,000	197.0	148.1
Mexico	3,600,000	11,000	478.0	8.4
Trinidad	2,200,000	5,000	159.0	12.4
Venezuela	14,000,000	42,000	3,370.0	1.7
United States	34,700,249	247,310	9,225.0	—2.4
Canada	9,424,170	50,299	1,750.0	14.0
Others	2,233,250	17,821	315.0	
Total	75,764,669	388,930	16,122.0	2.0
Total Non-Communist world	524,856,459	1,297,972	45,900.7	9.8
Communist world	103,000,000	735,400	9,312.0	4.5
Total world	627,856,459	2,033,372	55,212.7	8.8

Source: Oil and Gas Journal

energy requirements, and in Japan a massive 87 per cent of all energy sources, mainly oil, but some coal comes from abroad. In 1973, 55.2m barrels of oil were produced daily throughout the world, an 8.8 per cent increase on the previous year. Despite the production cutbacks, the Middle East contributed 21.3m barrels a day—an 18 per cent increase over 1972. In North Africa the Arab states of Libya produced just over 2m barrels a day and its neighbour, Algeria, produced slightly more than 1m barrels a day.

Transportation since the early years of the oil industry has been a vital element in the process of taking oil from the desert wells of the Middle East and moving it many thousands of miles to the consuming countries. About 50 per cent of world oil production, until the upheavals of 1973, was being transported around the world by the huge fleet of oil tankers which essentially form a constantly moving pipeline around the globe. Demand for transport increased more than the production warranted because of changes in the pattern of oil movements. In short, this amounted to a reduction in the short distance transportation from North Africa to Western Europe which has been more than compensated for by a substantial rise in demand for long-distance shipment from the Middle East to the west and particularly for the transportation of crude oil to the United States. In the 10 years 1963 to 1973 the world fleet of tankers increased from 65.1m tons dwt to 186m tons dwt with a sharp rise following the closure of the Suez Canal in 1967 from a capacity in that year of 94.1m tons to 114.3m tons in 1969. In spite of periodic fluctuations in the freight markets as a result of the movements in the volume of world trade, the tanker fleet has continued to expand steadily in line with the relentless expansion of crude oil production and consumption, which throughout the 1960s averaged about 7 per cent a year. Until the crisis, forecasts indicated a further huge requirement for additional tonnage to meet demand for oil in the consuming nations. During 1973, oil companies and the independent tanker owners (who play an important part in the energy transportation picture) contracted a vast quantity of new tonnage with world shipyards. At the beginning of 1973 the Shipbuilders Association of Japan suggested that in the five years 1976 to 1980 inclusive, total demand for a new tanker tonnage would be 160m tons dwt, an average yearly requirement of 32m tons. The events of the final quarter of 1973, however, must lead to a re-appraisal. The

Japanese forecast in fact represented, incredibly, 85 per cent of the existing world tanker fleet in the summer of 1972 which amounted to 188.4m tons.

The shipping industry in general, and the tanker owning sector in particular, make more demands on the world's money markets than almost any other. Vast sums of capital have been poured into the industry, boosted especially after the closure of the Suez Canal, which led to the development of the very large crude carrier (VLCC) and more recently of the ultra large crude carrier (ULCC) of more than 400,000 tons dwt. International currency crises, particularly over the period since 1971 have created problems for the industry, which has to service huge loans and funds. The oil companies, faced with a fourfold increase in crude oil costs, had to contend with demands from the independent tanker owners early in 1974 for an additional $300m on their existing charter contracts. Revenue on ships on long term charters of up to 20 years had been eroded by inflation at rates which had not been remotely contemplated at the time the charter was negotiated. Mr Erling Naess, chairman of a special working group of the International Association of Tanker Owners (Intertanko) warned that re-negotiation of numerous charters was a matter of the survival of a substantial part of the fleet owned by the members of the association. There was a suggestion that some owners could be faced with bankruptcy. The oil companies were therefore placed in a dilemma of either paying the extra demanded by the tanker owners or arranging new charters with other owners (if they could be found) at 1974 levels which would involve an estimated outlay of between $900m and $1,000m. With maintenance, operating and other overheads rising sharply, together with the likelihood that the higher costs of energy would prompt a slowdown in both world trade and economic activity, the shipping industry made it clear that the oil companies could no longer expect to obtain their transport requirements so cheaply. Prices for new construction in 1973 had risen sharply but the oil supply/price issue rebounded on shipowners with new ships on order from Japan. The Japanese invoked *force majeure* on delivery of some tankers and indicated that they would seek to re-negotiate original fixed price contracts.

The transformation of the oil industry has, as Mr Jamieson pointed out, changed the role of the international oil companies. They no longer have exclusive title to the bulk of the Middle Eastern reserves, a position that gave them a privileged position in Europe and Japan where the resources were so desperately required. The erosion of their power in the Middle East has also produced a change of attitude towards the energy crisis, and they have now joined the popular bandwagon of forecasting the exhaustion of oil supplies by the end of the century.

The major consuming nations are devoting considerable funds to research and development but, no matter how much money is spent, a significant increase in alternative supplies cannot be conjured up to take the burden off oil, at least for several years. New coal mines take years to sink and a new nuclear power station can take up to eight years from conception to commissioning. The conversion of industrial plant and power stations from oil burning to coal is an expensive process and will only be undertaken when alternative supplies can be guaranteed. The renaissance of coal could spark off more prospecting for supplies in the developing countries, as the opportunities for expanding the high cost reserves in Europe are limited. Coal in fact accounts for over 90 per cent of the world reserves of fossil fuels, and according to the United Nations Economic Commission for Europe only two per cent of total coal and shale oil reserves will have been depleted by the year 2,000. The bulk of these reserves lie in the Soviet Union but like Russian oil they are mostly in the remoter parts of Siberia. The United States has ample supplies of easily accessible coal but the coal owners' methods of strip mining have in the past raised violent environmentalist objections that make the exploitation of new reserves difficult. Certainly the old and cheap methods of the past will not be repeated.

The changing structure of the world oil industry that has given the producing nations control over large quantities of oil has already produced political problems in the consuming countries. The United States, Japan and the European Economic Community saw the dangers of individual countries competing against each other for supplies on a government to government basis and pushing up the prices at the same time. France, however, has followed a Gaullist course and concluded two major oil deals with the Saudi Arabians and the Iranians, and Britain also infuriated her Common Market partners by signing an industrial goods for oil deal with Iran. The period of unfettered expansion is over.

Saudi Arabia which at one time talked of increasing its output to an astonishing 20m barrels daily will be happy to consolidate its capacity at 10m barrels a day. The producers will be looking to use the higher revenues from stabilised outputs to establish an industrial base to their economies, and the most popular method appears to be the establishment of refineries and petro-chemical works close to the oil fields. If this objective is met, the industry will have gone full circle and will be back to the early days when refining took place in the producing countries and products were shipped to the main markets. The shipping and shipbuilding industries, which have pushed forward the bounds of ship construction technology in response to the requirements of the international oil industry to a point where the advent of the 1m tankers appeared imminent, may now have been checked.

There are certain parallels between the enforced transition of the present day oil industry from domination by the oil companies to control by the national oil companies established by the producer nations.

The transition of the oil industry from one dominated by seven large multi-national oil corporations to one where control rests largely in the hands of the national oil companies has implications far beyond a mere change in ownership of a major proportion of the world's crude oil reserves. The international companies made oil the biggest and most profitable business with their tentacles stretching from the Arctic wastes of Alaska to exploration off the coast of Australia. Their refineries, chemical plants and marketing chains circle the globe, and most people outside the communist bloc depend to a greater or lesser extent on the multitude of products that are derived from crude oil. The measure of control these companies had over crude oil reserves enabled them to act as a valuable buffer between the consuming nations and the oil producing countries. This has now disappeared. Decisions taken in Teheran, Kuwait City or Riyahd on the price, or availability, of oil will in future have ramifications as fundamental as the movement of the Wall Street stock market and the City of London.

Chapter Two
The Pioneering Years

The development of the international oil industry started with a discovery in Titusville, Pennsylvania by Colonel Edwin Drake in the summer of 1859. Drake, a former railroad conductor, whose knowledge of drilling techniques had been gained in the development of water wells, joined a New York lawyer, George H. Bissell, to test the lawyer's theory that kerosene could be produced more cheaply from crude oil rather than from coal.

Bissell had proved that kerosene could be made cheaply from the natural seepages of oil into shallow pits dug in the Titusville area. But he lacked the techniques for effective production.

At this time considerable quantities of kerosene were being produced from coal and shale under a process patented by a Scot, Dr James "Paraffin" Young. In the Middle East from the earliest days of civilisation, use had been made of natural seepages, and in Russia, as early as the thirteenth century, attempts were made to establish commercial production by digging pits and allowing oil to seep to the surface.

There are indications that the Chinese obtained small quantities of oil from shallow mines several thousand years ago and probably were the first people to move the product by ship. In the eighteenth century the Newchang junks of China are recorded as carrying oil in bulk, although they had only a capacity for fifty tons. There was considerable activity in oil trade on the river Volga where, from 1725 onwards, the carriage of oil in bulk had to conform with regulations laid down by Peter the Great.

Colonel Drake took charge of production for Bissell's company and to the amusement of the local population in Titusville began to set up a drilling derrick. Within a few weeks the well had reached 69.5 feet and crude oil began to bubble up to the surface. A pump was fitted to the top of the well and within a short time Bissell's company was producing 30 barrels of oil a day.

It was impossible to keep the discovery a secret. Titusville quickly became a boom town; thousands of dollars were paid for leases in the known oil bearing locations and other operators began to copy Drake's production techniques. The Titusville discovery quickly opened up other shallow reserves of crude in the Pennsylvania region.

Within two years kerosene refined from oil had replaced that made from coal in the United States of America and in 1861 exports of kerosene began.

Trouble on the Delaware

The first vessel to carry oil across the Atlantic was the 224 ton brig, Elizabeth Watts. The circumstances surrounding the loading of the vessel in Philadelphia were to be repeated many times in the following years. The crew discovered the nature of the cargo and deserted and a replacement crew had to be found from riverside bars along the Delaware.

Shipping of oil in barrels of 40-42 gallons capacity proved to be uneconomic because up to 50 per cent of the loading capacity of the vessel was lost.

A refinement of the barrel was the five gallon tin, packed in twos or fours which was widely used in the China trade where the tins found a multitude of end uses once they had been emptied.

The seaborne carriage of oil continued to be a hazardous business for the ships and their crews. Leakage from the containers led to highly dangerous gases permeating the cargo spaces and in effect created a floating bomb.

Despite the potential danger, exports of American oil to Europe continued to grow so that by 1864 exports of Philadelphia oil amounted to 7.6m gallons out of a total United States production of 31.75m gallons.

In 1863 the first iron hulled sailing tanker the Ramsay was built for an Isle of Man shipowner while in the August of the same year the Atlantic was launched on Tyneside and designed to carry oil in bulk "without the aid of casks".

The American Civil War gave further impetus to the development of international trade in kerosene. The Northern Government encouraged exports to earn foreign exchange to replace overseas revenues which were badly affected by the loss of the cotton trade.

The Pennsylvania oil industry was disorganised, fragmented and run mainly by speculators. There was little price stability and when new wells were discovered there was usually a glut of crude, and when the shallow reserves of other wells began to dry up there were often shortages. The refining industry was also in the hands of a large number of small, relatively inefficient operators.

Rockefeller and refining

Into this situation stepped John D. Rockefeller. He had established himself as a "commission agent" during the Civil War dealing in commodities of all kinds. Rockefeller found himself dealing in kerosene and set up his first refinery in 1863. The refining business centred on Cleveland, Ohio expanded rapidly and by the beginning of 1870 a joint stock company—the Standard Oil Company—was formed. The basic weakness of the infant industry was pinpointed by Rockefeller, who realised that the key to success lay in the control of the refining, rather than in gaining control of crude production.

Standard Oil began acquiring a number of small refining companies in Cleveland and after two years operation was probably the largest refiner in the United States.

It was the powerful railroad companies, however, which set Standard Oil on the road to success. The three largest railroads, the Pennsylvania, the Eyrie and the New York Central put forward a plan which effectively reduced competition in the carriage of oil by rail. The thirteen biggest refining companies formed themselves into an association and agreed to send all their shipments through the three railroad networks in return for lower freight rates than refiners outside their organisation. However, news of the agreement leaked out before it could be implemented and in a storm of public protest the scheme had to be dropped—but not before Standard Oil had earned itself a reputation for questionable business practices.

The overall expansion of refining in the United States led to considerable overcapacity with the result that by 1870 profit margins per barrel were down from almost 20 cents to just under 8 cents.

Then in 1873 the refiners were further hit by general economic depression and Rockefeller moved in to buy up his smaller competitors. By 1879 he had gained control of 90 per cent of America's refining capacity. In doing so he had acquired considerable influence over the pipeline and railroad companies.

His near monopoly position enabled him to command rail freight rates at almost half the level of those of his competitors. Standard Oil's monopoly power and influence over the whole industry soon brought legal actions against it. After a twenty-year legal battle the United States Supreme Court ordered in 1911 that the company be split up into a number of separate and independent corporations. Standard Oil New Jersey, which has now changed its name to the Exxon Corporation, remained with Standard's Esso brand name and is the world's largest oil corporation. Two of its other offshoots, Standard Oil of California and Mobil (formerly the Standard Oil Company, New York) rank among the major oil corporations. Other offshoots that have prospered in their independent role are Standard Oil of Indiana (Amoco) and Standard Oil of Ohio (Sohio) which is now in the protracted process of merging with British Petroleum.

In these early days the Americans were concerned with the development of their own vast oil reserves and took little interest in the exploration for oil in other parts of the world. They were however interested in exporting their products to compete with the growing European companies, led by the Royal Dutch Group that pioneered the development of a substantial oil industry in the Dutch East Indies (now Indonesia).

Shipping takes stock

While the expansion of the American oil industry continued together with exploration and development of oil reserves else-where in the world, demand in Europe for this new, cheap source of energy was growing rapidly each year. Without an indigenous industry of its own, Europe was obliged to import primarily from the United States. It was this requirement which prompted many European shipowners to diversify out of their traditional trades and with the shipbuilders of their various countries to pioneer vessels capable of carrying larger amounts of oil more safely.

In the years up to 1878 many wooden sailing ships were adapted to carry oil in bulk. The 794 tons deadweight Charles was the first vessel to be fitted with iron tanks (59 in all) each of 13 tons capacity which had to be laboriously emptied and filled by hand pumping. In that year (1878) a Swedish shipbuilding company built the Zoroaster designed to carry 250 tons of kerosene in 21 vertical and cylindrical tanks. She was the first of many tank steamers that were used in the oil trade but it was not until 1884 that the concept, that the hull of a ship should form part of the cargo tanks, gained wide scale acceptance. The remaining six years of that decade marked a critical period in the development of tanker design.

After a series of 'experimental' tanker types had appeared, the 3000 ton dwt. Gluckauf, launched in 1885 for the German American Oil Company by Armstrong Mitchell & Co. of Newcastle-upon-Tyne provided the prototype design for tankers which were to follow for many years later.

A year after the Gluckauf was launched there were about a dozen steam tankers engaged in the petroleum trade from the United States. By 1891 their number had grown and between 80 and 90 were operating on the Atlantic service alone. The size of the steam powered tanker fleet increased almost monthly but they remained a subject of some scepticism with the more conservative shipow-ners. As the oil industry developed momentum it also provided employment for many sailing ships in the years to the end of the nineteenth century, since speed was not considered a vital requirement.

Suez, Samuel and Shell

The potential of the Suez Canal for oil transportation was realised by Marcus Samuel, the son of a London merchant who was to form in 1897, Shell Transport and Trading. Five years before Shell Transport and Trading emerged, his first tanker, the 4,500 ton Murex, became the first specialist oil carrier to negotiate the canal after loading in the Black Sea and eventually discharging her cargo in Singapore and Bangkok. Samuel had negotiated a concession with the canal authority which was to give him a tremendous advantage since this concession was not extended to others in the tanker trade until 1898.

Shell Transport and Trading built up marketing outlets in Europe and the Far East, and had an up to date shipping fleet to support it, but Samuel lacked the enthusiasm and drive that distinguished many of the other early founders of the oil industry. His British-owned company lacked secure sources of crude and in 1902 he formed an association with Royal Dutch, a group with ample crude reserves from their Indonesian fields. The agreement covered refining and marketing in the Far East but left the two partners free to compete in other parts of the world.

Royal Dutch under the energetic Dutchman, Henri Deterding, continued to build up its production facilities in the Far East. At the same time, Shell Transport and Trading continued to suffer from lack of crude oil and when the prolific Spindletop well in Texas began to decline in 1902, the company was faced with an even more serious crude shortage. It was forced to withdraw from the European markets creating a gap that was eagerly filled by Royal Dutch.

Samuel was eventually forced to offer to amalgamate with Royal Dutch on a 50/50 basis in order to solve the inherent weaknesses in the Shell organisation. But Deterding was fully aware of Shell's short-comings and was able to negotiate a 60/40 agreement in favour of the Dutch company. Deterding then began an aggressive world wide expansion programme. He acquired new reserves in Rumania and Russia and in 1914 took control of his first reserves in the United States—just two years after he had inaugurated a marketing venture in competition with the established American companies. He then moved south signing up reserves first in Mexico and then Venezuela before the oil bonanza really got under way.

Spindletop

The discovery of the now famous Spindletop well near Beaumont in Texas in January 1901 marked another milestone in the development of the international industry. The well, just south of the town, in its first year produced an equivalent to the entire output of close on 40,000 wells in the eastern United States. But output from the first Texas well slumped dramatically before the end of 1902 and, although there were fears that the industry would collapse, new reserves were discovered within months in other parts of the State, with further finds made in Oklahoma and Louisiana.

The growth of the industry in Texas provided opportunities for companies to challenge the monopoly established by Standard Oil based on the earlier oil finds. Texaco and Gulf both had their origins in Texas. Spindletop also coincided with the decline in the use of kerosene for lighting and heating and the introduction of the internal combustion engine. On a very small scale, fuel oil was being used to replace coal for steam raising in large industrial units, locomotives, and ships. Motor cars were multiplying weekly and in the United States, in the ten years 1902-1912, increased from 23,000 vehicles to more than one million. Petrol sales soared accordingly.

The navies of the world were rapidly changing from coal to oil for steam raising and at the outbreak of the 1914 war, Winston Churchill, then First Lord of the Admiralty, negotiated a long term contract for Anglo Persian to supply the Royal Navy with fuel oil. At the same time the British Government invested £2m in the company to become its largest stockholder.

Anglo-Persian, which changed its name to British Petroleum in

1954, had in 1913 completed a 400,000 ton annual capacity oil refinery at Abadan and it was the nationalisation of this refinery in 1951 which gave impetus to a radical change in the whole pattern of international oil movement. During the war Anglo Persian began to build its own tanker fleet.

In the early part of this century the Texas oil discoveries and later the Middle East finds gave further incentive to shipowners and shipbuilders to develop more effective vessels in which oil could be carried.

Many of the early oil carrying vessels had suffered from serious structural weaknesses. The hazardous nature of the cargo and its tendency to expand and contract, to "slosh" in the tanks, and to produce dangerous gases all added to the difficulties faced by designers. It was not until 1920 that a radical change in tanker design occurred with the introduction of a combined system of transverse and longitudinal bulkheads. The effect of this design (drawn up by Sir Joseph Isherwood) was that it reduced the net weight of a vessel of a given cargo carrying capacity and had the additional advantage of imparting extra strength to the hull.

This development marked the start of a significant movement towards larger ships although this trend took place only gradually. In the period up to the outbreak of World War II the average size of tankers had settled at about 12,000 tons dwt. This remained by and large the familiar size during the period from 1918 to 1939, although at the end of World War I the Eagle Oil Company placed orders for six 18,000 ton dwt oil tankers.

Britain in the Middle-East

As a result of the huge effort made by the United States to produce war material, consumption by 1920 was more than double its pre-1914 levels at 455 million barrels. Prices were also rising sharply and were three times their 1913 level. The situation provoked the now familiar warnings of an impending "energy crisis". It came from Dr George Otis Smith the director of the United States Geological Survey who told the United States that unless it cut down on the use of oil products, imports on a large scale would be inevitable. In practical terms this would have meant giving British companies an even firmer foothold in the American market. Shell had already established a retailing group in the United States, but American companies had not achieved the same penetration in Europe, neither had they gained control of any significant sources of foreign crude.

The American Government already suspected that the British were trying to exclude American companies from the development of concessions granted to British companies by the defeated Turkish Empire in places such as Iraq and Palestine. They felt their suspicions were confirmed when, in 1919, the British authorities in Palestine prevented the Standard Oil Company of New York from resuming exploration activities that had started before the First World War. While the Americans were ejected from Palestine, Shell was given permission to step up its exploration effort in Iraq.

The prospect of British control, either directly or indirectly, of the major known oil fields outside the United States and the most promising exploration areas, prompted the American Government to bring seven of the largest American oil corporations into a single syndicate with the objective of obtaining concessions in the Middle East. The Americans were not slow to point out that it was a joint allied effort which had won the First World War and that it was for all the victors to share in the spoils—in this case the former Turkish empire.

Intense diplomatic activity on the part of the Americans eventually persuaded the British Government that American participation in the Middle East was desirable. It was strongly believed, but never officially confirmed, that Standard Oil of New Jersey had threatened to cut off supplies to its British subsidiary, Anglo American, (now Esso Petroleum) if the United States consortium did not get a fair deal in the Persian Gulf. At that time Anglo American was second only to Shell in the British retailing field.

British and French oil interests were keen to undertake large-scale development in Iraq but realised that nothing of value could be decided until the question of the American position was settled. The American diplomatic offensive, combined with this desire to start work in Iraq, led in 1922 to the US syndicate being invited to negotiate a stake in the Turkish Petroleum Company.

However, the negotiations were to have far more widespread effects than just fixing the share holding in the now Iraq Petroleum Company; eventually they were to decide how the international oil industry would carve up the huge empire previously controlled by the Turks. In the negotiations over the shareholdings, Shell and the French Compagnie Française Des·Pétroles were determined to curb the power of Anglo-Persian, in which the British Government held a 50 per cent stake and with the support of the Americans they forced Anglo-Persian to abandon its demand for a 50 per cent share in Turkish Petroleum and agree to each of the four main parties being given 23.75 per cent of the shares, with Calouste Sarkis Gulbenkian taking the remaining 5 per cent. Gulbenkian had been among the first to realise the potential of Iraq and made the first approaches to the Turkish Government.

Gulbenkian and the Red Line

Outside Iraq, the British and the Americans favoured a free for all policy in obtaining new oil concessions which, with their greater size and resources, would have ensured that the French were largely excluded. Gulbenkian too was opposed to this idea. But the French Government brought pressure to bear on the other parties and in 1927 the "Red Line Agreement" was drawn up. The French circled in red pencil the area which they claimed constituted the old Turkish Empire. This included the whole of Saudi Arabia, Jordan and Syria but excluded Kuwait. Although the British disputed the accuracy of the marking they eventually accepted the French demarcation. Under the agreement the companies undertook not to compete for concessions. They were also obliged to seek the permission of the other oil corporations if they wished to acquire exclusive concessions within this area.

As the Red Line Agreement was being negotiated the first well drilled in Iraq was nearing completion. On October 27th 1927 the drilling team hit the biggest "gusher" the world had yet seen, at Baba Gur Gur close to Kirkuk. This area had been chosen for the first well as it was close to the "Eternal fires" of Nebuchadnezzar's Biblical fiery furnace. Oil men felt that these fires must have been stoked by natural seepages from an extremely large deposit.

The Baba Gur Gur well proved capable of producing 12,500 tons a day but already the world oil industry was beginning to lose interest. The negotiations to settle the future of the Middle East had started at a time when oil was in short supply throughout the world but at their conclusion the industry was moving into a period of surplus. In particular the American syndicate became less interested in international expansion and, by the time the final agreement on carving up the Middle East was signed, only Standard Oil of New Jersey and Standard Oil of New York were left out of the seven original partners.

One of the factors that had diverted American interest and contributed to the growing surplus of oil was the development, much closer to the American market, of oil in Venezuela. In December 1922 Shell made a major find close to Lake Maracaibo. Several American groups also held concessions in the same area and with the aid of extremely generous terms from the Venezuelan Government production raced ahead and by 1928 exceeded 100 million barrels a year. At this stage Venezuela was second only to the United States as an oil producer.

As Venezuelan production reached new high levels addtional new and very large deposits were found in eastern Texas in 1930—a discovery which led to a glut of oil on the American market.

Texas also proved to be a prodigious source of natural gas and at the start of the 1930s the United States had begun to develop this natural resource. The potential of natural gas as an industrial and domestic fuel had been known for many years and in the New York town of Fredonia wooden pipes had been used to bring supplies from a small local source to the community as early as 1824. Natural gas however proved to be less popular than coal gas which can be manufactured close to the consumer. As new oil discoveries were made, communities close by made use of the gas but it was not possible to pipe it over long distances. To move gas efficiently it is necessary to subject it to high pressures which requires strong, thin walled steel pipeline. The development of acetylene welding in the 1920s made it possible to begin a network of gas lines that by 1930 extended over 1000 miles of the United States. There are now almost 250,000 miles of natural gas lines in the United States serving every State with the exception of Alaska and Hawaii.

The Gulf and gold

While the discoveries in Iraq concentrated most of the oil industry's efforts in this area, a number of experts felt that similar finds could be made in Kuwait, Bahrain, and Saudi Arabia. Kuwait fell outside the Red Line agreement, but in the other areas the signatories successfully prevented their development. Gulf Oil which had been obstructed in its plans for the development of reserves in Bahrain, resigned from the Iraq Petroleum Group and began to look at the possibilities of exploiting Kuwait and in 1933 agreed with Anglo Persian to set up a jointly owned company—the Kuwait Oil Company. Production however began on a small scale in 1938. Saudi Arabia at this time suspected that Britain was trying to undermine Ibn Saud's attempts to unify the country. The King was offering a country-wide concession for £50,000 in gold and favoured the Standard Oil Company of California—free from any connection with the British or the British influenced Iraq Petroleum Group. This company countered with an offer of £30,000 in Sterling but Standard Oil of California produced the full £50,000 in gold and secured the world's most valuable oil concession.

The granting of this concession however generated a bitter dispute between the French and Gulbenkian on one hand and the American partners in Iraq Petroleum on the other. The Americans were anxious to curtail Middle East production and prevent further erosion of their margins from serious overproduction. Development of Saudi Arabia posed a threat to this policy. Standard Oil New Jersey and Standard Oil of New York offered to buy California Standard's Saudi Arabian production but were vetoed by the French and Gulbenkian. The French were not interested in containing production and keeping prices high. Their principle concern was low cost imports to aid the French economy and they saw rapid expansion in Saudi Arabia as a way of achieving this. Standard California's first move to break the deadlock was to sell a half interest in the concession to Texaco. The outbreak of the Second World War changed the situation completely as CFP and Gulbenkian were labelled as enemies and the Red Line Agreement was dissolved. Standard Oil of NewJersey and Standard Oil of New York opened negotiations for a stake in the company and in 1947 agreement was reached on the formation of the Arabian American Oil Company (Aramco) whose partners are Standard

California, Texaco, and Standard New Jersey, each holding 30 per cent, and Standard New York (later to become Mobil) the remaining 10 per cent.

Between the two World Wars there was a steady although not particularly spectacular growth in the use of oil products. World use of mineral oil increased from 200m. tons in 1920 to 255m. tons in 1938. The use of motor cars and commercial vehicles continued to expand rapidly and industrial usage also increased. New markets appeared including aviation and specialised lubricating applications. Despite the growth there was never any danger of oil challenging coal as the principal energy source—or so it seemed. World War II accelerated the trend towards increased use of oil products. Personal usage was curtailed but the war effort underlined the role which oil was to play in the post-war era. It also demonstrated the vulnerability of major industrial nations to any threat to their supply lines.

Changing patterns of trade

During World War II, with the emphasis on the carriage of refined products, the tendency in the development of the oil industry up to the outbreak of hostilities had been to locate refineries close to the oil fields rather than in the consuming countries. The size of tankers had remained relatively small in contrast to many of the vessels now engaged in oil transportation. A new and larger breed of oil industry workhorses made their appearance during the War and typical of these was the so-called T2 tanker of 16,600 tons dwt which had an average speed of 14.5 knots.

American shipyards constructed a total of 620 T2 tankers during the war. These vessels were then classed as supertankers. Tankers were still engaged primarily in the carriage of refined products and the design characteristics enabled the pre-World War II tankers to carry a number of different grades of fuel on a single voyage. The tanker fleet, which at the end of World War I numbered 467 vessels (over 2,000 tons dwt) aggregating just short of 3.7m tons and rose to more than 1,500 ships totalling 16.6m tons dwt, remained small in terms of average size. Nevertheless, this gave these ships a flexibility both in the variety of cargoes they could carry and in their ability to follow the

Chart 2/1: Economies of scale derived from large tankers

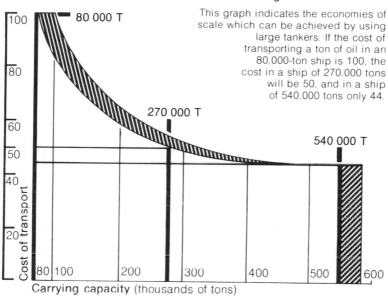

This graph indicates the economies of scale which can be achieved by using large tankers. If the cost of transporting a ton of oil in an 80,000-ton ship is 100, the cost in a ship of 270,000 tons will be 50, and in a ship of 540,000 tons only 44.

Source: Shell

international pattern of trade in oil, which at that time was markedly different from the situation today. Only a very small part of the total tanker fleet was engaged in crude oil deliveries, with by far the majority engaged in product delivery.

In the pre-World War II period 80 per cent of oil carried was in the form of refined oil products with the balance of plus or minus 20 per cent in the form of crude. In the post-1945 period these proportions were totally reversed. The distance between the major oil producing nations, the main consuming areas for oil and its products, together with the steadily growing demand, has ensured a spectacular rise in the tonnage of merchant shipping engaged in this trade.

The change in the proportions of crude oil and products carried, which took place after World War II, reflected the transfer by the oil companies of their policy in establishing new refineries in locations close to the major markets. This was brought about for a variety of reasons.

Techniques used in refining had progressed sufficiently to enable oil to be produced which was more closely linked to the local market requirements, while demand for oil in all the major industrial countries rose steeply. The technical advances also meant that the amount of unusuable waste to be disposed of from a cargo of crude oil was substantially reduced while on the political front the nationalisation of the refineries of the Anglo-Iranian Oil Company (formerly Anglo-Persian Oil) gave a further push to the already evident oil company strategy of locating their new refineries in more secure consuming countries. The overriding factor, however, was the steeply rising demand that enabled the consuming countries to absorb all the products from large refinery units.

These spectacular growth rates were the result of a change from coal to oil across the entire range of industry. New power stations began to use heavy fuel oil as a boiler fuel, the railways of Europe and America switched from coal burning locomotives to diesel and electric trains on a large scale, manufacturing industry saw the advantages of using a fuel that was clean, easy to handle and store. Householders on a more limited scale began using oil for central heating.

In addition, civil aviation became a reality on a scale hardly envisaged before the War. The oil companies also began looking for new outlets for what had previously been thought of as unsaleable refinery by-products. Out of this search grew the modern petro-chemical industry. The coal industry of Europe, ravaged by the war and suffering from severe under-investment could make little response to the aggressive marketing techniques of the oil companies who were selling a much more easily handled product at more competitive rates.

All the coal owners could do was to close uneconomic pits, and from this moment the supremacy of oil was assured.

Against the background of the surge in demand from these sources, was the implicit requirement for larger ships to ensure that oil remained a competitive source of energy, since transportation costs form such an important element in the final cost of crude oil at its eventual destination. The Suez crises of 1956 and 1967 made this abundantly clear and the trend towards the larger oil tanker was beginning to emerge in the early years after the war. Essentially, the larger the vessel, the lower the building costs per ton of deadweight and lower operating costs per ton mile provide a lower transportation cost. Thus the shipping industry saw the arrival of tankers of 20,000 tons deadweight soon after the war with a series of 24,000 ton deadweight vessels built for Norwegian owners providing an insight in to what the future would hold.

Chapter Three
The Ascendancy of Oil

Two separate events on different sides of the world in the late 1940s and the early 1950s marked the beginning of the end of international oil companies' reign as the unchallenged masters of the oil industry. The venue for the first event was in Venezuela where for the first time the companies were forced into ceding a larger share of their profits to the host government—a move that was to lead to similar demands from other oil producers and set the basis for the current world crude oil pricing system that guarantees huge revenues to governments. This was followed in 1952 by the nationalisation of the Anglo-Iranian Oil Company (now British Petroleum) and the protracted dispute that resulted in the re-organisation of the oil industry in Iran. At the time, neither event may have been seen as a shattering blow for the industry as a whole, but for the first time it was demonstrated that the oil companies could not resist the demands of governments. The heyday of the majors as producers of cheap oil and gigantic profits for their shareholders was to continue for many years after the initial repercussions of these happenings had died down, but their operations were never again to be as soundly based and, as was later demonstrated, had little intrinsic political or economic bargaining strength behind them.

But it was the nationalisation of the Anglo-Iranian Oil Company in Iran that attracted world wide attention. It had all the ingredients for a first-rate international political and human drama—the rise of the radical politicians, the exile of a young ruler and the expulsion of a large and powerful British oil company. Iran, perhaps more than any other of the oil producing countries, was ripe for staging this drama. Unlike most of its oil producing counterparts, Iran has a long and distinguished history. It considered itself one of the cradles of western and eastern civilisations, and although it had slipped from its ancient days of greatness, the Iranians still retained an individuality throughout years of domination by other cultures.

After World War II, when the country had been occupied by the British and Americans and the pro-German Shah Reza had been forced into exile, the Iranians were again being dominated by outside forces, as Anglo-Iranian had a stranglehold on the economy. This single company controlled the entire Iranian oil production and provided the bulk of the country's revenues.

Mossadegh

In this atmosphere the fervent nationalism of Dr Mohammed Mossadegh prospered and received widespread support from all classes in Iran. Mossadegh led the opposition in the Iranian Mahjlis (parliament) at a time when the right wing Government had been trying to negotiate a peaceful settlement of Iranian demands for higher revenues from Anglo Iranian's production.

The Iranians had seen the Venezuelans squeeze the companies and win a 50/50 split in profits. While the South Americans were making more from their oil, Iran had suffered a restriction of its own income because of the peculiar nature of its agreement with the British company. Iran's revenues were related to dividend payments made by Anglo-Iranian to ordinary shareholders and at this time all UK corporation dividends were subject to restraint by British Government order. The Iranians refused a straight cash payment in compensation and began negotiating a 50/50 profit sharing deal. The two sides eventually agreed on royalties of six shillings (30p) a ton with a guarantee that revenues would never fall below £4m in a single year. A sum of £5m compensation for dividend restraint in the UK was also agreed.

Mossadegh, however, was opposed to the agreement and used his position in the national assembly to force the Government to renounce the deal negotiated with Anglo-Iranian. As a result, the British company again suggested further talks and was evidently prepared to discuss a 50/50 profit sharing agreement. But Mossadegh's success in blocking the original agreement increased his power within the national assembly and his proposals for outright nationalisation of Anglo-Iranian were passed. Attempts by the young Shah to reach a compromise solution failed and the country faced threat of a complete economic and social break-down. Mossadegh was appointed prime minister and a nationali-sation bill received the Royal Assent.

Mossadegh was now at the height of his power and rejected, out of hand, a series of compromise solutions put forward by Anglo-Iranian, and the British Government. This would have recognised Iran's right to nationalise the company, but would have ensured that British expertise played a major part in the continued development of the oil fields and that Britain's principal source of crude oil remained open to them. On October 3, 1952 the last of the British staff employed by Anglo-Iranian left the country and Iran prepared to run the oil installations herself.

From this point Mossadegh's nationalisation strategy ran into serious trouble. The Iranians were able to keep the oil flowing but the British Government had made it clear that it would try to prevent Iran selling her output on the international market. With this backing Anglo-Iranian took court action against several Japanese and Italian companies who bought cargoes from the Iranians and after this the world demand for Iranian oil suddenly dried up.

Mossadegh had over-estimated Britain's dependence on Iranian supplies. While Anglo-Iranian took the bulk of its crude from Iran, it also had interests in the Kuwait Oil Company and Iraq and Qatar and expanded production in these areas to fill the gap left by Iranian crude. Iran on the other hand had no alternative to the revenues received from Anglo-Iranian. In the two years following the nationalisation total sales by the nationalised oil company amounted to only 132,000 tons compared with 54 million tons in the two years preceding the State take over. Despite the serious nature of the economic slump within Iran, Mossadegh declined outside offers of help. The Shah tried unsuccessfully to force Mossadegh out of office and was forced to flee the country. But the Prime Minister's popular support had evaporated and a military coup returned the Shah to power.

Immediate negotiations began, aimed at restoring the flow of oil and revenues. The following October the solution had been reached. The nationalisation of the Anglo-Iranian concessions was recognised and a consortium of international oil companies was formed to operate them on behalf of the National Iranian Oil Company. Production was sold to the individual members of the consortium according to their stake in this group. Profits were shared equally between the companies and the Government.

Anglo-Iranian, which during the dispute had changed its name to British Petroleum, received a 40 per cent stake in the consortium and the remaining equity was shared between eight of the major international oil companies. In 1955 a grouping of American independent oil companies obtained a 5 per cent holding in the consortium through the Iricon agency. The major groups involved in the consortium were Royal Dutch Shell (14 per cent) Standard Oil of California, Esso, Mobil, Gulf and Texaco (7 per cent each) and Compagnie Française des Pétroles (CFP) with 6 per cent.

At the end of the dispute Iran still had not gained a better deal than the 50/50 profit sharing agreement that was the basic cause of the dissatisfaction that led to nationalisation. The oil companies had initially opposed the 50/50 sharing agreement in Venezuela as they rightly guessed that other oil producing nations would demand similar treatment, but it did provide them with side benefits that made the imposition of the system in other parts of the oil producing world less unpleasant.

Royalties could not be offset against taxation in the oil company's home country. Royalties remained at the same levels and the 50/50 profit split was achieved through increasing the taxation, which under the complex double taxation agreements enable the companies to offset tax paid in the producing countries against tax liabilities in their home country.

To make the system workable the companies needed a basic level on which to calculate their tax liability. The Arabian American Oil Company (Aramco) set the ball rolling in Saudi Arabia in 1950 by "posting" publicly the prices at which they would export crude oil. Aramco then deducted the cost of production and royalty payments and paid half the remaining sum to the Government in the form of income tax.

The introduction of the posted price system marked a new period of prosperity for both oil companies and producer nations. World demand for oil was rising and the Korean War had put pressure on crude supplies and had stimulated demand for tankers.

At the same time American imports of oil were growing—mainly because the smaller independent US-based oil companies were beginning to look outside the United States for cheap supplies. The independents searched for concessions alongside the valuable territories held by the majors. In doing so, the way was opened for the producing nations to impose more favourable terms under which new territory for exploration would be distributed.

Aminoil, a group owned by Phillips, Signal and several other independents scored the first major success in 1948 by gaining a concession in part of the Neutral Zone, an area between Kuwait and Saudi Arabia. Aminoil won the concession in the part governed by Kuwait. Getty Oil acquired the rights on the Saudi side of the line in the following year—for the first time the independents were in competition with the majors. The decision to allow the American Iricon group (Atlantic Richfield, American Independent Oil, Signal, Getty, Continental and Sohio) a stake in the Iran operators' consortium gave these companies a status that they had never had before.

Mattei of ENI

French and Italian companies had also joined the race for concessions and like the American independents were not concerned if their agreements gave the producer nations slightly better terms than could be obtained by the majors. There was little concern within the majors since the independents faced considerable risks entering new and unproven reserves.

French oil companies were principally concerned with the exploration and exploitation of new reserves found in Algeria and it was left to the Italians to take the really aggressive stand against the established order. Enrico Mattei, the guiding light of ENI, the Italian state energy concern, proved the biggest thorn in the side of the majors. During the isolation of Iran following the nationalisation of Anglo-Iranian, Mattei's first instinct had to be step in and snap up part of the production. He was persuaded to abide by the oil industry embargo on Iran and in return had expected that his restraint would be rewarded by a share in the operating consortium, formed after that dispute had ended. ENI was excluded from the initial consortium and to add insult to injury was forced to stand by and watch the American independents gain a valuable share of the Iranian oil play in 1955.

Always a maverick, Mattei entered negotiations with the National Iranian Oil Co for new concessions outside the rich areas held by the consortium. In 1957, ENI and NIOC evolved the first of a new breed of concession agreements in which the state oil company entered as a working partner. ENI would meet all the initial exploration costs and would only recover a half share from NIOC if a successful find was made. In addition, the Iranian Government would take 75 per cent of the total profits of the joint company which was known as the Société Irano-Italienne des Pétroles (Sirip).

ENI failed to find oil but the precedent had been set and Standard Oil of Indiana took up an offshore concession on similar terms and across the Gulf, the Arabian Oil Co, a Japanese-owned group, acquired an offshore concession in the Neutral Zone which gave the Governments of Saudi Arabia and Kuwait each a ten per cent share in the equity of the operating company.

The majors had not been idle during this time. BP's exclusion from its Iranian source of crude had forced the crash development programme in Kuwait, Iraq and Qatar. Between 1950 and 1957 production in Kuwait increased from 345,000 barrels a day to 1,140,000 b/d; from 136,000 b/d to 452,000 b/d in Iraq and from 34,000 b/d to 138,000 b/d in Qatar during the same period.

Governments in the producing countries encouraged the gradual erosion of the majors' position by granting concessions to the independents. There was still no real major unrest about their overall position in relation to the oil companies.

World oil consumption was also beginning to surge forward. In Europe the first signs were appearing that governments might be prepared to drop their protection of high cost coal industries to make way for cheaper oil supplies and in Japan the economic explosion was being kindled and, as in Europe, the Japanese were attracted by the prospect of low cost oil. When Britain, France and Israel went to war with Egypt in 1957 and the Suez Canal was closed a really serious threat was posed to the entire economic growth of the principal manufacturing nations.

Along with overall growth, the producing nations were beginning to reap the benefits of the widespread implementation of the 50/50 profit sharing agreements. Their revenue from each barrel of oil exported rose sharply, as illustrated in Saudi Arabia where the state income from each barrel of crude oil exported by Aramco rose from only 17 cents in 1946 to 28 cents in 1950. After reaching 96 cents a barrel in 1955, it settled at 80 cents in 1957. With the American owners of the consortium continually opening up new production areas, output increased from 579,000 barrels a day in 1950 to 990,000 barrels a day in 1957. Government revenues from oil soared from $59m to $298m in 1957.

Significance of Suez

The importance of the Suez Canal to the international shipping industry, and particularly to the oil industry, since its opening in 1869 cannot be over emphasised. Marcus Samuel was quick to realize the economic benefits in terms of reducing the voyage time between Europe and the Far East. The Canal has exercised a huge influence on the development of both the oil and shipping industries, but just as the Canal offered advantages to the oil companies in the transport of their oil from the major producing nations in the Middle East, it has also had a profound effect on international trading patterns.

Following its opening in 1869 the attractions of the high latitude great circle routes was reduced dramatically and heralded the decline of the sailing ship era. The distance between London and Tokyo for instance via the Cape of Good Hope is some 14,600 miles but via the Canal the distance is only some 8,600 miles.

The Canal also reduced the distance between the UK and Australia by about 1,000 miles and brought Bombay 4,000 miles closer. It was inevitable that shipowners would switch their growing fleet of steamships away from the route round the Cape of

Good Hope and as a result of this change the ports of the Mediterranean once again were brought on to one of the major routes of
international trade.

Indeed, so important was the Suez Canal to the international
shipping industry that for almost a century shipowners built few
vessels which exceeded its draught limits which were increased
by less than 3 feet over the fifty years 1908 to 1958. The closure of
the waterway during the Arab-Israeli conflict of 1956-57 was to
exert a massive influence on the whole established pattern of the
international oil transport system, of sizes of ships (particularly
the birth of the very large crude carrier) with their consequent
demands on new technologies and developments.

The movement to the larger ships had already begun on a small
scale. Doubts about the future of the Canal located in a highly
politically sensitive area promoted the major oil companies and
the independent owners to evaluate the requirements for ships
passing south round the Cape of Good Hope. Implicit in this
requirement was the need for larger vessels if oil was to remain a
competitively priced source of energy.

In the post-World War II period vessels of 20,000 tons dwt made
their appearance and with the shift in refinery locations about 75
por cent of tanker tonnage in the late nineteen-forties and early
nineteen-fifties was switched to carry crude with the balance
engaged in products trading. The fact that tankers were no longer
required to carry a varied assortment of products, limited by
market requirements accelerated the trend towards the larger
ships. Vessels with ten cargo tanks and later with only five (split
into fifteen compartments) and greater deadweight capacities
began to emerge so that in 1951 80 per cent of vessels in the
tanker fleet were less than 17,000 tons dwt but five years later
more than half the total fleet were in excess of this tonnage. In
1955 Shell placed orders for a series of tankers in the 38,000-
42,000 tons dwt range which at the time ranked as the largest
merchant ships ever built in a British yard while under construction at the same time was the largest ship ever to be built for the oil
trade, the Spyros Niarchos of 47,750 tons dwt.

These and other ships were soon afterwards eclipsed by orders
placed in Japan by the Ludvig Group which contracted two tank-.

ers of 82,000 tons dwt. But until the closure of the Canal the growth·
in tanker size suffered from two major constraints apart from the
overriding factor that, for most purposes, there was no real incentive to increase size while the Canal remained open. First were the
practical difficulties involved in constructing unloading terminals
in Europe and elsewhere capable of accommodating large tankers at the rate which the Arab Israeli conflict was later to demand.
Secondly the Suez Canal had a draught restriction of some 36 feet
limiting access to ships of less than 45,000 tons dwt.

The Suez closure in 1956, however, was to change the whole
concept and thinking of the oil and shipping industries and
accelerate the trend towards the larger ships. Closure of the
Canal meant that tankers had to be re-routed south via the Cape of
Good Hope and some of the independent owners, notably Onassis, Niarchos and Livanos were in a position to capitalise on the
crisis. Onassis, for instance who in the early part of the 1950's had
found himself in difficulties with the oil companies, had been
forced to lay up ships because he was unable to obtain new
charters as the old ones expired. Closure of the Canal, however,
led to a veritable scramble for ships and freight rates rose
astronomically.

The United States Government considered that during the closure
of the Canal double the amount of tonnage would be required to
ensure the continued flow of oil. Shipowners like Onassis who had
foreseen the requirement for the larger ships and with tankers idle
were in a position to plug the tonnage gap. Others sought to
re-negotiate existing charter contracts in order to exploit the
sharp rise in rates. Onassis himself estimated that his profits
alone arising out of the Suez crisis were valued at between $60m
and $70m.

This heady situation was not to last, however, but its repercussions were to set the pattern for the development of the oil transportation industry for many years ahead. The Canal's closure,
however, did remove the major constraint on the already percep-
tible movement of the shipping industry toward larger ships. In
1956 a considerable volume of orders were placed for ships of
more than 100,000 tons. The era of the supertanker had arrived.
By 1963 ships of 130,000 tons had appeared and three years later
tankers of 150,000 tons had emerged. This acceleration toward

much larger ships was also given impetus by the development of ports in Europe capable of accepting such large ships and also by the introduction of refineries constructed adjacent to deep water.

Over supply

The oil and shipping industry had perhaps to some extent over-reacted to the Suez debacle. Large quantities of new tonnage had been constructed, and it was widely believed that the now nationalised waterway could not be run by the Egyptians and that the time required for the clearing of the canal after the sinking of blockade ships would ensure that rates would remain high. This proved to be erroneous.

So buoyant had been the independent owners that some had contracted vessels on charter to oil companies at the prevailing high rates which the oil companies were forced to accept since they too shared similar doubts about the ability of the Egyptians to run the canal efficiently. Charters covering a period of years were fixed on ships which were not due to enter service until 1960.

But the Canal took only a few months to clear with the result that there was a glut of tonnage available and the bottom fell out of the market. The oil companies which had entered into long term charters with the independent owners on rates prevailing at the peak of the crisis were paying in some cases double the rate which applied when the ships entered service while the tanker owners were unable to find employment for them in the carriage of oil. Some had to be converted to carry grain and others were laid up. About 1 million tons of tanker tonnage was laid up between 1959-66 and a substantial number of older ships were scrapped.

It was not only in the tanker market that there was a substantial over supply problem. The efforts of the independent oil companies to develop the concessions they had won were proving far more successful than even they had hoped in their wildest dreams. The French exploration effort in Algeria proved highly effective and despite the revolutionary war, these finds were quickly put into production. Between 1957 and 1967, Algerian output rose from low volumes to 39m tons a year. Across the

Sahara, Nigeria was emerging as a major oil producing state. Shell and BP operating as a consortium had poured millions of pounds into the exploration effort since the end of World War II. Long years of disappointment were rewarded in 1956 when the first of a series of major discoveries was found and by 1958 the first oil was exported and by 1967 exports went up to almost 17m tons. In the Persian Gulf the small sheikhdom of Abu Dhabi was undergoing a dramatic transformation as a group led by British Petroleum found oil in the desert and offshore.

Suez had also concentrated the oil companies' attention on finding new sources of supply outside the Middle East. Success in Algeria stimulated the exploration effort in neighbouring Libya. By the ninteen-sixties preparations were made for large-scale production. Output in 1961 was less than a million tons a year but by 1967 it had soared to over 83m tons a year.

But immediately after Suez most of these new oil provinces were not contributing significantly to world production. Product prices rose in the United States and the oil companies responded in the Gulf by increasing posted prices. At this stage posted prices represented the real export cost and in these circumstances it seemed logical that higher product prices led to higher posted prices. But once the posted prices had risen it became apparent that the oil companies had misjudged the situation. Sizeable discounts largely wiped out the effect of higher product prices and the only real effect of the posted prices was to increase the revenue of the producer Governments.

With large new parcels of oil production scheduled to come on the market the companies were faced with the prospect of finding new outlets for their crude or suffering the hardship caused by a major glut in the market place. European consumption had been gathering pace and by 1960 had topped 200 million tons annually. Japanese consumption was beginning to reflect the headlong rush to convert industry and electricity production to oil burning. Imported oil accounted for just over one third of that country's 86 million tons coal equivalent energy requirements.

OPEC arrives

The discounts offered on the posted prices began to grow larger and at this stage the American Government took the important step of placing mandatory controls on crude oil imports. The Eisenhower Administration's decision in 1959 wrecked the oil companies' plans to replace high cost indigenous production with low cost imports. The Americans had seen the effects of disruption of oil supplies on the European economy and was growing anxious that moves to further imported supplies would make American oil as vulnerable as its European counterpart.

In imposing the import restrictions the Americans preserved their own high cost oil fields but created a world surplus of oil that ultimately led to the formation of the Organisation of Petroleum Exporting Countries (OPEC). Without the American markets the independents turned their attention to finding alternative outlets for their new sources of crude. In Europe they entered the market in competition with the major companies and their efforts to secure a foothold put considerable pressure on product prices.

To add to the problems in Europe caused by the intervention of the independents, came small quantities of oil from the Soviet Union. The free operation of the market demanded that prices should be reduced but the companies were hesitant since this would have meant a further cutback in posted prices. In 1959 under pressure from the consuming governments the oil companies had reduced posted prices, and in doing so the revenues of the producer governments. Despite protests the prices stayed down but the companies recognised the disruptive effect this had on their relations with governments and would only repeat the process as a last resort. But in 1960 they could not resist market pressures and the promptings of the European governments any longer and for the second time reduced the posted prices.

Threatened with new losses of revenue representatives from Venezuela, Iran, Kuwait and Saudi Arabia met in Iraq to discuss their problems. From this meeting grew OPEC. The oil companies partly restored the cuts but they had taken heed of the dangers posed by the Iraq meeting and the formation of OPEC, and have never made any new attempts to reduce posted prices. The result has been that these posted levels have become purely tax reference prices and the actual export price of crude can be up to 40 per cent below the posted price.

Chart 3/1: 'Breakdown' of average barrel in W. Europe

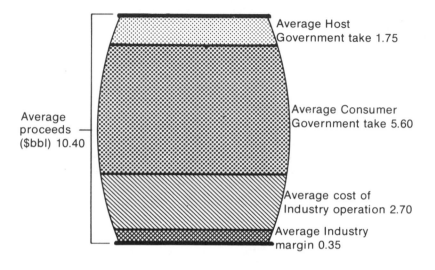

Average Host
Government take 1.75

Average
proceeds
($bbl) 10.40

Average Consumer
Government take 5.60

Average cost of
Industry operation 2.70

Average Industry
margin 0.35

Table 3/1: Payments per Barrel, Seven Countries, 1957-1970

(cents, U.S.)

Year	Kuwait*	Saudi Arabia*	Iran	Iraq	Others	Total P. Gulf	Libya	Venezuela
1957	79.6	88.2	86.8	93.1	91.3	85.7	—	103.0
1958	81.7	81.7	89.0	88.9	92.4	84.8	—	111.6
1959	77.8	75.8	83.6	82.4	89.1	79.8	—	98.4
1960	76.4	75.0	80.1	78.6	88.7	77.7	—	89.2
1961	74.4	75.5	75.8	76.5	87.2	75.8	62.7	92.9
1962	74.8	76.5	74.5	76.7	83.4	75.9	64.7	97.2
1963	74.3	78.7	79.7	80.7	79.2	77.9	65.0	98.6
1964	76.9	82.0	81.8	80.1	58.4	78.4	62.9	95.4
1965	78.9	83.2	82.9	81.7	57.7	79.5	83 8	95.6
1966	78.4	83.4	83.2	81.3	81.0	81.1	87.0	95.8
1967	79.3	84.8	82.5	85.2	81.5	82.6	101.6	102.2
1968	80.5	87.8	83.7	90.7	84.1	85.0	100.7	101.4
1969	80.8	87.1	80.9	91.4	87.0	84.3	100.0	103.6
1970	82.9	88.3	80.8	94.2	88.7	85.8	109.0	109.2

  * Including half Neutral Zone.

Source: Petroleum Press Service, Sept. 1971, p. 327

The large discounts that were available to users of crude oil strengthened the swing away from the use of coal in the major industrial nations. In 1960, coal still accounted for more than 50 per cent of the world's energy requirements of 3,058 million tons of oil equivalent. Europe gained 61 per cent of its fuel requirements from coal and only 32 per cent from oil and in Japan coal accounted for 54 per cent and oil 36 per cent. Only in North America did oil dominate the market providing 44 per cent of the requirements compared with 23 per cent by coal.

In just five years oil accounted for almost all the growth in energy demand and at the same time made considerable inroads into coal's traditional markets. The change from solid to liquid fuels was most pronounced in Japan where oil consumption almost trebled during this period to account for almost 59 per cent of the country's energy needs. Expressed in real terms, the Japanese consumption of coal moved ahead very slightly but its contribution to the overall energy mix slumped dramatically. The European switch to oil was rapid but nowhere near as pronounced as in Japan. By 1965 oil burning accounted for 48 per cent of Europe's energy consumption and coal had fallen to just under 45 per cent.

The developing nations stayed outside the scramble to convert to oil and in the United States the fuel mix remained almost unchanged, with oil and natural gas dominating the market and coal accounting for just over 20 per cent. Whether this no-change situation would have occurred if US consumers had been given access to cheap imported oils is debatable. During this period the international oil industry had no problems in meeting all the demands made on it and with new fields coming into production almost daily, capacity remained consistently at 20 per cent above the soaring demand.

Freight ups and downs

While the shipping industry had continued to experience relatively low freight rates following the 1956 Suez closure and the consequent overtonnaging which followed, the growth in the consumption of oil had continued so that by 1964 oil represented about 50 per cent of total world seaborne freight. The 640m tons transported in 1962 represented an increase of approximately 40 per cent on the previous three years. Voyage charter rates in mid-1964 were at Worldscale 50 but by the end of the year had reached Worldscale 105 dropping sharply again by the middle of 1965 and rising again to Worldscale 120 at the turn of the year.

Although the decline which then took place continued with a slight rise again in the autumn of 1966, the overall trend was downwards reaching a low of Worldscale 40 in March 1967. It was 1963 when the Japanese shipbuilding industry—which now dominates the world's construction capacity for large tankers and bulk carriers—presented the world with a foretaste of what was to come. In the Spring of that year, the Japanese shipbuilding industry quoted prices sufficiently low to shock its competitors. This was a reflection of the tremendous rationalisation of the country's shipbuilding industry promoted by the Japanese Government in the late 1950s which has resulted in the reduction in the major shipbuilding groups from about 50 to 13. The Japanese, appreciating the benefits of the economies of scale in the operation of large units building standard design ships on a series production basis, introduced their lower prices both as an inducement to ordering and to meet the growing demand for larger tankers.

Closure of the Suez Canal as a result of the 1967 Six Day War produced a predictable reaction in the freight markets but at the same time ushered in a dramatic alteration in the pattern of oil transportation.

Tankers transporting crude from the Persian Gulf to Europe faced a round trip of about 22,000 miles and lasting some 65 days via the Cape of Good Hope while the round trip via Suez required only 40 days and involved a total distance of 12,500 miles. The freight rates continued to rise sharply soon after the outbreak of hostilities and continued their upward movement well into the second part of that year.

Indeed, within a few days the rate of £1.15 per ton for voyages via the canal to Europe from the Persian Gulf rose to a level of £10 per ton for the journey round the Cape. Rates, however, did not achieve the same peak which had been experienced during the previous crisis when spot rates reached a high of 253 per cent above the flat rate. In the 1967 crisis the spot rate at its peak was only just over 90 per cent higher. The reason for this apparently paradoxical situation was that at the beginning of 1967 a large section of tanker tonnage was available, whereas in the previous period tankers had been in short supply.

Although the canal has remained closed—though recently schemes have been advanced for its re-opening and improvement—rates declined once again and dropped to their spring 1967 level in the early part of 1969. The effect of these high tanker freights on market prices was cushioned from the oil companies point of view by the imposition of special Suez surcharges of products in some countries.

Later that year the margin between supply and demand for tankers had disappeared and at the end of 1969, as a result of the growth in consumption throughout the world for oil demand for tonnage increased again. The Six Day War with the second closure of this vital waterway within a decade, underlined the requirement for much larger ships to transport the crude from the Persian Gulf to Europe and the United States. Contracts for ships whose draught was considerably in excess of that in the Suez Canal flooded into the world's shipyards.

At the start of the Arab-Israeli war in 1967 throughout the world there were orders for 30 ships of 200,000 tons deadweight or more. But within a few months the number of VLCCs of 200,000 tons plus was 90 and in 1968, there were 125 tankers of this size either on order or under construction. By the end of 1969 approximately 80 per cent of the total tanker tonnage on order consisted of ships of this class.

The operation of the VLCC round the tip of South Africa despite the longer voyage more than offsets the previously traditional route through the canal with its draught limitations. Since the 1967 crisis the growth in tanker size has continued although a number of operators anxious to preserve flexibility of operation have opted for 250,000 tonners which could make a return voyage to the Persian Gulf in ballast.

Teheran, a turning point

The formation of OPEC curtailed the power of the oil companies in a very limited way. But on September 1, 1969 a young army lieutenant, Muammamor Gadaffi, led an army coup that overthrew King Idris of Libya and set in train a series of events that ultimately led to the restructuring of the whole oil industry in the Middle East and North Africa, and to the $20 barrel of oil. The first action against the oil companies by the new Libyan regime came in May 1970. Gadaffi had been agitating for an increase in posted prices for some time and to support his claim he ordered the companies to reduce production by 800,000 barrels of oil a day and issued his first threat that Libya would not baulk at nationalisation if its demands were not met. Gadaffi was helped in his initial campaign against the oil companies by an event at the other end of the Mediterranean. A bulldozer working close to the Trans Arabian Pipeline (Tapline) in Syria "accidentally" sliced through the line reducing the flow of Saudi Arabian oil to the terminal on the Mediterranean coast by 500,000 barrels a day. In normal circumstances, pipeline fractures can be repaired within a few days, but the Syrian Government waited nearly eight months before it allowed technicians to move in and repair the damage.

The loss of 500,000 barrels a day of short haul crude from the east Mediterranean, coupled with the almost simultaneous loss of 800,000 barrels of Libyan crude put considerable pressure on tanker capacity, pushing up rates by 2 to 2½ times. The Libyans, who had always been able to command a higher price for its crude because of the shorter journey needed to transport the oil to the European markets, incorporated the higher Persian Gulf freight rates into its argument for higher prices. The oil companies countered that this was an exceptional situation and posted prices could not be recalculated on the basis of a freight situation that would not last indefinitely. At the back of their minds was the realisation that if the Libyan freight differential rose sharply, then they would be faced with claims for re-adjustment of prices from the Persian Gulf countries once the freight market eased. Two companies were involved in the negotiations with the Libyans at this stage. Exxon, representing the major company attitude although at this stage not negotiating on behalf of the other groups, offered a two part adjustment in prices: 10 cents a barrel plus a freight differential of 11 cents that could be adjusted according to movements in the freight market. The initial offer was rejected but the Libyans seemed to accept the principle and further talks were planned.

One month later, the Libyans, for the first time successfully exploited the basic difference in interests between the major oil companies and the independents and signed a new pricing agreement with the independent companies led by Occidental. Between them the independents controlled about half the production in Libya and agreed to increase the posted price by 30 cents a barrel. Annual escalations in the posted price and an increase in the 50 per cent income payment rate by between 4 to 8 per cent was also agreed. At this point, the majors could have stood firm and reiterated their policy that such an agreement would only lead to a counter-claim for higher revenues from the Persian Gulf States. In the tight supply situation that faced Europe, the majors were not prepared to test Colonel Gadaffi's nationalisation threat and they agreed to similar terms in October. The companies with interests outside Libya were right in thinking that the Libyan agreement would have repercussions in the Gulf. Iran set the pace by demanding a 16 cents a barrel increase in posted prices, an adjustment in the posted price for heavy crudes and a new 55 per cent income tax rate. Again the companies felt they could not resist the demands.

Success in Libya and Iran boosted the confidence of all the oil exporters and when they met in Venezuela in December 1970 demands were made for an all-round increase in posted prices and rises in the tax rate. The Venezuelan Government set the pace by unilaterally increasing the tax rate from 50 to 58 per cent which in turn spurred Libya to submit a new set of demands to the companies. While OPEC was using its combined negotiating strength, the companies were hampered by their inability to negotiate as a co-ordinated group. The fear of anti-trust legislation in the US kept the companies negotiating as separate entities. The leading companies sounded out the US State Department on its attitude to joint company negotiations to counter the group approach of the producer nations. A favourable ruling by the Justice Department's anti-trust division led to thirteen oil companies with interests in North Africa and the Middle East asking for joint negotiations with OPEC. The original 13 were joined later by another eleven companies. From this action grew the London Policy Group under the chairmanship of Mr Joseph Addison, general manager of Iranian Oil Participants (the consortium of companies operating in Iran). Mr George Piercy, a senior vice-president of the Exxon Corporation, told a US senate foreign relations sub-committee on multi-national companies in February 1974, that the principal function of the London Policy Group was to establish the terms of reference for the teams negotiating separate price deals in Teheran and Libya, since it had become apparent that there was no opportunity of conducting one set of negotiations with all the producers. The group also helped in the selection of technical experts to accompany the negotiators and liaise with a similar policy making group in New York. Mr Piercy denied that it was a secret organisation and emphasised that "at all times each company retained its individual freedom of action to pursue its individual course".

Once the negotiations with the producer states in the Gulf began in January 1971, the companies made it clear they wanted more than just an agreement covering prices. The long term objective was a stable price system that would not be subject to "leapfrogging" if other countries signed subsequent agreements. The companies offered the Gulf states a 15 cents a barrel increase and the Gulf states countered with a claim for 54 cents. A compromise agreement of 35 cents a barrel with annual upward adjustments of 2½ per cent to compensate for inflation and an annual five cents per barrel a year annual increase over the five years of the agreement. Immediately afterwards, the companies' negotiating team moved to Tripoli and concluded an agreement, which, as the companies had hoped, did not spark off new demands for similar terms from the Gulf producers. Both the Teheran and Tripoli agreements were modified to take account of two devaluations of the dollar that hit the producer nations' oil revenues.

The success of the OPEC nations in the Teheran and Tripoli price negotiations came as something of a shock to the producer states. They had expected a stronger response from the companies and some kind of support for their position from the United States and European governments. But the time for government intervention passed once the Teheran agreement had been signed. OPEC had proved its strength and as the world oil supply situation became even tighter they prepared a new offensive—this time a campaign to win a stake in the concessions of the major oil companies. The major break-through came when the Aramco consortium conceded the principle of Government participation in Spring 1972 but an agreement giving the Government a 25 per cent stake rising to 51 per cent by 1982 was not finalised until the end of the year. Qatar, Abu Dhabi and Kuwait also signed similar agreements, but the Kuwaiti National Assembly refused to ratify the contract with British Petroleum and Gulf Oil. Meanwhile, Libya had resumed its pace-setting role and demanded immediate 51 per cent participation, and again split the companies' united front by concluding an agreement on these lines with Occidental and the other independents operating in Libya. This time, the majors decided to resist the Libyans as acquiesence to the Occidental-type deal would have re-opened the whole question of participation in the Middle East at a time when BP and Gulf were trying to re-negotiate participation without writing off the previous agreements with Saudi Arabian, Abu Dhabi and Qatar. The Libyans had already demonstrated they would take over company installations and in 1972 had nationalised British Petroleum's half share in the Sarir oilfield in retaliation for the UK's failure to prevent the occupation of the Tumbs Islands in the Gulf by Iranian troops. Libya arbitrarily took a 51 per cent stake in the major operations in Libya in 1973, an action which led to threats of legal action from the oil corporations against buyers of the oil.

By early 1973, Kuwait's decision to conserve its production by limiting production to 3m barrels a day, combined with further cutbacks in Libya, had produced the first real signs of a serious supply crisis. The United States was suffering selected shortages and the margin between supply and demand in Europe was wafer-thin. Small amounts of participation oil began to seep on to the market at close to the posted price for Gulf oil—20 to 30 per cent above the tax paid cost of supplies. The Gulf countries called for a radical re-negotiation of the Teheran agreement, and the London Policy Group was re-convened in an effort to save the prices pact. At a series of meetings in Vienna the companies offered a 45 cents a barrel increase in posted prices and a new formula for compensating for the effects of inflation. The OPEC nations demanded a $3 a barrel (100 per cent increase) also subject to a new inflation formula. The companies called for a two week adjournment to reconsider their position—it was in fact the last time the two sides met jointly to discuss the world prices structure.

Chapter Four
The Supply Crisis

Egyptian commandos and tanks began to roll across the Suez Canal to attack Israeli positions on the Bar Lev line on October 6, 1973. Simultaneously, Israeli forces, entrenched on the Golan heights, came under fire from the Syrians and were driven back. The apparently invincible Israeli armed forces were caught unprepared, and the initial successes of the Arab armies captured headlines around the world. Even before the Israelis halted the Arab advance, it was obvious that the fourth Middle East conflict in twenty-five years was to be protracted and bitterly fought, unlike the earlier routs of the Arabs in 1967 and 1956. For months beforehand there had been speculation that the Arab nations would use their "oil weapon" against the United States, in particular, and other nations sympathetic to the Zionist cause. The speculation was well founded. On the day following the outbreak of war, the Iraq Government (which had despatched troops to fight alongside the Syrian Army) fired the first shot in the "oil war" by nationalising the American interests in the Basrah Petroleum Company. This, and the events that followed, precipitated the most fundamental change in the relationship between the oil producers, the oil companies and the Governments of the major oil consuming countries in the history of the oil industry.

Basrah Petroleum, operating in the south of the country, had escaped the attention of the Iraq Government when it nationalised the Iraq and Mosul Petroleum companies in June 1972 and March 1973 respectively. The Basrah concern was an affiliate of IPC, with identical shareholders. The American stockholders were Exxon and Mobil, which together held a 23.75 per cent share. Iraq's Baathist Government, amongst the most militant in the Middle East, left no doubt that the American companies were being punished because of the United States' support for Israel. The other shareholders in Basrah, British Petroleum, the French oil company CFP, Partex, the organisation which represented the Gulbenkian interests, and Shell were left untouched, although later in October, Iraq also nationalised 60 per cent of Shell's holding in BPC—the equivalent of the Dutch stake in the group. According to the Iraqis, this was further evidence of their intention to limit their action to those companies based in countries supporting Israel. The Iraq National Oil Company took over the Exxon, Mobil and Royal Dutch interests in BPC, which had been producing an average of 786,000 b/d in September, and agreed that the expansion of the southern Rumaila and Zubair oilfields could proceed to reach BPC's target of producing 1.6m b/d by 1976. The two American companies and Royal Dutch were told that they would be compensated for the takeover of their assets.

The Iraqis were also the first to suffer any loss of oil revenues because of the war. On the day it nationalised Exxon and Mobil, the loading of Iraqi oil piped through Syria to the 700,000 b/d capacity Banias terminal on the Mediterranean coast was suspended because of threats to the security of the installations. The fears were well justifed when, four days later, an Israeli naval force, supported by air cover, bombarded the terminal and put half of its twenty-four storage tanks out of action. The Israelis carried out a similar raid on the Syrian terminal at Tartus, the main export point for 100,000 b/d of Syrian oil, and destroyed the country's only refinery at Homs. Aramco's subsidiary company, Tapline, the operator of a 500,000 b/d pipeline for moving oil from Saudi Arabia to the Sidon terminal in Lebanon, was forced to reduce the flow of oil by half. The line runs close to the Golan Heights, and there was acute danger of the line being breached in the fighting. Iraq's other principal pipeline taking 450,000 b/d to Tripoli in the Lebanon, remained untouched. The immediate loss of exporting capacity to the southern European nations who relied upon Middle Eastern supplies piped through the war zone was about 1m b/d. Although the Tripoli and Sidon terminals in the Lebanon remained open, the number of oil companies and shipowners who were prepared to risk their vessels in these waters was comparatively few. Freight rates, which had been improving steadily throughout 1973, rose even higher in the early weeks of the conflict, which tended to increase demand particularly for single voyages. Rates for single voyages on the Mullion World Scale Index rose from W396 in the first week of October to W440 three weeks later.

The oil weapon

While the fighting continued in Sinai and on the Golan Heights, the leaders of the Arab oil producing nations were investigating the best ways to use their powerful "oil weapon". Before revealing their strategy to the world, the Arab members of the Organisation of Petroleum Exporting Countries (OPEC) were committed to a revision of crude oil prices. The Arab members in the Persian Gulf, together with Iran, met in Kuwait. The six nations—Saudi Arabia, Kuwait, Iraq, Abu Dhabi, Qatar and Iran—had been pressing the International oil companies operating in the Gulf area for a revision of the five year Teheran pricing agreement signed in 1971. The producing nations had seen the prices for the oil they had acquired under the participation agreements exceed the revenues from the supplies lifted by the major oil companies under the posted price system as regulated by the Teheran agreement. The first request for a fundamental redrafting of the agreement was made at a meeting at OPEC headquarters in Vienna early in October. The oil companies had been shocked by the size of the OPEC demands and had requested a fortnight's break in the negotiations to allow them time to study the implications of the new demands on the world oil pricing structure.

OPEC was unhappy with this response. A number of States thought the companies were merely playing for time and, in unofficial discussions, began to work out a new unilateral pricing policy that would make individual countries directly responsible for their own crude oil prices, and to exclude the oil companies from any part of this cost fixing exercise. The companies were unaware of this change in attitude by the producers and went ahead with their detailed study of the implications of higher prices. They were caught completely unawares by the OPEC announcement from Kuwait on October 16 that crude oil prices would rise by more than 70 per cent as a result of unilateral price-fixing arrangements that would replace the Teheran pact.

Table 4/1: Posted Prices and Government Take

(US dollars per barrel)

		Posted Price		Government Take	
		Oct. 1	*Oct. 16*	*Oct. 1*	*Oct. 16*
Arabian Light	34 °	3.011	5.119	1.77	3.05
Iranian Light	34 °	2.995	5.091	1.75	3.02
Iraq Basrah	35 °	2.977	5.061	1.74	3.00
Kuwait	31 °	2.884	4.903	1.71	2.94
Abu Dhabi Murban	39 °	3.084	6.045	1.82	3.58
Qatar Dukham	40 °	3.143	5.343	1.81	3.15
Libya	40 °	4.604	8.925	2.83	5.45

The prices in this table include premiums for low sulphur crude and in the case of Libya a "Suez Canal Closed" element and a freight premium.

Source: Petroleum Economist

The Kuwait meeting decided that the market price for Arabian light crude should be $3.65 a barrel—17 per cent above the best prices obtained by the State oil companies in sales of participation crude. It was decreed that the posted price, on which government tax revenues are calculated, should be 40 per cent above the market price as this was the differential between the market price and the posted price at the time of the Teheran agreement. The Algerians quickly followed the example of their OPEC partners, and Venezuela implemented a 56 per cent rise in its tax reference prices on November 1. Nigeria raised its posted price to $8.310 a barrel, including a low sulphur premium of $1.30 a barrel, a Suez factor of 15.1 cents and a freight premium of 39.2 cents. This move was followed in November by Indonesia, which increased the sale price of all its crudes to $6.00 a barrel, with the exception of supplies from the Tarakan field which was raised to $6.23 a barrel. Pertamina, the state oil company, controls the entire production in Indonesia and the posted price system is not in operation.

The international oil companies were horrified at the prospect of unilateral pricing. Although none of them was publicly critical of the new arrangement, in private they pointed out that higher

Table 4/2: Crisis cutbacks

Millions of Barrels per Day	Sept. 1973	Oct. 1973	% Change Oct. vs. Sept.	Nov. 1973	% Change Nov. vs. Sept.	Est. Dec. 1973	% Change Dec. vs. Sept.	Est. Jan. 1974	% Change vs. Sept.
Saudi-Arabia (Aramco)	8.3	7.6	— 9	6.1	—27	6.4	—23	7.7	— 7
Kuwait (KOC)	3.2	2.8	—13	2.4	—26	2.3	—28	2.5	—22
Neutral Zone	0.6	0.5	—15	0.4	—24	0.4	—23	0.5	—17
Arab States	2.6	2.5	— 4	2.1	—19	2.0	—24	2.3	—12
Algeria	1.1	1.0	— 7	0.9	—20	0.9	—22	0.9	—18
Libya	2.3	2.4	— 4	1.8	—23	1.8	—23	1.9	—17
Iraq	2.2	1.7	—21	2.0	— 7	2.1	—1.0	2.1	— 5
Other*	0.4	0.2	—50†	0.1	—75†	0.2	—50†	0.4	0
Total Arab production	20.7	18.7	—10	15.8	—24	16.1	— 22	18.3	—12

* Egypt, Syria and other North African Arab.
† Affected by war damage.

Source: Esso Petroleum

prices had been based on the return for participation oil which accounted for only 2.5 per cent of production in the Middle East. Some oil company executives found it difficult to believe that after more than sixty years of operations in the Persian Gulf, the oil companies no longer had any role to play in the price fixing machinery. Stunned by this action, the companies were to receive another body blow. The following day the Organisation of Arab Petroleum Exporting Countries (OAPEC), also meeting in Kuwait, held a short formal meeting and then announced that its members would cut oil production by a minimum of 5 per cent on the September output level and make further 5 per cent cuts at monthly intervals. They said, in an official statement, that the production cutbacks would continue until Israel withdrew its forces from all the Arab territories occupied in June 1967 and restored "the legal rights of the Palestinian people". Saudi Arabia set the pace and reduced its output by 10 per cent—a lead that was followed by all the major Arab exporting countries with the exception of Iraq. An embargo was also placed on all oil exports to the United States and to Holland. A 10 per cent cutback represented slightly less than 2 million b/d combined with the 1 million b/d that was also lost through the Mediterranean terminals.

Tanker chaos

The unprecedented measures implemented by the Persian Gulf area producers wreaked havoc with the tanker markets. Indeed, the use of the "oil weapon" brought about the most calamitous fall in rates ever experienced. This came as a most unwelcome reversal to the shipping industry which, despite periodic ups and downs, has benefited from the relentless expansion in oil consumption throughout the world. Eighteen months before the shipping industry was thrown into turmoil, rates in many trades had reached a nadir and the prospect of a sharp improvement appeared most unlikely. However, in the autumn of 1972 world trade began to expand in response to increased economic activity in the major developed nations and, as a result, freight rates began to rise. In the tanker sector, the oil supply situation in the United States towards the end of 1972 and early 1973 gave further impetus to tonnage demands and during the first ten months of 1973, single voyage rates for medium sized tankers (those up to 100,000 tons dwt) rose from Worldscale 115 to Worldscale 450

Chart 4/1: Tanker market freight index

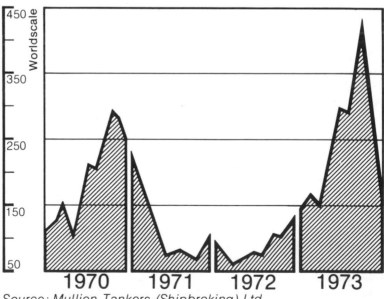

Source: Mullion Tankers (Shipbroking) Ltd

for a voyage from the Persian Gulf to the UK and Europe. Rates for very large crude carriers rose from Worldscale 80 at the beginning of January to Worldscale 420 by October.

A similar pattern was followed in the market for clean tankers—those carrying refined products—and in the final three months of 1973, rates reached Worldscale 800 for a Mediterranean-Black Sea, voyage to Britain-Europe-United States. During the year, a large number of tankers were fixed on three to five year time charters with rate levels for medium-sized ships rising from $3.00-3.500 at the beginning of the year to more than even $6.00 six months later. Rates for very large crude carriers doubled over the same period from $2.50 to $5.00.

The boost given to rates in the early part of the year stemmed from the lifting of import restrictions into the United States. Although the USA generally imports only about 15 per cent of its energy requirements, President Nixon's energy message unleashed American companies on to the market in a desperate attempt to secure early tonnage. The sharp increase in freight market indices also reflected the requirement of the major oil importing countries to replenish stock levels and also, to some extent, their concern over possible interruptions to the output of short haul crude from Libya. Congestions in the Gulf during July did depress single voyage rates for a brief period, but the upward climb was underlined by the general purpose Average Freight Rate Assessment (AFRA) index—based on all rates in any one month—which between May and August rose from Worldscale 143,9 to Worldscale 210.9 and reaching Worldscale 266 in November. The October war and the price increases and production cutbacks, however, were to change the situation almost overnight.

Western Europe imports around 70 per cent of its annual energy consumption, while the proportion imported by Japan is even higher at about 87 per cent. They are therefore extremely vulnerable to reductions in availability of oil. Implicit in this scenario is the reduced requirement for tanker tonnage, particularly since both major oil consuming blocs generally employ about 80 per cent of tanker capacity. The renewal of hostilities pushed single voyage rates to Worldscale 440 during the third week of October. This is equivalent to a cost of some $44.0 in the shipping of a ton of oil from the terminal at Ras Tanura, Saudi Arabia, to Rotterdam. Yet the rate prevailing for the same voyage in April 1972 was $5.40. The realisation of the extent of the production cuts and export embargoes to the United States and Holland led to the market for tonnage virtually disintegrating by the end of the month. Within a matter of days, the tanker market was faced with a surplus of tonnage and rates slumped. Worldscale rates from the Persian Gulf fell to around 120 and later slid to Worldscale 80, and during the first two weeks of December fell to Worldscale 47.5. Owners then had to face up to both shortages and steep price increases for bunker fuels.

Before the production cutbacks imposed by the OAPEC at their October meeting in Kuwait began to be felt in the main consuming countries, a second Ministerial meeting of the Organisation had been summoned for November 4, again in Kuwait. The consumers were still getting their normal deliveries of crude, since the tanker journey from the Gulf to Europe takes over one month, while the voyage to Japan is a little shorter. The ten nation organisation, which represents all the Arab countries with an interest in production or transportation (with the exception of Dubai and Oman) were called to discuss the use of the "oil weapon" to break the deadlock in the ceasefire negotiations on the Suez front. The more militant nations were angry at the intransigence of the Israelis and had no trouble in persuading their partners to step up the production cutbacks to 25 per cent below the September level. The embargo on supplies to Holland and the United States was reaffirmed. Only one country, Iraq, stood out against this policy. Iraqi representatives told the meeting that production cutbacks were "self defeating" since it was impossible to differentiate between friendly, neutral or hostile nations. Their country had already lost sizeable revenues as a result of the closure of the Mediterranean terminals and with an expensive industrialisation programme under way, Iraq could ill afford to lose more oil revenues.

OPEC warning

As well as cutting production by 25 per cent, the meeting warned the consuming countries that there would be further monthly cuts of 5 per cent until progress was made towards a political settlement that recognised the rights of the Palestinians. The cutback meant that production in November averaged 15.8m b/d compared with 20.7m b/d in September. These figures disguise the true situation. Oil companies had been planning to increase their liftings from the September level to meet the increased demand in the peak consumption months of January, February and March. In Saudi Arabia, the Aramco consortium, which had invested in new production and loading facilities, had been scheduled to increase its November output to 9.1m b/d from the 8.2m b/d in September. Instead of higher output, it only lifted 6.1m b/d in November. During that month the only Arab country that did not fulfil its obligation to reduce production by 25 per cent was Iraq. The tanker terminals, damaged by the Israeli raids at the beginning of the war, had been repaired and, with the ceasefire, vessels which had been deterred from entering eastern Mediterranean waters were queueing to pick up cargoes. By the end of the month Iraqi production was back to the 2m b/d output reached before the war. At this stage the only supply shortage in the eastern Mediterranean stemmed from the closure to export traffic of the Israeli pipeline running from Eilat on the Gulf of Aqabar to Ashkelon on the Mediterranean. The 600,000 b/d pipeline was starved of crude as a result of the Arab blockade of shipping through the Bab-el-Mandeb Straits at the entrance to the Red Sea. In December, Saudi Arabia made a further 5 per cent cutback in production but the other OAPEC members continued to hold output at 25 per cent of the September level.

Sheikh Ahmed Zaki Yamani, Saudi Arabia's oil minister, and M. Belaid Abdesselem (his Algerian counterpart) were briefed at the Kuwait meeting to undertake a tour of the principal consuming countries to explain OAPEC policies. The two ministers were accorded receptions normally reserved for Heads of State during their whistle-stop tour of the capital cities of the United States, Japan and Europe. The pair advanced the Arab case with disarming eloquence. The host Governments, who were beginning to feel the cutting edge of the "oil weapon", used the opportunity to point out the damage being inflicted on their respective economies, regardless of whether the nations were classed as friendly, neutral or hostile. Saudi Arabia had already classified its oil customers into these three categories, and nations considered friendly to the Arab cause were given preferential treatment, hostile countries suffered complete embargoes and the neutrals were left in the middle taking what oil was left after the friendly countries secured their share.

The friendly list consisted of Britain, France, Spain, all the Arab states of the Middle East and North Africa, Turkey, Pakistan, Malaysia, India, Brazil and the black African states that had severed diplomatic relations with Israel. Apart from the United States and Holland, a number of other countries were placed on the embargoed list. These included Portugal, South Africa, Rhodesia and South Yemen. The embargo also applied to Caribbean countries with refineries which supply refined products to the United States, or act as trans-shipment centres for crude oil to the United States. The position of Canada was ambiguous, as a proportion of its requirements were shipped through the United States and part of its crude oil imports were refined and the products exported to the United States.

The effect of the production cutbacks on the developed nations made a considerable impression on the two Arabs, and as a result they made the case for a relaxation of the restrictions on output. When the OAPEC members met again at the end of December, the consuming countries had expected the Arabs to announce tightening of the production curbs to 85 per cent of the September output levels. After the intervention of Sheikh Yamani and M. Abdesselem, it was agreed to reduce the restrictions to only 70 per cent of the September level. After the Saudi Arabians had raised their production from 6.1m b/d to 6.4m b/d in December overall production among the Arab states was about 4.6m b/d below the September output and 6.3m b/d below the level of output originally planned by the companies for December. In world terms this was equivalent to an 11 per cent shortfall on the 53m b/d needed by non-Communist countries. The easing of the restrictions in January trimmed production cuts to 2.7m b/d below the September average.

A friendly gesture

OAPEC's friendly gesture in relaxing production restrictions was followed over the Christmas holidays by a meeting of the major producers in the Gulf, including Iran which, like Iraq, had not reduced its daily output. Again the subject was prices. The curb on oil output in the Arab states had played havoc with the prices of the relatively small amounts of oil that were available on the free market. OPEC members had taken advantage of sellers' market conditions and put participation oil up for auction. Reports that Nigeria had placed small parcels of oil on the market and had received bids of more than $20 a barrel were received with incredulity. But, it was pointed out that there was no embargo on supplies from West Africa, and companies in the United States facing massive penalty clauses through failure to deliver were prepared to meet these levels. The strength of the free market was tested by the Iranians, who placed a substantial parcel of oil on the auction lists and received bids of $17 a barrel. Only two years earlier the asking price had been $1.80 a barrel.

Using Saudi Arabian crude as the basis for revising prices, the OPEC countries calculated that the prices being obtained on the free market warranted a 130 per cent increase in the price of crude to the oil companies taking the bulk of Middle East supplies under long term arrangements. The posted price of Saudi Arabian light crude was increased to $11.651 a barrel from the $5.119 set on October 16. Iran, a non-Arab country which had not suffered any fall-off in its income through not taking part in the production cutback, had put the case for even higher prices. This was rejected by the other Gulf countries. However, the task of announcing this unwelcome news to the consumer nations fell to the Shah of Iran. He said that the second major increase in prices

---

Table 4/3: Posted Prices (US Dollar per Barrel)

| | | Oct. 1 | Oct. 16 | Jan. 1 |
		1973	1973	1974
Arabian light	34°	3.011	5.119	11.651
Iranian light	34°	2.995	5.091	11.875
Iraq Basrah	35°	2.977	5.061	11.671
Kuwait	31°	2.884	4.903	11.545
Abu Dhabi Murban	39°	3.084	6.045	12.636
Qatar Dukham	40°	3.143	5.343	12.298
Libya	40°	4.604	8.925	15.768

within two months meant that the cost of crude oil was related to the estimated minimum cost of obtaining energy from alternative sources such as shale oil, tar sands and the extraction of oil from coal.

As the squeeze on deliveries to the consuming nations began to tighten, so the pressure on the international oil companies increased. Apart from Saudi Arabia, which had produced its friendly, neutral and hostile list and had largely taken the job of deciding where the oil was to be shipped out of the hands of the companies, none of the other Arab states gave any guidance other than warning on the perils of breaking the embargo. The companies faced a dilemma. They were urged by the more influential consuming countries, such as Britain, France and Germany, to maintain a high level of deliveries in order to minimise the effects of the crisis on industrial production. But the large multi-nationals had marketing outlets throughout the world, and compliance with these requests would have meant that deliveries to smaller countries would have been cut by up to 50 per cent.

Supply equalisation

Mr Frank McFadzean, Chairman of Shell Transport and Trading, and Deputy Chairman of the Managing Directors of the Royal Dutch Shell Group outlined the company's philosophy in the authoritative Europa supplement, published simultaneously by The Times and three other influential European newspapers in January 1974. He claimed that the oil industry had warned Governments in Europe and Japan that a crisis of supply was likely, although the industry had not foreseen it arising in this particular fashion.

"We do not regard it as being a function of a multi-national enterprise such as ourselves, to start allocating in scarce conditions. . . . On the question of Arab oil we have complied strictly, as we are bound to do, with the destination controls imposed upon us. Where we have got non-destination controlled oil, we will use that to meet the needs of the countries that would otherwise go short. And I don't think that an international enterprise such as ourselves has any alternative," he said.

Table 4/4: Crude Oil Imports by Area of Origin

Half-year figures in thousand metric tons

	Jan-June	Iran	Middle East	North Africa	Other Africa	Carribean Area	Soviet Bloc	Others & Unspecified	Total	% incr. (decr.)
Total										
West Germany	1972	4 588	15 834	21 298	5 255	2 118	1 284	277	50 654	
	1973	6 556	19 653	20 981	5 202	1 174	1 209	167	54 952	
France	1972	3 460	33 336	11 781	6 952	843	728	76	57 226	
	1973	5 906	42 424	9 975	7 181	844	1 754	117	68 201	19.2
UK	1972	6 280	29 230	8 615	5 253	2 957	115	2 940	55 390	
	1973	11 740	27 927	7 796	4 338	2 137	147	2 913	56 998	2.9
Italy	1972	7 849	33 796	12 322	853	666	3 668	154	59 308	
	1973	9 000	33 620	13 000	200	500	2 750	250	59 620	0.5
Netherlands*	1972	6 655	27 943	3 386	5 012	82	—	—	43 078	
	1973	10 000	32 350	2 000	5 500	150	—	—	50 000	16.1
Belgium-Luxg	1972	2 260	11 566	2 093	778	326	224	2 863	20 110	
	1973	2 980	9 970	1 397	486	380	338	3 204	17 957	(—7.1)
Denmark	1972	724	3 634	40	927	—	—	—	5 325	
	1973	988	3 243	196	592	—	—	—	5 019	(—5.7)
Sweden	1972	161	2 150	105	1 705	588	391	67	5 167	
	1973	984	1 314	569	1 392	758	94	—	5 611	8.6
Spain*	1972	1 338	12 268	4 433	888	728	280	—	19 935	
	1973	2 000	14 300	3 000	500	900	300	—	21 000	5.3
Total of above	1972	33 315	169 807	64 073	27 623	8 308	6 690	6 377	316 193	
	1973	50 154	184 811	58 914	25 391	6 843	6 592	6 653	339 358	7.3
Percentage shares	1972	10.5	53.7	20.3	8.7	2.6	2.1	2.0	100.0	
	1973	14.8	54.4	17.4	7.5	2.0	1.9	2.0	100.0	

* Estimated for 1973, on the basis of incomplete official figures

Source: Petroleum Economist

In spite of Mr McFadzean's defence of the oil company policy of sharing out all supplies as fairly as possible through the use of non-embargoed Iranian and Nigerian supplies, countries that have felt themselves deprived of their normal deliveries of crude from these sources, have criticised this policy. The most vocal criticisms have come from Europe, where the shortages caused by the productions restrictions were first experienced. Western Europe relies on the Arab countries for more than 70 per cent of its oil requirements and major consumers, such as France, Italy and Spain are even more dependent on supplies from this source with over 80 per cent of their oil deliveries originating from Arab terminals. Imports from Nigeria and Iran amounted to 7 per cent and 15 per cent respectively of the 14m b/d that were imported from all sources before the crisis.

Central to Europe's oil needs is the Dutch port of Rotterdam and the associated refineries and storage facilities at Europoort. In 1972, the last full year in which figures for normal activity are available, 132m tons of crude oil and products were moved into the port, while 48.8m tons were shipped out again. Rotterdam is the hub of the refining and distribution network for the whole of Northern Europe. A pipeline from Rotterdam—the Rotterdam-Rhine pipeline—moved 19.4m tons of crude oil into West Germany and a further 10m tons were piped from the port to the Belgian refineries around Antwerp. Another pipeline moved about 7m tons of refined products into German industrial centres. The Arab decision to place Holland on the embargoed list was a bitter blow for the whole of Europe. Of the 130m tons of crude imported during 1972 some 94m tons (72.3 per cent) arrived from Arab countries. After allowing for the ever-growing internationally-bonded storage facilities in the area total crude supplied to Holland in 1972 was 77.6m tons. The Dutch market, including oil for ships' bunkers, absorbed 35m tons and the remainder was exported. From the Dutch point of view, the embargo posed serious problems for the industrial life of the Rotterdam area. Although comparatively few people were employed in the five refineries around Rotterdam, more than 80,000 out of a total workforce of almost 400,000 were involved in the associated petro-chemical industry. But for the rest of Europe the situation was equally grave. The huge surplusses in the refining capacity of Rotterdam served Germany, Belgium and Denmark, and helped to balance the range of products in Britain, France

and a number of smaller countries which theoretically had sufficient refining capacity of their own to meet domestic requirements. Capacity of the five refineries is about 92m tons a year but
during 1972 they were running considerably below capacity and
produced only 66m tons. Following the embargo, the Dutch Government suspended publication of production levels, although
the oil companies' equalisation policy meant considerably
larger quantities of Iranian and Nigerian crude being processed
for Dutch domestic consumption. The entrepôt trade was considerably eased by the OAPEC decision to allow crude oil to pass
through Rotterdam to other European destinations, providing
guarantees were given that none of the supplies would find their
way into the Dutch distribution network.

Sunday driving ban

The Dutch, at the centre of the European crisis, were the first to
introduce a ban on Sunday driving, which the Government estimated would save about 10 per cent of weekly petrol consumption. Deliveries of other fuel oil to customers was reduced by 15
per cent. Rationing was not necessary in the initial stages as
Holland had substantially more than the 65 days of stocks
required by the European Economic Community (EEC). The dangers emerging from the embargo forced the Dutch Government
into a serious re-appraisal of its whole energy policy. A Government memorandum proposed a switch-over from oil to natural gas
that would reduce national oil consumption by between 12 and 13
per cent in 1974. The conversion programme was to cost Dutch
florins (D.fl.) 12,000m and would involve the consumption of an
additional 1,500 cubic metres of gas during the first four
months of 1974, rising to 1,800m cubic metres at the end of the
first six months. The Government also earmarked D.fl.
450,000m for expanding indigenous natural gas production
facilities and internal pipelines that would make a further 7,200m
cubic metres of gas available in 1975. Dutch gas consumption,
mainly from the huge Groningen field, was more than 36,000m
cubic metres in 1973. The Government's decision to replace oil
with gas caused some surprise, as only one year earlier experts
had down-graded the gas fields' annual output by 20,000m cubic
metres to 82,500m cubic metres a year. As a result of this down-
ward revision, the Dutch gas concern, Gas Unie, in partnership

Table 4/5:   Oil Movements to and from West European

Half-year figures in thousand metric tons

	Crude oil January to June		Light oils (a) January to June		Medium oils (b) January to June	
	1972	1973	1972	1973	1972	1973
IMPORTS into:—						
W. Germany (d)	50 654	54 952	3 608	4 336	557	547
France	57 226	68 201	988	841	26	26
UK (f)	55 390	56 998	2 762	4 054	783	839
Italy	59 308	59 620	507	523	60	32
Netherlands (e)	43 078	50 000	1 309	2 500	267	250
Belgium-Luxembourg	20 110	17 957	490	450	53	60
Denmark	5 325	5 019	485	571	314	343
Irish Republic (e)	1 180	1 500	140	200	180	150
Total EEC (g)	292 271	314 247	10 289	13 475	2 240	2 247
Sweden	5 167	5 611	1 501	1 489	188	194
Switzerland	2 265	2 760	843	823	16	28
Austria (h)	2 542	2 805	351	519	—	—
Norway	3 027	3 851	372	432	260	215
Finland	3 966	4 018	14	15	18	14
Portugal	1 641	1 552	37	36	—	—
Iceland	—	—	23	35	34	51
Total EFTA (j)	18 608	20 597	3 141	3 349	516	502
Spain (k) (e)	19 935	21 000	37	50	1	1
Total W. Europe	330 814	355 844	13 467	16 874	2 757	2 750
EXPORTS (l) from:—						
W. Germany	—	—	1 023	1 214	39	54
France	—	—	1 255	1 502	312	338
UK (f)	1 430	1 522	1 014	960	625	500
Italy	—	—	2 610	2 780	1 000	1 200
Netherlands (e)	8 880	12 000	3 472	3 750	1 446	1 400
Belgium-Luxembourg	15	165	990	1 250	250	325
Denmark	—	—	312	374	11	18
Irish Republic (e)	—	—	—	—	—	5
Total EEC (g)	10 325	13 687	10 676	11 830	3 683	3 840
Sweden	—	—	246	214	18	6
Switzerland	—	—	—	—	—	—
Austria	—	—	—	—	—	—
Norway	860	909	176	193	—	—
Finland	—	—	51	47	—	—
Portugal	—	—	—	—	42	43
Total EFTA (j)	860	909	473	454	60	49
Spain (k) (e)	—	—	487	600	83	60
Total W. Europe	11 185	14 596	11 636	12 884	3 826	3 949
NET IMPORTS	319 629	341 248	1 831	3 990	—	—
NET EXPORTS	—	—	—	—	1 069	1 199

(a) Mainly gasoline and naphtha, but also including white spirits in some cases.
(b) Mainly kerosine and jet fuel. Figures for UK, Sweden and Norway also include white spirits.
(c) Gas/diesel and fuel oils.
(d) Including shipments of products from East Germany.
(e) The latest figures are estimated on the basis of incomplete official returns.

Source: Petroleum Economist

Countries

Lubricating oils January to June 1972	1973	Black oils (c) January to June 1972	1973	Total crude and major products January to June 1972	1973	Net imports January to June 1972	1973	Per cent incr. (decr.)
51	47	13 007	13 241	67 877	73 123	64 799	69 749	+7.6
25	28	3 496	2 412	61 761	71 508	55 653	65 388	+17.5
250	293	6 415	6 318	65 600	68 502	55 545	60 632	+9.2
115	96	2 070	1 834	62 060	62 105	48 840	49 016	+0.4
265	100	1 549	1 750	46 468	54 600	18 057	21 800	+20.7
213	323	2 495	3 050	23 361	21 840	19 358	16 985	(−12.3)
48	46	5 093	4 962	11 265	10 941	10 120	9 590	(−5.2)
18	—	1 150	1 500	2 668	3 350	2 368	3 145	+32.8
985	933	35 275	35 067	341 060	365 969	274 740	296 305	+7.8
91	74	6 627	6 473	13 574	13 841	12 607	12 969	+2.9
21	26	3 203	2 800	6 348	6 437	6 286	6 330	+0.7
44	50	850	896	3 787	4 270	3 716	4 195	+12.9
31	31	1 165	1 209	4 855	5 738	2 891	3 650	+26.3
40	40	1 446	1 365	5 484	5 452	5 431	5 342	(−1.6)
12	9	172	174	1 862	1 771	1 800	1 712	(−4.9)
3	3	201	233	261	322	261	322	+23.4
242	233	13 664	13 150	36 171	37 831	32 992	34 520	+4.6
31	70	98	130	20 102	21 251	17 627	18 081	+2.6
1 258	1 236	49 037	48 347	397 333	425 051	325 359	348 906	+7.2
184	188	1 832	1 918	3 078	3 374			
311	204	4 230	4 076	6 108	6 120			
365	343	6 621	4 545	10 055	7 870			
110	109	9 500	9 000	13 220	13 089			
308	150	14 305	15 500	28 411	32 800			
151	140	2 597	2 975	4 003	4 855			
9	8	813	951	1 145	1 351			
—	—	300	200	300	205			
1,438	1 142	40 198	39 165	66 320	69 664			
30	36	673	'616	967	872			
2	2	60	105	62	107			
70	74	1	1	71	75			
11	10	917	976	1 964	2 088			
I	I	I	02	60	110			
20	16	—	—	62	59			
134	139	1 652	1 760	3 179	3 311			
14	10	1 891	2 500	2 475	3 170			
1 586	1 291	43 741	43 425	71 974	76 145			
—	—	5 296	4 922	325 359	348 906			
328	55	—	—	—	—			

(f) Crude oil figures include "partly refined petroleum for further refining".
(g) For both years, this includes the full membership as from January 1973.
(h) Crude figures include "products for further treatment".
(j) For both years, includes only the remaining members as from January 1973.
(k) Including Canary Islands and Ceuta.
(l) Excluding bunker deliveries to foreign-flag vessels (where known).

with a number of other European utilities successfully bid for 1,700m cubic metres of gas a year from the Ekofisk discovery in the Norwegian sector of the North Sea. It was also involved in negotiations to import liquefied natural gas from Algeria. Installing additional wells on the Groningen field will make the additional gas available, but ultimately will reduce the life of the field. The Government was also anxious to encourage the exploitation of gas fields found in the Dutch sector of the North Sea which could yield between 6,000m-12,000m cubic metres of gas annually. However, it became clear to the Dutch that there would be no early removal of the embargo and that additional measures would be needed to curb domestic consumption until the full benefits of the additional gas supplies could be introduced. The ban on Sunday motoring, well received by the Dutch public, was removed and replaced by full-scale rationing of petrol, which lasted from January 12 to February 5, 1974.

Typical of smaller countries hit by the supply crisis in Rotterdam was Sweden which had operated on the policy of buying oil products in both Eastern and Western Europe—a policy that produced low prices at times when there was a surplus of crude oil and products in Europe. But in the crisis surplus supplies completely disappeared, and Sweden, which only refines about 40 per cent of its light fuel oil requirements, was forced to make major savings. The country has a high consumption of energy on a per capita basis, and the reduction of 25 per cent in domestic oil deliveries led to serious privation for the Swedes, most of whom have oil-fired central heating systems in their homes. Industrial oil and petrol deliveries were reduced by 10 per cent.

German reaction

West Germany's pipeline links for both crude oil and refined products with Rotterdam produced initial fears of a major economic recession because of oil shortages. The fears, however, proved groundless, and West Germany, without a major home-based international oil company, has fared extremely favourably from the oil companies' equalisation policy. The even-handed treatment from the international oil companies has, to some extent, quelled longstanding German concern that, in the event of a supply crisis, the international oil companies would give preferential treatment to their home countries. Nevertheless, the German Government has pushed ahead with its plan to create a major German presence in international oil circles by combining the oil interests of the Gelsenberg and Veba companies.

The Germans followed the Dutch lead and introduced a Sunday driving ban and speed restrictions. The Sunday ban was lifted after it was found that the new lower speed limits produced sufficient savings to meet the 5 to 6 per cent shortfall in petrol supplies. The German Government estimated that supplies of middle distillate and fuel oil would fall 15 per cent short of normal deliveries from the first part of 1974. More serious problems arose from the shortages of naphtha needed as a petro-chemical feedstock. Crude oil deliveries increased by 7.3 per cent in spite of the crisis and that sales moved ahead at the rate of 6.8 per cent. However, between January and October 1973 there had been an 8.6 per cent increase in sales, part of which was accounted for by stockpile building on the part of many consumers. As a result, undistributed stocks of crude and products at the end of the year had only been reduced to 23.8m tons from the level of 25.8m tons at the end of September. The crisis produced a more significant effect on prices than on deliveries. Oil companies faced allegations of profiteering, but the Federal Government declined to introduce price controls. Instead, it announced a subsidy of between Deutsche Marks (DM) 100 and DM 300 to about three million low-income families who were affected by the rises in central heating oil prices.

The recovery of German industry since World War II has been largely fuelled by oil. Many of the fears about Germany's lack of its own major oil company were stoked by the rapid penetration that oil made in the energy balance. Total consumption of energy rose by 26.4 per cent between 1966 and 1970 while oil consumption during the same period rose by 46.5 per cent. This meant that about four-fifths of the total increase in primary energy consumption was accounted for by oil. Much of the growth was accounted for by the rapid rise in demand for light fuel oil while the percentage of refinery output channelled into production of petrol slumped significantly. The German coal industry has declined, but indigenous production of natural gas rose rapidly from 3,200m cubic metres in 1966 to almost 20,000m cubic metres in 1973, while imports, principally from Holland and the Soviet

Table 4/6: West Germany, Oil and Natural Gas

OIL (million metric tons)

		1970	1971	1972	1973 (e)	% change 1972/73
Supply:						
Crude: production		7.5	7.4	7.1	6.6	−7.0
from Middle East		33.9	41.0	43.1	54.8	+27.1
from Libya		40.9	30.0	28.7	24.7	−13.9
from other Africa		17.2	23.0	23.8	26.3	+10.5
from Venezuela		3.4	2.8	3.7	2.1	−43.2
from USSR		3.4	3.3	2.9	2.8	−3.5
from Norway		—	0.1	0.4	0.4	
	Total	106.3	107.6	109.7	117.7	+7.3
Refinery throughput		105.5	106.6	109.6	116.5	+6.3
Products: output (net)		97.8	98.9	101.7	108.2	+6.4
Imports (a)		32.5	35.4	39.1	42.3	+8.2
	Total	130.3	134.3	140.8	150.5	+6.9
Disposal:						
Inland sales:						
Motor gasoline		15.5	17.2	18.1	18.7	+3.3
Diesel fuel		9.6	9.7	10.2	10.8	+5.9
Light fuel oil		43.6	46.1	48.3	51.6	+6.8
Heavy fuel oil		26.3	26.3	28.4	29.7	+4.6
Other products		19.4	19.7	21.0	23.8	+13.3
	Total	114.4	119.0	126.0	134.6	+6.8
Military requirements		1.6	1.6	1.9	1.9	
Ocean bunkers		3.8	3.8	4.0	3.9	−2.5
Exports		8.7	8.5	7.8	8.3	+6.4
	Total demand (b)	128.5	132.9	139.7	+6.5	
Undistributed stocks (c)		19.1	23.0	22.7	23.8	+4.8
NATURAL GAS (th mill cu m)						
Production (d)		12.7	15.4	17.7	19.7	+11.3
Imports		3.9	6.4	10.1	15.0	+48.5
	Total	16.6	21.8	27.8	34.7	+24.8.

(a) Including deliveries from East Germany.
(b) Excluding refinery fuel (about 8.3 mill tons in 1973).
(c) Crude and products (including those in pipelines) at end of years shown.
(d) Including casinghead gas.
(e) Provisional.

Source: Esso AG.

Union, soared from 50m cubic metres in 1966 to 15,000m cubic metres in 1973. By 1975 it is thought that imports will equal the level of domestic production. The Federal and Provincial Governments and industry have decided to support a DM1,500m energy research programme between 1974 and 1977. Significantly the biggest portion of the funds, DM 616m, will be poured into research on coal gasification and hydrogenation, while coal production technology research will receive DM 330m. The programme will also make DM 270m available for investigations into energy transformation, transmission and storage; DM 174m for new techniques for oil and gas exploration and DM 56m on methods of energy conservation.

French Independence

Of all the European nations, France has perhaps pursued the most fiercely independent and nationalistic policies towards maintaining its sources of imported oil. Her position at the top of the Arab list of "friendly" European countries should have provided the French Government with near normal deliveries. The oil companies' policy of equalising supplies dashed these hopes and brought vehement criticism from the Administration that its policy in the Middle East had been largely nullified. At one stage, leading executives from the French subsidiaries of the major oil corporations operating in France were told that their licences to refine and market, could be endangered by failure to accede to Government demands that supplies should not be affected by the equalisation policy. Like most European countries, France has very small indigenous oil reserves, which account for less than 2 per cent of the country's requirements. Crude imports for the first ten months of 1973 were 113m tons—a 17.6% rise on the same period of 1972. Of this total, over 30 per cent was shipped round the Cape of Good Hope from the Middle East, while another 30 per cent emanated from Middle Eastern sources via pipeline to the East Mediterranean. Algeria and Libya, which at one stage met almost 40 per cent of the country's import requirements only accounted for 17.6 per cent, mainly because of successive reductions in output by the Libyans.

Between 1966 and 1970, France followed the example of Germany, Belgium and Holland and ran down its coal industry in the

Table 4/7: French Energy Per Sector (Million Tons Coal
           Equivalent) 1972

Sector	Coal	Oil	Gas	Elec-tricity	Total
Iron and steel	14.0	3.5	2.0	3.4	22.9
Other industries	4.5	31.0	7.5	22.0	65.0
Domestic and services	9.0	44.5	8.0	16.5	78.0
Agriculture	—	4.0	—	—	4.0
Transport	—	41.0	—	2.0	43.0

Source: French Government Statistics

wake of cheaper supplies of crude oil from the Middle East. Oil's
share of total energy consumption during this period rose from 47
per cent to 59 per cent, a trend that continued over the following
three years, working towards a target of two-thirds of the energy
market by 1975. Most of this growth stemmed from increased
industrial demand for middle distillates and residual fuel oils.
France also has small but valuable deposits of natural gas
located in the south west of the country. By 1975 domestic output
of gas should level out at something under 12,000m cubic metres
a day but may be exceeded by imports of gas from Holland, the
Soviet Union and Algeria. Imports are scheduled to reach
14,000m cubic metres in 1980.

The Government's initial insistence that its position as a "friendly"
nation in the Middle East would ensure adequate supplies led to
numerous statements that consumers would be unaffected by the
crisis. But, by December 1973, the Government was forced to
announce measures to cut petrol consumption in the light of
declining Arab deliveries. Speed restrictions were imposed,
some air services were reduced, and regulations to control space
heating and television programmes were also introduced. A special "delegate general" for energy was appointed with comprehensive powers to allocate and ration all sources of energy. At
the same time, the French, in breach of the spirit of the EEC,
began talks with the Saudi Arabians and eventually signed a
long-term agreement under which France received 800m tons of
oil over 20 years in return for French capital investment in new
industry and arms. Similar negotiations were initiated in Kuwait.

Italian shortages

Italy has built up a refining industry that, like Rotterdam, is geared largely to meeting the requirements of other countries. Independent refiners developed the concept of service refineries to process "job lots" of oil for the major marketing groups and these operated principally on supplies from North Africa and Middle East crudes shipped in from the East Mediterranean terminals. More than 70 per cent of the country's energy requirements are met by oil, with locally produced natural gas accounting for a further 9 per cent. Imports of oil, for both domestic consumption and re-export as refined products, grew at an average of 10 per cent up to 1973 while the gas industry made provision for Dutch and Soviet imports as well as buying liquefied natural gas from Libya. Agreement has been reached to construct a pipeline under the Mediterranean to transport 11,000 million cubic metres of Algerian gas a year to Italy from 1978. With its heavy dependence on East Mediterranean crude oil, Italy was immediately affected by the fall off in supplies from these terminals at the beginning of the war. Together with Spain, it was driven into introducing export restrictions. A Government order banned the sale of products to countries outside the EEC, a move that had immediate repercussions in Switzerland and Austria, both of whom took large amounts of oil from Italy. The export restrictions were necessary, since Italy was already faced with a critical shortage of heating oil before the East Mediterranean terminals curtailed deliveries of crude oil. Stocks were 25-30 per cent below those of the previous year, reflecting, as the oil companies claimed, the lack of profitability from operating in the Italian market. State control of prices led to British Petroleum's selling its refineries and marketing chain to the Monti Group in 1973, and in January 1974 Shell disposed of its Italian interests in AGIP, the oil industry division of Ente Nazionale Italiana (ENI).

British frustration

British diplomacy during the build-up to the October 1973 war was intended to woo the Arabs, a policy that came into the open with the outbreak of fighting and was successful insofar as it put Britain on the Arab oil producers' "friendly" list. But, as with France, the British Government found their diplomatic offensive had been thwarted by the oil companies' equalisation policy. The Government took the view that British based companies had an obligation not to frustrate national policy, and there were a number of acrimonious exchanges between ministers and senior oil company directors before the equalisation strategy was grudgingly accepted. While actual shortages in Britain as a result of allocations of petrol and industrial oils were no more serious than other European countries, there was a rush of panic buying in October and November that forced petrol stations to close and led to a massive transfer of stocks of oil company reserves into the storage held by industry and to the tanks of the petrol stations.

Britain also had the frustration of knowing that in the long term she had an excellent chance of becoming almost self-sufficient in providing her energy requirements, thanks to North Sea oil and gas. No other European country with the exception of Norway could hold out this prospect, but in the short term the crisis in Britain was much more serious than in any other European nation. Britain's 250,000 miners began a ban on overtime working in mid-November that had an immediate effect on deliveries to power stations. The run down of the coal industry in Britain has not reached the massive proportions of the European retrenchment, and the State controlled electricity network provides a captive market for its products. Power stations in the UK are dependent on coal for some 70 per cent of their electricity generating capacity, and as the miners had proved during the strike of 1972, are extremely vulnerable to any curtailment of coal supplies during the peak winter months.

During the first twelve weeks of the overtime ban, almost 9m tons of coal were lost. To compensate, the Government declared a state of emergency and, after restrictions on the use of shop lighting and advertisements, put most of industry on to a three day week in 1974. A daily electricity savings target of 25 per cent was set, and television transmissions were shortened to encourage householders to make 10 per cent reductions in the use of electricity in the home. Following an all-out ballot of its members, the National Union of Mineworkers began an all-out strike on February 10—despite the fact that two days earlier Parliament had been dissolved and a General Election campaign had started. On March 4 a minority Labour Government took office and four days later industry began to return to five day working after agreement was reached on the miners' pay claim.

Britain's friendly status with the Arabs paid dividends. Early in January, the Saudi Arabian Government agreed to make an additional 200,000 barrels of oil a day available to Britain because of the special difficulties posed by the miners' overtime ban. These supplies enabled the oil companies to increase oil deliveries to the power stations, but sparked off further Governmental criticism of the equalisation policy. It was forcibly pointed out that if the Saudi Arabians recognised that Britain was a special case because of the miners' dispute, then the companies, which generated profits and had shareholders in Britain, could have taken a similar attitude.

One of the sectors of industry that was exempted from the three day working regulations, were companies supplying equipment for the North Sea oil production programme. Interruptions in imports, combined with the quadrupling of crude oil costs, made the development of indigenous oil reserves a project of the highest priority. In 1972, Britain had consumed 327.7m tons of coal equivalent, with oil providing 194.3m tons of coal equivalent (48.1 per cent) almost entirely through imports. Coal consumption slumped from 138.7m tons in 1971 to 120.9m tons (36.9 per cent) while gas, the bulk of this from the North Sea, filled the remainder. First oil from the British sector of the North Sea is due in late 1974 and appreciable quantities should be flowing by 1976. Official Government estimates put oil production at 100m tons a year by 1980, although these Whitehall forecasts may be too conservative.

Table 4/8: UK Primary Energy Supplies 1972

Million therms

		Coal	Petroleum	Natural gas*	Nuclear power	Hydro power	Total
Used by primary fuel producers		332	2 641	23	—	—	2 996
Directly consumed		8 085	28 634	6 617	—	—	43 336
Input to secondary fuel producers		22 208	8 796	3 598	2 450	463	37 847
	Total	30 625	40 071	10 238	2 450	463	83 847·

* Including colliery methane.

Table 4/9: Final Consumption by Sectors

Million therms

	Industry	Domestic	Transport	Others	Total
Coal (direct use)	3 047	4 209	30	799	8 085
Coke and other solid fuels	3 128	1 188	2	294	4 612
Coke oven gas	441	—	—	—	441
Town gas	458	2 217	—	538	3 213
Natural gas (direct use)	3 230	2 292	—	458	5 980
Electricity	2 511	2 960	92	1 451	7 014
Petroleum (direct use)	11 383	1 523	11 962	3 766	28 634
Others	72	—	—	—	72
Total	24 270	14 389	12 086	7 306	58 051

Source: United Kingdom: Energy Statistics. HMSO

Bilateral deals

There are also parallels between the British and French reactions to the energy crisis. Both countries resented the oil companies' even-handed treatment of all their customers; both ignored the wishes of the EEC and sought government-to-government oil deals. While the French were negotiating with Saudi Arabia, a trade mission led by senior officials from the Department of Trade and Industry was finalising a barter deal in which British goods, notably chemicals, synthetic fibres, paper and steel, were to be sold to the Iranians in return for 5m tons of crude.

French and British government-to-government oil deals with Saudi Arabia and Iran tested the patience of their partners in the EEC. A conference of Common Market government heads in Copenhagen during December faced considerable pressure from the Arabs for joint European action against Israel. Internally, the Dutch and the Germans called for Community action to ensure fair shares of oil for all the partners, while Britain and France made it obvious that they had no intention of throwing away their new found "friendly" status in the Arab world. The outcome of the conference was a compromise. The Arabs were told that the Community was in favour of Israel's territorial withdrawal from Egyptian and Syrian territory occupied during the 1967 war and of a political solution that took account of the rights of the Palestinians. The EEC Commission was instructed to draw up a policy that would allow "the orderly functioning" of a Common Market for energy and would enable the members to solve jointly the prob-

Chart 4/2: Primary requirements in OECD Europe

Million tons of oil equivalent

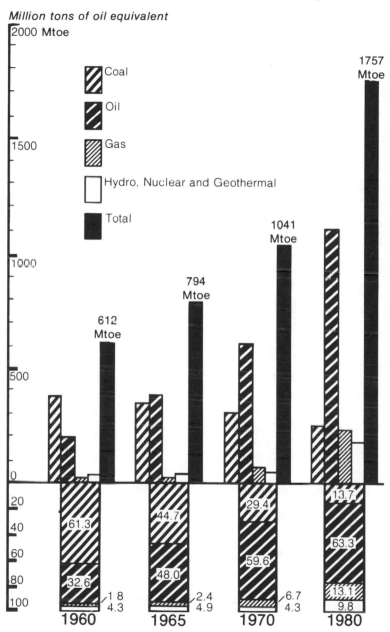

Source: OECD

lems raised by the energy crisis. The Commission was also asked
to adopt provisions "to ensure that all member States introduce,
on a concerted and equitable basis, measures to limit energy
consumption". Progress has been slow because the British Government used the energy crisis as a bargaining counter in its
moves to ensure favourable implementation of the Community's
proposed Regional Fund.

Japanese vulnerability

The most vulnerable of all the industrialised nations to the Arab
production cutbacks was Japan. All the industrialised countries
of Europe are heavily dependent on imported oil, but still have
significant reserves of indigenous coal and natural gas to call on.
Japan, on the other hand, imports between 85-87 per cent of all its
energy requirements. Oil accounts for 75 per cent of energy
needs, while a further 12 per cent is met from imported coal and
only 4 per cent comes from indigenous coal reserves. Hydro-
electric power contributes 6 per cent, and nuclear power, natural
gas and imported liquefied natural gas a further 1 per cent each.
The current Japanese energy "mix" is a complete reversal of the
situation which appertained in 1960. At that point, coal
accounted for 54.8 per cent of a much smaller energy requirement, with imported oil holding a 36.4 per cent share of the market
of 86.2m tons of oil equivalent. By 1970, the market had grown to
265.7m tons of oil equivalent, with oil meeting 73.4 per cent of
this. Domestic coal production had slumped from 41.1m tons of
oil equivalent to 25.6m tons of oil equivalent, while imports of
solid fuel soared from 6.1m tons to 35.6m tons.

After an intensive diplomatic effort in the Persian Gulf to improve
the Japanese image in the area, the Tanaka Government was
surprised to find itself only rated as a "neutral country" by the
Arab oil producers. Hard won Japanese concessions in Abu
Dhabi and the Neutral Zone were ordered to make the full 25 per
cent cutbacks, which prompted fears that the shortfall in
deliveries from the Gulf could be as high as 30 per cent in 1974.
The Japanese supply situation was slightly eased when the
December meeting of OAPEC decided to give it special treatment
but still failed to classify Japan as "friendly". The new classifica-
tion, said the Arabs, would give Japan similar treatment to those

Chart 4/3: Primary energy requirements in Japan

Million tons of oil equivalent

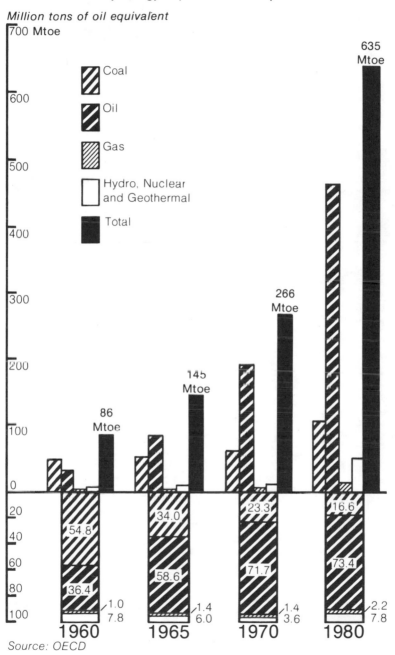

Source: OECD

Table 4/10: Japan's Primary Energy Requirements

	1960	1961	1962	1963	1964
Total requirements	86.2	96.6	104.0	118.9	134.3
Indigenous production	49.2	50.1	49.2	50.9	50.8
Coal and lignite	41.1	40.6	39.8	40.2	40.3
Oil	0.5	0.7	0.8	0.8	0.6
Natural gas	0.9	1.0	1.4	1.9	2.0
Hydro	6.7	7.8	7.2	8.0	7.9
Nuclear	—	—	—	—	—
Net imports	37.0	46.5	54.8	68.0	83.5
Oil	30.9	38.0	47.3	59.7	73.8
Solid fuels	6.1	8.5	7.5	8.3	9.7
Natural gas	—	—	—	—	—

Source: OECD

Table 4/11: Japan's Oil Products Consumption Pattern

Year	Motor Gasoline		Aviation Fuels Kerosenes and other products*		Gas/Diesel Oil	
	Million tons	%	Million tons	%	Million tons	%
1960	4.0	14.7	2.9	10.7	5.2	19.1
1961	4.8	14.1	3.8	11.2	5.3	15.6
1962	5.5	14.3	4.6	11.9	6.4	16.6
1963	6.5	12.1	7.7	14.4	7.6	14.2
1964	7.0	9.9	13.2	18.6	8.6	12.2
1965	7.7	9.3	16.7	20.2	9.7	11.7
1966	8.7	9.2	20.4	21.6	11.3	11.9
1967	10.7	9.5	25.4	22.6	12.9	11.5
1968	11.4	8.9	31.0	24.3	14.6	11.5
1969	13.1	8.6	39.3	25.7	16.5	10.8
1970	14.9	8.1	54.6	29.9	19.5	10.7

Of which Naphtha:	Million tons	% of total
1967	8.8	7.8
1968	11.1	8.7
1969	15.3	10.0
1970	18.7	10.2

Source: OECD

				Million tons of oil equivalent		
1965	*1966*	*1967*	*1968*	*1969*	*1970*	*1980*
144.5	163.2	188.7	205.5	237.8	265.7	635.7
48.3	49.9	49.6	47.4	45.3	39.5	82.9
36.9	37.9	38.7	35.5	33.4	26.3	25.6
0.7	0.8	0.8	0.8	0.8	0.8	2.3
2.0	2.1	2.2	2.6	2.6	2.7	5.3
8.7	8.9	7.7	8.2	8.3	8.6	10.1
—	0.2	0.2	0.3	0.3	1.1	39.6
96.2	113.3	139.1	158.1	192.4	226.2	552.8
83.9	98.7	120.1	134.2	162.1	189.6	464.0
12.3	14.6	19.0	23.9	30.3	35.6	79.8
—	—	—	—	—	1.0	9.0

Fuel Oil		*Total all Products*		*Total all Products percentage increase over previous year*
Million tons	*%*	*Million tons*	*%*	
15.1	55.5	27.2	100	—
20.1	59.1	34.0	100	25.0
22.0	57.2	38.5	100	13.2
31.7	59.3	53.5	100	39.0
42.0	59.3	70.8	100	32.3
48.7	58.8	82.8	100	16.9
54.2	57.3	94.6	100	14.2
63.3	56.4	112.3	100	18.7
70.5	55.3	127.5	100	13.5
84.0	54.9	152.9	100	19.9
93.9	51.3	182.9	100	19.6

% increase over previous year

—
26
38
22.2

Table 4/12: Japanese Crude Oil Imports

	Thousand Metric Tons *April 1972-* *March 1973*	*% share*
Iran	78 961	37.5
Saudi Arabia	35 267	16.8
Kuwait ,	18 010	8.6
"Neutral Zone"	17 573	8.3
Abu Dhabi	12 565	6.0
Oman	4 892	2.9
Dubai	1 026	0.5
Iraq	248	0.1
Qatar	56	0.0
Middle East	168 598	80.7
Indonesia	28 988	13.8
Brunei	5 274	2.5
USSR (Sakhalin)	363	0.2
Australia	188	0.1
Far East	34 813	16.6
Nigeria	3 677	1.7
Cabinda	1 098	0.5
Libya	327	0.2
Africa	5 102	2.4
Venezuela	518	0.3
USA	56	0.0
Brazil	55	0.0
Western Hemisphere	629	0.3
Total, all sources	209 142	100.0

other nations on the "friendly" list. The initial cutbacks during November and December had a catastrophic effect on industrial confidence and morale in Japan. The Ministry of International-Trade and Industry forecast that from December 1973 Japan could expect "zero to negative economic growth" reducing the increase in the Gross National Product in that financial year from 9.5 to less than 5 per cent. The Government had already announced a fuel saving programme that it hoped would curb consumption by between 10 and 12 per cent. Direct burning of crude oil in power stations was forbidden; the export of refined products was strictly regulated; the use of motorways was restricted. The electricity utilities, which generate 77 per cent of Japan's electricity, through oil-burning plants, led the lobby for all round reductions in power consumption. Implementation of the power cuts affected the operations of the iron and steel, ship-building and aluminium industries, while a shortage of naphtha presented serious difficulties for the chemical industry.

The relief that followed the OAPEC decision to upgrade the status of Japan was shortlived. The oil producers' subsequent decision to double prices for the second time in two months had disastrous implications for the Japanese balance of payments situation. In mid-January, 1974, new and tougher restrictions on the use of energy were introduced. Public transport and food processing industries had to reduce their consumption by 5 per cent, news-papers and broadcasting by 10 per cent, and the rest of industry had to cut consumption by 15 per cent.

The American crisis

The United States of America was well on the way to a fully-fledged energy crisis long before the first Egyptian soldier cros-sed the Suez Canal. In the winter of 1972 petrol stations had run short of supplies, and in a number of States heating oil was also difficult to acquire. The reversal in America's oil fortunes had been dramatic. When the 1967 Arab-Israel war disrupted the international supply pattern, the USA made an additional 1m barrels of oil available from its domestic sources to help out its NATO allies in Western Europe. Critics of the oil industry in the United States Congress had blamed the companies for this change round, but not all the blame can be laid at the door of the

Chart 4/4: Primary energy requirements in N. America

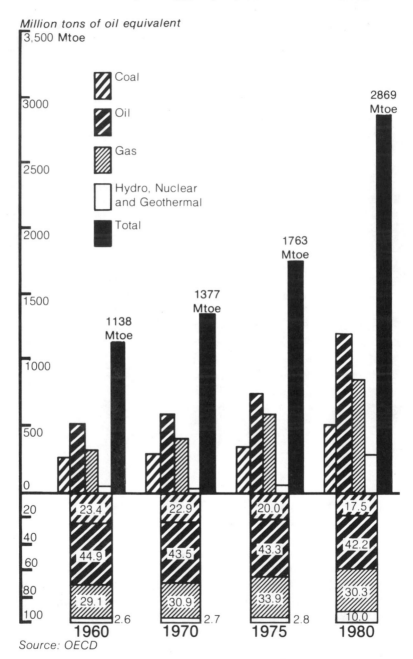

Million tons of oil equivalent

Source: OECD

oil corporations. US Government policy in the face of declining indigenous production and steeply-rising demand at home has been indecisive. Before the 1973 Middle East conflict, the USA was importing 35 per cent of its oil requirements, with the Arabs making a 10 per cent contribution.

Table 4/13: US Production

	Crude Oil (a) (thousand barrels per day)	Natural Gas (b) (million cubic feet per day)
1938	3 507	8 386
1946	5 074	16 959
1950	5 906	23 231
1955	7 579	32 109
1960	7 965	34 989
1965	9 014	43 944
1966	9 579	46 895
1967	10 219	49 784
1908	10 628	52 793
1969	10 827	56 708
1970	11 297	60 057
1971	11 155	61 625
1972	11 211	62 767
1973 (c)	11 077	61 643

(a) Including lease condensate and natural gas liquids.
(b) Marketed production excluding field use.
(c) Estimated.

Source: Petroleum Economist

A number of factors conspired to exacerbate a difficult situation. The Alaskan North slope discoveries were not brought into production, as the pipeline needed to move the oil across the Arctic tundra to the ice-free port of Valdes in Southern Alaska was delayed by environmental objections to the scheme. Approval has now been given for construction work to begin, but the oil will not arrive until 1976. Exploration in the Gulf of Mexico has also

suffered from environmentalist objections, and it is perhaps significant that, since petrol has gone into short supply and the
effects of the crisis have made themselves felt, the wave of objections to almost any new development by the oil industry in the
United States has subsided to a ripple. Much needed regulations
governing the amount of sulphur in atmospheric emissions from
power stations and industry were introduced before the United
States refining industry was in a position to meet the new regulations. The result was a shortage of refinery capacity equipped to
handle some of the higher sulphur indigenous crudes and, as a
result, refiners entered the import market for low sulphur oils that
would enable them to continue production in their existing plants
without expensive modifications.

Table 4/14: US Crude Oil Imports From Arab States

(*barrels per day*)

	1971	1972	First half 1973
Abu Dhabi	79 523	73 624	72 011
Algeria	12 835	86 994	153 756
Egypt	18 969	8 468	16 066
Iraq	10 772	3 602	1 696
Kuwait	29 178	36 178	44 574
Libya	53 221	109 778	143 044
Qatar	—	3 460	506
Saudi Arabia	114 989	174 317	349 320
Tunisia	3 284	6 904	19 226
Total	322 771	503 325	799 199

The energy market in the United States has always been something of a contradiction. Private enterprise in the form of the oil
and coal companies, and the electricity and gas utilities, dominate the field, but gas prices are not subject to the free enterprise
laws of supply and demand, while the domestic oil industry has
been sheltered by restrictions on imports. The principal difference between the market in the United States and the other main

industrial nations is the longstanding balance achieved between the three major primary fuels. Oil and natural gas have commanded a sizeable share of the market since World War II, and coal was not subject to a rapid displacement because of cheap imports from the Middle East in the 1950s and the 1960s. The oil industry coined a wise catch-phrase: "A country that runs on oil cannot afford to run short." But that was just what the Americans allowed themselves to do. The domestic oil and gas industry stagnated after years of continual expansion, and the oil industry's warnings of impending disaster were seen by influential Congressmen as a ploy to speed up the Alaskan pipeline issue. Concern over future Government policies on the import of crude oil, combined with environmental objections, held up new refinery capacity. In 1973 the American Petroleum Institute estimated that the operating capacity of US refineries was 13.6m barrels a day. Daily consumption during the year averaged 17.2m barrels a day, while indigenous production was only 10.9m barrels a day. The balance was made up by a 46 per cent increase in crude imports to 3.2m barrels a day and a 16 per cent rise in product imports to 2.9m barrels a day. Following the lifting of import restrictions in Spring 1973, refiners announced plans to install an additional 2.1m barrels a day of capacity, decisions that came too late to make any significant difference to the nation's energy prospects before the end of 1974.

The announcement of the first mandatory allocation to ensure fair distribution of oil products through the winter of 1973 came on October 2, a few days before the outbreak of the Middle East War. The allocations covered certain types of fuel oil, including heating oil, diesel oil, jet fuel and kerosene. The most immediate effect was a cutback in scheduled flights by airlines—up to 10 per cent in some cases. Allocations were followed by exhortations to Americans to conserve fuel. They were told that 2.7m barrels a day could be saved by turning down their heating thermostats by three degrees, limiting the speed of cars and carrying more passengers per vehicle; filling more seats on scheduled aircraft and making more efficient use of energy in industry and com-, merce. On top of this difficult supply situation came the Arab oil embargo. During the first half of 1973, almost 800,000 barrels a day of crude from Arab sources arrived in the United States and Arab supplies were also fed into offshore refineries supplying refined products.

Table 4/15: North America's Primary Energy Requirements

	1960	1961	1962	1963
Total requirements	1 137.9	1 152.2	1 206.5	1 258.5
Indigenous production*	1 053.3	1 066.1	1 116.9	1 172.9
Coal	281.9	276.2	286.0	306.9
Oil	412 4	417.8	433.7	448.8
Of which : NGL	(35.2)	(36.9)	(39.3)	(41.8)
Natural gas	329.2	341.4	364.3	384.4
Hydro	29.6	30.1	32.1	31.7
Nuclear	0.2	0.6	0 8	1.1
Net Imports	84.6	86.1	89.6	85.6
Oil	98.8	100.8	105.6	108.2
Coal	—15.8	—16.0	—18.0	—24.2
Natural gas	1.6	1.3	2.0	1.6

*Stock changes with indigenous production.
†Co-ordinated estimates submitted by Canadian and United States Delegations. There is

Source: Statistics of Energy, OECD

Table 4/16: North America's Oil Products Consumption

Year	Motor Gasoline		Aviation Fuels Kerosenes and other products*	
	Millions tons	%	Millions tons	%
1961	185.2	39.8	102.1	22.0
1962	192.5	38.2	114.9	22.8
1963	198.9	37.7	132.0	25.0
1964	206.0	36.4	150.7	26.7
1965	211.6	35.6	163.6	27.5
1966	221.8	35.4	175.9	28.0
1967	228.9	35.6	175.8	27.3
1968	243.6	25.9	192.0	28.3
1969	255.0	35.0	208.3	28.6
1970	267.3	35.1	211.5	27.9

*Of which Naphtha:	Millions tons		Annual percentage change
	1967	1970	
Special naphtha	2.9	3.6	7.4
Naphtha jet fuel	13.2	10.7	—5.8
Petrochemical feedstock	5.9	6.7	4.4
Total	22.0	21.0	—1.4

(Assuming 8.5 barrels per metric ton)

Source: OECD Oil Statistics

1960-1980

					Million tons of oil equivalent		
1964	*1965*	*1966*	*1967*	*1968*	*1969*	*1970*	*1980†*
1 317.5	1 378.0	1 458.0	1 504.1	1 599.7	1 683.6	1 762.3	2 869
1 224.5	1 272.2	1 347.1	1 400.6	1 476.4	1 522.1	1 632.1	2 408
321.2	338.0	353.2	347.3	360.0	369.7	389.7	544
460.8	473.0	497.2	529.1	554.8	575.8	597.8	731
(44.6)	(47.2)	(49.6)	(52.1)	(57.2)	(61.1)	(63.3)	n.a.
407.2	424.0	458.0	482.0	517.9	558.5	594.9	845
34.1	36.0	36.9	40.0	39.9	44.0	43.8	58
1.2	1.2	1.8	2.2	3.8	4.1	6.0	230
93.0	105.8	110.9	103.5	123.3	131.5	130.2	461
114.9	127.3	131.1	124.8	144.9	157.1	164.9	478
—22.8	—22.8	—22.3	—22.6	—22.8	—26.8	—37.7	—42
0.9	1.3	2.1	1.3	1.2	1.2	3.0	25

some degree of diversity among the experts in estimating the extent to which the United States will be importing oil by 1980. The figures shown reflect the latest Department of the Interior estimates

---

Pattern 1961-1970

Gas/Diesel Oil		Fuel Oil		Total all Products		Total all Products percentage increase over previous year
Millions tons	*%*	*Millions tons*	*%*	*Millions tons*	*%*	
103.8	22.3	73.8	15.9	464.9	100	—
111.2	22.0	85.8	17.0	504.4	100	8.5
113.6	21.5	83.4	15.8	527.9	100	4.7
114.8	20.3	93.7	16.6	565.2	100	7.1
119.3	20.0	100.5	16.9	595.0	100	5.3
122.7	19.6	106.3	17.0	626.7	100	5.3
126.3	19.7	111.7	17.4	642.7	100	2.6
132.9	19.6	110.1	16.2	678.6	100	5.6
139.5	19.1	125.9	17.3	728.7	100	7.4
143.6	18.9	137.5	18.1	759.9†	100	4.3

†Of which non-energy :	1970	
	Thousand barrels/day	*Millions tons*
Lubricants	135	(7)
Asphalt and road oil	440	(26)
Petrochemical feedstocks	818	(40)
Other	201	(9)
Total	1 594	(82)

Table 4/17: US Supply Demand Estimates For 1974

Calendar Quarter	1st	2nd	3rd	4th
Total demand	20.0	18.1	18.0	20.2
Supply				
Domestic	11.2	11.2	11.2	11.1
Imports	4.9	4.5	4.6	5.0
From inventory	1.2	—0.7	—1.0	0.7
Total supply	17.3	15.0	14.8	16.8
Shortfall	2.7	3.1	3.2	3.4
(per cent of total demand)	(13.6)	(17.0)	(17.7)	(16.6)

Source: Federal Energy Office

From Washington the Government took a pessimistic view and produced forecasts that substantiated the 2.7m barrel a day earning savings figure in the first quarter of the year with even more depressing estimates for the remaining nine months. In the event, the situation was not as serious as predicted. The public took heed of the conservation warnings; the weather was unseasonably mild, and Libyan and Iraqi crude began to slip through the embargo, mainly as refined products via the Caribbean refineries. Nevertheless, the mandatory allocations were extended to all products, and plans for full-scale petrol rationing were drawn up.

While the Arabs have borne the brunt of public criticisms for the deterioriation of the energy situation, they did no more than accelerate at the rate at which the impending crisis was felt by the American public. In a roundabout way, they have done the Americans a favour; the administration has found it easier to enlist support for its "Project Independence" aimed at removing the country's reliance on foreign supplies of energy by 1980.

East European problems

The Eastern bloc countries have not escaped unscathed from the production cutbacks. Rumania imposed speed limits and reduced supplies to vehicles owned by the state in order to save

1.5m tons of oil a year. Rumania produces about 14m tons from its own resources but was importing 2m tons a year from Iran which stopped when the Eilat to Ashkelon pipeline was closed. Russia has traditionally supplied most of East Europe's oil needs, but there has been a tendency to acquire supplies from the Middle East under barter deals and buy disputed oil from fields nationalised by host nations and where the international oil companies were threatening legal action against purchasers. Bulgaria cut electricity consumption to save oil, and Yugoslavia was affected by the disruption of deliveries of Iraqi oil through the eastern Mediterranean terminals. Planned increases in Soviet production have failed to materialise on the scale predicted. A Government announcement indicated that in 1973 production rose by 26m tons to 420m tons which was just short of the 424m tons target for the year. The objective of producing 496m tons by the end of the current five year plan in 1975 has been downgraded to 480m tons. Most of the increases in production result from the development of oilfields in Western Siberia and the opening of large pipelines to bring the oil to the main consuming areas. Western Siberia is undoubtedly very rich in oil and gas reserves and proposals have been put forward by the Japanese and the Americans for assisting the Russians with the development of these resources.

Table 4/18: USSR: Crude Oil Production

Million metric tons

	West Siberia	Other Areas	Total
1970	31.4	321.2	352.6
1971	44.2	327.8	372
1972	62.7	331.3	394
1973	86.5	333.5	420
1974 (a)	115	335	450
1975 (a)	145	over 335	over 480
1980 (a)	270-300		

(a) Target figures according to latest official indications.

Bunkers

While governments and the oil companies grappled with the new situation, the shipping industry itself was facing supply difficulties of bunker fuel. The tanker freight market was just beginning to recover from the chaos of companies releasing substantial tanker tonnage onto the market in the form of re-lets, when the bunker situation began to emerge as a major constraint early in November. It was inevitable that prices would not only increase steeply, but also that a black market would develop. The supply difficulties and high prices were felt by all sectors of the shipping industry. In December 1973, the monthly journal, Seatrade, reported a London-based Greek owner being offered a minimum 1000 tons of bunkers in Philadephia on December 12 at a price of $26.30 a barrel or $176.00 a ton.

The major oil companies, in an attempt to introduce a level of sanity into the situation, decided that their customers should be allocated bunker supplies on the basis of between 22-25 per cent of the quantity supplied in the first nine months of 1973. Forecasts that the bunker crisis would reduce international trade by 20 per cent with consequent laying up of tonnage began to emerge. The shipping industry reacted in many trades by companies ordering their ship captains to cut speeds by between 10 and 15 per cent, and as supplies of bunkers dried up at some of the major ports of the world, companies and ships' masters sought to pick up supplies when and where they could. Japan and South Africa were particularly badly hit, and the oil companies, who were being accused in Britain at least, of failing to provide UK refineries with their requirements as a result of their equalisation policies, were also accused by the shipping industry of favouring particular customers.

In mid-December the international shipping industry grasped the nettle and sought to achieve "total reciprocity" on bunker supplies. Mrs Helen Bentley, Chairman of the United States Federal Maritime Commission, embarked on a European tour with the objective of persuading the major shipping nations of Western Europe to share their information and resources and to reach some agreement for the orderly allocation of available supplies. Her overtures were supported by the Japanese Shipowners Association, and particularly by the UK Chamber of Shipping.

Its President, Mr Ian Denholm, stated: "This country cannot survive physically without imports, nor financially without exports, and well over 90 per cent of both are carried by sea. If world shipping is to continue to serve any country, it must be sure that if its ships go to a particular port, they will be able to get the fuel needed to go on their way again." Oddly, the UK shipping industry had been excluded by the British Government from the priority fuel list in the early stages of the crisis, and when this situation was remedied, the Chamber of Shipping established an emergency committee with representatives from the Government and the oil companies to ensure that the wheels of international trade continued to be oiled. But in December the UK could only supply about 6m tons of bunkers from a total annual foreign trade requirement for the UK of around 15m tons.

The prices for bunkers used in computing world scale rates, however, had become totally divorced from the level of prices being paid on the open market. On the black market, cases were reported of diesel changing hands at rates of $250 a ton, compared with $50 before the crisis. But the forecast heavy build-up of tonnage made idle because owners could neither find bunkers or were not prepared to pay extortionate rates failed to materialise on any scale, although there was a rise in tonnage idle

Table 4/19: Scheduled Price Increases for Bunkers (US Dollars)

	Fuel Oil		Diesel		Gas Oil	
	Oct. 1	Mid. Dec.	Oct. 1	Mid-Dec.	Oct. 1	Mid-Dec.
UK, N. Europe Atlantic Islands	29.90	43.40	63.96	93.46	68.76	98.26
West Africa (Dakar)	29.58	43.08	62.70	92.20	67.32	96.82
South Africa, Far East (Durban)	27.02	40.52	48.44	77.94	53.60	83.10
Middle East	20.96	34.46	36.24	60.24	39.80	63.80

Source: Seatrade

at the beginning of 1974 to 160 vessels, totalling 837,000 tons gross, from 151 ships, totalling 688,000 tons the previous month. This was the first rise for 19 months.

By the middle of January, however, the prices which had rocketed in the two previous months began to show signs of declining once more, although in the Far East the shortage continued to be felt more acutely. There were suggestions that seeing the high prices, the Arab embargo had been discreetly eased, while the oil companies had also been building up their stocks. What was clear, however, was that bunker prices would not fall back to the levels before the October upheavals and that that shipping industry would have to reconcile itself to the reality.

As the shipping industry, oil companies and the Governments of the major consuming nations began to adjust themselves to the new situation, the political settlement in the Middle East moved a little closer. The efforts of the peripatetic Dr Henry Kissinger, flitting between Cairo, Tel Aviv and Damascus, brought results, with a phased withdrawal of Israeli troops from the west bank of Suez and by the Egyptians from the opposite bank. Implicit in the withdrawal was the earnest desire of the Egyptian Government to go ahead with the long proposed Suez-Mediterranean pipeline (SUMED) and the dredging, clearing and re-opening of the Suez Canal, which had remained closed since the 1967 war. Once again, the Canal, which had so dramatically altered the pattern of world trade in general and the oil industry in particular in its early years, was poised to exert its influence once more on world trade.

Chapter Five

Ships, Builders and Finance

The Canal re-opens?

Early in February 1974, one month ahead of the date originally scheduled following the Kissinger mission to the Middle East, parties of Egyptian Army engineers began the task of clearing the Suez Canal, and its adjacent areas, of mines and other explosives which had accumulated since 1967. The work of the army units was the preliminary to the Egyptian cabinet's decision to press ahead with a complete restoration of the waterway to its pre-1967 state and, ultimately, to expand the capacity of the Canal to accommodate the vessels which the oil and shipping industries had been forced into building, following its closure seven and a half years earlier. The shipping industry, thrown into turmoil by the ripple effect of the Middle East war, was therefore placed in a position of having once more to evaluate its entire strategy and to re-appraise building and financing policies.

The Egyptian Government, despite its ambitious plans for the Canal, was keen to stress that their full implementation depended on a successful and lasting peace settlement being brought about. Israel, too, was anxious that the Canal should be restored since, in the view of Israeli leaders, the restoration of Canal operations would provide some form of guarantee against the possibility of a future Egyptian initiative across the waterway. The Egyptian Government, appreciative of the economic effects of a re-opened Canal, announced a three-stage programme to achieve its objective. Under the first phase, the Canal was to be cleared of obstructions and dredged to a depth of 38 feet, which would enable vessels of 60.000 tons dwt to pass through. Egyptian experts considered that this could be completed by the summer of 1974, while it was considered that the second phase—deepening and widening of the Canal to accommodate vessels of up to 150,000 tons dwt—could be completed by late 1976. Beyond that point, and always conditional upon a peace settlement acceptable to the Egyptians, the waterway would be expanded further to a state where it could accept very large crude carriers in the 250,000-260,000 tons dwt class. The cost of the reclamation work was estimated at £75m for the first phase, with a total estimated cost of £500m.

Restoration of the Canal to its pre-1967 state would provide the Egyptian Government with a revenue of about £59m, but the more ambitious development projects, likely to take at least six years, would require financial aid from a number of major oil consuming countries. The combined effect of the aftermath of the oil price/supply crisis and the re-opening of the Canal could have a deleterious effect on international shipping. Faced with a slow down in the level of activity in the industrialised countries, the shipping industry was confronted with the inevitability of a reduction in the rate of demand for tonnage. The Canal has exerted an enormous influence on the pattern of world trade and on the development of the shipping industry. In 1966, the year before the Six Day War, close on 14 per cent of the world's seaborne trade passed through the Canal. Tankers provided the Suez Canal Authority with nearly 75 per cent of its revenue, a reflection of the fact that 85 per cent of ships sailing northward through the Canal were tankers, while a similar position applied for vessels passing through southbound.

A boost for the giants

The impact of the enforced closure of the waterway was underlined by the reaction of the shipping industry, which was then faced with the need to ship oil from the Persian Gulf south around the Cape of Good Hope. When the Canal was closed in June 1967, world shipyards held orders for tankers totalling 27.8m tons. Six months later the order book had swollen to in excess of 40m tons. Oil companies, independent shipowners, and financial institutions have been involved in diverting vast sums of money into the development of the world tanker fleet since 1967. While the increase in tankers' size, and in total tanker tonnage, has been

boosted by the closure of the Canal, the relentless growth in the
amount of world oil production entering seaborne trade has been
the over-riding factor. This has risen steadily, particularly in the
period after World War II, rising from 49 per cent in 1960 to 60 per
cent in 1970 *(United Nations Monthly Bulletin of Statistics)* while
the share of long distance inter-regional oil movements (as
defined by British Petroleum) increased from 53 per cent in 1970
to 57 per cent two years later. During the 1960s, the rising share
was largely accounted for by increased levels of imports in the
European and Japanese economies, although over the 1970-73
period imports into both areas grew at a slower rate than world oil
production. The proportion of tankers in the world fleet has
reflected the growth in oil consumption, and the requirement for
its transportation.

Chart 5/1: World fleet total

(452,472,000 tons dwt)

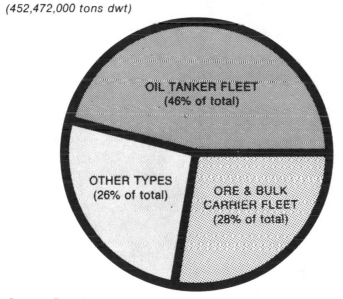

Source: Brandts

In 1972 world energy consumption rose by 5 per cent *(Fearnley &
Egers Chartering Review, 1972)* continuing the pattern of the
average annual rate of increase over a period of several years,
with the seaborne transportation of so-called "energy cargoes"
rising at a rather greater rate. During 1972 some 1,440m tons of oil

and oil products were moved by sea, while ships also transported a total of 100m tons of coal—mainly for steel making—an indication of the dependence of the major industrialised blocs on imported forms of energy raw materials, resulting from their own limited resources. Before the October crisis of 1973 it was clear that the already evident energy problems being experienced, particularly in the United States, would result in a huge surge in demand for the importation of energy materials. Although import restrictions were lifted early in 1973, America has now been forced to accelerate the development of its own substantial energy resources.Distances involved in transporting oil have tended to increase, with the average for inter-regional movements between 1960 and 1970, rising from 4,300 to 5,500 nautical miles. Average distances rose further over the 1970-72 period to 6,100 miles as a result of expanded American imports from the Persian Gulf, and the switching by European countries to long haul crude supplies from the Middle East, from short haul supplies from North Africa.

Oiling the wheels of industry

Responding to the booming economies in the major industrialised countries of the world, the volume of world trade in 1973 continued to grow and, with these nations increasingly dependent on oil to fill their respective energy gaps, trade in oil also rose. In 1971, on a tonnage basis, world trade grew at a rate of about 5 per cent, rising the following year to between 7 and 8 per cent. In 1973 the rise was even more pronounced, at an estimated 11 per cent on a tonnage basis. Expressed in ton miles, a more meaningful guide, the increase was at a slightly higher rate. The expansion of world trade was particularly pronounced in the first nine months of the year, and the volume of growth in the oil trade increased to about 11 per cent on a tonnage basis—rising above the ten year average level of about 10.5 per cent—while on a crude oil ton-mile index the expansion was calculated at a rate of about 14 per cent, although there was a slow down in the rate of growth in longer average hauls.

Over the three years 1970-73 there has been a rapid increase in the size of the world tanker fleet in proportion to the total world merchant fleet. Tanker tonnage in service increased by 95m tons

Table 5/1: World Seaborne Trade 1962-1973 Tonnes

Figures in million metric tons (tonnes).

	Total trade Estimate	Crude oil	Oil products	Iron ore	Coal	Grain	Other cargo Estimate
1962	1250	366	170	102	53	53	506
1963	1350	424	158	107	64	59	538
1964	1510	482	170	134	60	71	593
1965	1640	552	175	152	59	70	632
1966	1770	607	195	153	61	76	678
1967	1860	672	193	164	67	68	696
1968	2040	768	207	188	73	65	739
1969	2240	871	209	214	83	60	803
1970	2480	995	245	247	101	73	819
1971	2580	1068	247	250	94	76	845
1972	2750	1179	254	247	96	89	885
1973 Est.	3040	1310	275	285	107	99	964

Notes: Estimates for 1973 are based on statistics for the nine first months of the most important countries plus estimates for the rest of the year as regards the specified commodities. Total trade estimates and other cargo estimates for 1973 are based on world trade growth as indicated by official sources.

Table 5/2: World Seaborne Trade 1962-1973. Ton-Miles

Figures in MMM ton-miles.

	Total trade Estimate	Crude oil	Oil products	Iron ore	Coal	Grain	Other cargo Estimate
1962	4356	1650	650	314	170	272	1300
1963	4704	1850	600	348	202	304	1400
1964	5353	2150	620	456	199	378	1550
1965	5849	2480	640	527	216	386	1600
1966	6238	2629	700	575	226	408	1700
1967	7230	3400	730	651	269	380	1800
1968	8372	4197	750	775	310	340	2000
1969	9374	4853	760	919	385	307	2150
1970	10654	5597	890	1093	481	393	2200
1971	11729	6554	900	1185	434	406	2250
1972	13072	7670	950	1156	442	454	2400
1973 Est.	14800	8750	1020	1330	495	505	2700

Source: Fearnley & Egers Chartering

dwt over the three year period to a total of 243m tons dwt, while other types of ship over the same period rose by 19m tons dwt to 209m tons dwt.

Chart 5/2: History of world fleet—tankers and non-tankers

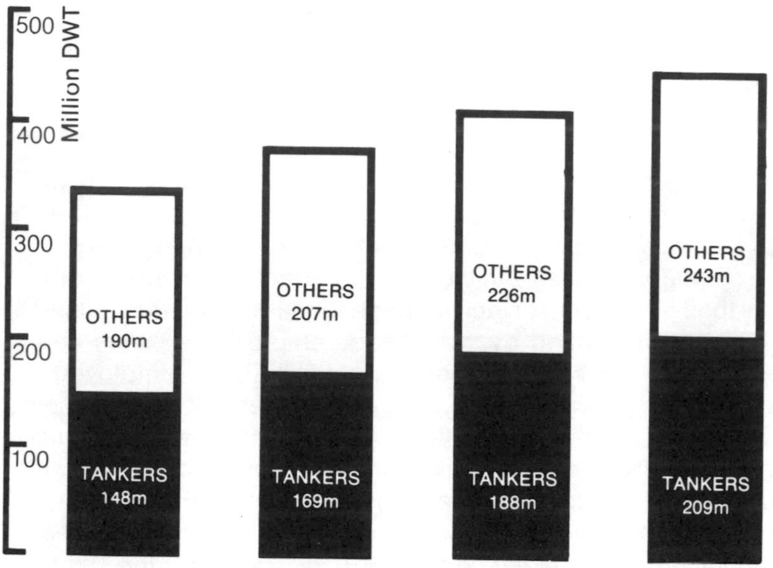

Source: Brandts

Combined carriers

There has also been a steady increase in the size of the combined carrier fleet, those vessels which are able to transport oil, ore and bulk cargoes, either independently or in 'mixes'. Generally speaking, most combined carriers are used in the oil trade but they offer owners a greater degree of flexibility than the conventional tanker insofar as the combined carrier can be switched into dry bulk trades if market conditions alter. There was a significant switching of tonnage in the aftermath of the October war when, although the tanker voyage market collapsed, the dry cargo market remained relatively stable. In 1963 there were 69 combined carriers with a total tonnage of 1.9m tons dwt. Five years later, in 1968, the combined carrier fleet had increased to 153 ships totalling 7.7m tons dwt. In the following five year period there was a huge increase in both numbers and tonnage of combined carriers employed in the world merchant fleet, with 352 ships totalling 36.6m tons dwt in service at the beginning of 1974, indicating not only the growth in the size of the fleet but also the size of individual ships as a result of owners seeking to obtain similar economies of scale to those which have applied to crude oil tankers.

Tanker fleets

Cwnership of the world's tanker fleet is roughly divided in a ratio of 2 to 1 in favour of independent tanker owners compared with tonnage controlled by the international oil companies. Generally, the oil majors operate on the basis of direct ownership of rather less than 50 per cent of their tonnage requirements, with about 25 per cent represented by the tonnage employed by them under long-term charter arrangements and the balance employed on spot or voyage charters. This arrangement enables the oil companies to enjoy a degree of flexibility, and facilitates adjustment of the size of the fleet operating to their accounts, according to the fluctations in world trade and to the seasonal peaks and troughs of oil demand. Against the background of the sharp increases in the total tanker tonnage engaged in world trade over the 1963-73 period, almost all is attributable to growth in individual tanker size, since the total number of ships employed in the oil transportation business, although it has increased, has risen only slightly. The number of tankers in service in 1963 was 2,650 totalling 65.1m tons dwt.

The whole raison d'etre of the spectacular increase in tanker size over the past decade has been the importance of ensuring that oil remained competitive. The closure of Suez provided a real boost to the acceleration in tanker size in order to keep down the final cost. Out of the final cost of crude oil delivered to northwest Europe from the Persian Gulf south round the Cape of Good Hope, some 30 per cent is accounted for by transportation costs at Worldscale 70. At the end of 1970 a 30,000 ton dwt tanker delivering Gulf crude to Rotterdam could do so at a cost of $9.93 per ton while the rate for the same oil carried by a 70,000 tonner was $7.45 per ton. A very large crude carrier of about 250,000 tons dwt employed on the same route could perform the same voyage at a cost per ton of cargo of $5.44.

Chart 5/3: World tonnage on order

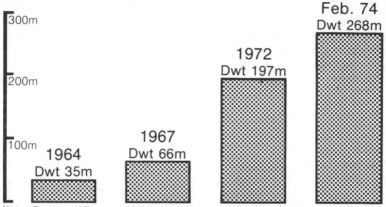

Note: Tonnage of Passenger Ships, Ferries and Miscellaneous Vessels excluded, as figures not available.

Source: "Ships on Order", Fairplay, 1974

There has therefore been a huge emphasis by the oil companies and shipowners on the construction of large oil tankers and combined carriers to cater for the steadily-increasing demand for crude oil. In 1973 the world's cargo carrying fleet increased by about 12 per cent or by about 47m tons dwt (net of scrappage) while new building deliveries during the year rose by 8m tons dwt on the 1972 level to 52m tons dwt. This increase was largely attributable to deliveries of new tanker tonnage, which increased from a steady 20m tons over the three previous years to 28m tons dwt in 1973 (1973 Review, Fearnley & Egers Chartering). The rate of contracting for new tonnage of all types, but particularly for tankers during 1973, reached new peaks, with the world order book at the end of 1973 almost 50 per cent greater than a year earlier and totalling 128,889,862 tons gross.

Tankers—The Rising Sun

The volume of new orders contracted by the world's shipbuilding industry during 1973 amounted to 74m tons gross, with Japan, which dominates the international shipbuilding industry, increasing the size of its order book by 9.7m tons during the final quarter of the year to produce a year end figure of almost 60m tons gross. The volume of tanker tonnage in the world order book fell just short of 100m tons gross and represented 75.7 per cent of the total, while bulk carriers and general cargo ships represented 14.3 per cent and 4.5 per cent respectively. The output of the Japanese industry has expanded dramatically over the period 1964-1973, rising from 4.08m tons gross to 15.7m tons gross last year. The construction of very large crude carriers have formed the basis of the Japanese shipbuilding industry for many years. By virtue of their design, these ships, relative to other merchant ships, such as container ships and liquefied gas carriers, are simple to build. They enable shipyards to establish series production which provides the builder with similar economies of scale to those enjoyed by the shipowner who will operate them. While more than half of the Japanese industry's annual production has in recent years been devoted to the construction of vessels for export, the shipbuilding industry, under the Government sponsored construction programmes, has also been responsible for the massive expansion of the Japanese merchant fleet vital to securing the supplies of raw materials on which the Japanese economy depends.

It was Japan, which ahead of most other major shipbuilding nations, foresaw the likely trend in the pattern of demand for oil tankers and, influenced by her own domestic requirements, invested massive sums of capital in the provision of facilities for the construction of these ships. As the size of vessels demanded by the oil industry increased, it became less economic to construct vessels on the traditional slipway. Many major shipyards engaged in the production of large oil tankers and other similar vessels now construct these ships in large building docks involving the assembly of large prefabricated block sections. In Europe, the Swedish yard of Gotaverken was among the early pioneers of large tanker construction. At its Arendal yard near Gothenburg, the company employed the extrusion principle, where tankers are constructed—the after end first—and then squeezed out of the construction facility (rather like toothpaste from a tube). It is a system which has been employed, with certain modifications, by a number of other shipbuilders. The vast majority of major Japanese shipbuilders, most of whom are building large quantities of tonnage for the independent tanker owning fraternity, now have additional large building docks either in operation or planned for the future. Indeed, the constant renewal and expansion of Japanese capacity has been a source of considerable disquiet and concern for European shipbuilders. Until the ordering boom, which began in the autumn of 1972 and

Chart 5/4: World fleet by flag

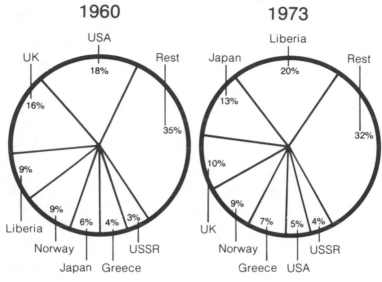

Source: Brandts

continued unabated until the end of 1973, and in which they also shared, most European builders considered that Japan was simply pursuing a policy directed towards achieving total hegemony of the international shipbuilding industry, and that the relentless expansion of capacity could only produce a severe oversupply situation by the end of this decade. The fear was that such a situation would rebound unfavourably on the European shipbuilding industry which historically has been unable to offer delivery dates and prices as competitive as its Japanese counterpart.

The Japanese industry's productivity and technological advances have ensured that despite the huge investments made, it is able to compete effectively in world markets. The Japanese have always justified their expansion on the basis of more optimistic forecasts of future demand for tanker tonnage than those advanced by the Europeans. The Japanese industry, under the watchful eye of the Japanese Ministry of Transport, began a huge expansion of its productive capacity in 1969. Mitsubishi Heavy Industries invested £70m in a new yard at Koyagi near Nagasaki, which began construction of large oil tankers in the autumn of 1972. It is designed to produce between six and seven vessels in the 250,000-350,000 tons dwt class every year. Ishikawajima-Harima Heavy Industries (I.H.I.) and Hitachi ship-building and Engineering, introduced new facilities capable of accommodating ships up to 1m tons dwt at Chita and Ariake in the summer of 1973. Three other shipbuilders, Kawasaki, Mitsui and IHI all added new docks to their existing facilities at Sakaide, Chiba and Kure in the course of 1973. A number of other major shipbuilders had, at the end of last year, other expansion plans under consideration, although the events following the October war will almost certainly lead to their being shelved, in view of the catastrophic effect of the Arab "oil weapon" on the Japanese economy.

During 1974 it is estimated that Japanese shipbuilders will com-mence work on 18.3m tons gross of merchant tonnage and will complete some 17m tons gross. This is likely to rise in the follow-ing year to a commencement figure of 20.8m tons gross and a completion level of 18.5m tons. Almost certainly, these estimates, made at the end of 1973, will be revised downwards. Against the background of expansion already under way and plan-ned—involving 13 new shipyards and new docks with six of the new yards able to accommodate ships up to 1m tons dwt—Japanese shipbuilding experts at the end of 1973 indicated that even without further new projects, output of the Japanese industry could rise to more than 20m tons gross by 1976. A huge proportion of the inflow of orders into the Japanese industry in recent years has fallen broadly into two categories: those for tankers trading between the Persian Gulf and Japan through the Malacca Straits with a draught restriction of about 20 metres and ranging in size from 230,000 tons dwt to 250,000 tons dwt; and those for trading from the Gulf via the Cape of Good Hope to Europe where there is no draught limitation and where the size demanded has been in the range of 250,000 tons dwt to 280,000 tons.

Ultra large crude carriers

The announcement in 1973 that the facilities at Europoort would be developed to accommodate ships of up to 22 metres draught led to a demand early in 1973 for ships of up to 300,000 tons dwt (ULCC or Ultra Large Crude Carrier) and later, with the introduction of designs incorporating an extra wide beam for the same draught, ships of 400,000 tons began to emerge during 1973 particularly for the routes from the Persian Gulf to Europe. In Japan there are at least eight shipbuilding yards capable of constructing these behemoths—a further illustration of Japan's bold attitude towards catering for the needs of the tanker and oil industry. European yards which shared in the demand for new tonnage in 1973, particularly in the tanker field, provided a counterbalance to at least part of the Japanese dominance in the ULCC sector. A Norwegian yard secured orders for a series of 420,000 tonners and the Uddevallavarvet yard in Sweden obtained orders for tankers of 485,00 tons dwt.

Even larger ships are in service and on order. Two of these, the Globtik London and Globtik Tokyo of 483,939 tons dwt and 483,664 tons dwt, built in Japan for operation between the Persian Gulf and Japan through the Lombok Straits in loaded condition, are already in service. Shell has two ships of 540,000 tons scheduled for delivery in 1976 and 1977 from the French yard of Chantiers de l'Atlantique, which is also building a similar size ship for a French oil group. In Japan the Hitachi company has orders for two 500,000 tonners. In spite of these contracts, however, it seems likely that tanker size will stabilise predominantly in the 260,000 ton dwt range with the ships of beyond 400,000 tons being used in specific trades.

Finance for shipping

The vast demand for tonnage, particularly for tankers, has placed enormous stress on the financial institutions of the world. The constant inflation throughout all the major developed countries and the constant fluctuations of the major currencies have provided the industry with enoromus problems. Prices for new construction began to edge upwards in the final quarter of 1972. The shipping industry, in the belief that prices would continue to rise steadily upwards, rushed to the world shipyards to secure early delivery berths. By the end of 1972 most Japanese and European builders were fully committed for their deliveries up to 1976. Early in February 1973 the US dollar was devalued by 10 per cent, and was followed soon afterwards by the floating of the Yen. The fluctuation of currencies continued throughout the year, with the effects of inflation being particularly felt in Japan.

The US dollar devaluation produced further substantial currency differential losses for the Japanese shipbuilders. It was estimated that the fitfeen major members of the Shipbuilders Association of Japan incurred losses totalling Yen 165,000m on their existing order book at that time. This was the second heavy loss to be sustained by the Japanese, who were also hit badly by the Smithsonian agreement of December 1971 on currency parities, since before the spring of 1970 almost all of Japan's export contracts had been booked in dollars. The Smithsonian agreement altered the Yen/US dollar exchange rate from Yen 360 to Yen 308 to the US dollar, while the February 1973 devaluation reduced the exchange rate still further to Yen 264 to the US dollar. The currency parity changes in the early part of the year provided some check on the rate of ordering in Japan, although European yards benefitted considerably as a result, and by the spring the "sellers' market" had been confirmed. Shipbuilders began to open their order books for deliveries into 1977, although European builders were keen to negotiate cost escalation clauses and were followed by the Japanese who, beginning to appreciate the full ramifications of the Arab oil cutbacks, were forced to follow suit. Since its rebirth after World War II, the Japanese shipbuilding industry has remained attractive to shipowners because of its fixed price contracting ability, and the guarantee of prompt, if not earlier than scheduled, deliveries.

During the third quarter of 1973, authoritative sources (R. S. Platou A/S) calculated that during the period, orders were placed throughout the world for merchant tonnage toltalling 46m tons dwt and out of this total, more than 41m tons was in the form of tankers. This in fact represented approximately 20 per cent of the tanker fleet in service at that time.

The prices spiral

The upward movement in ship prices began at the latter end of 1972, and during 1973 the price of all types of ships rose by between 40 and 60 per cent compared with the previous year, with the most significant increase being the price for tanker tonnage. Owners were prepared to pay vastly inflated prices as a result of premiums on ships with an early delivery against the backcloth of the steadily strengthening freight market (see Chapter Four). In this situation a very large crude carrier (providing that there were no long term contract arrangements with an oil company) which had been ordered in 1970 or 1971 at a cost of about £11m could realise a price of between £25m and £30m. The Globtik Tokyo, which was delivered in February 1973 and cost some £21.5m, was clearly a bargain when compared with the price levels which prevailed during 1973 on contracts for new tonnage. Orders placed with Uddevallavarvet for 485,000 tons tankers for delivery in 1978 had a price tag of between £38m and £42m. Apart from the increasing buoyancy of the tanker market during the first nine months of the year, shipbuilders were also able to jack up prices in the face of the prospects of a vastly-increased requirement for tonnage to ship the additional quantities of oil to meet the United States shortfalls.

The huge influx of orders, and the establishment of a "sellers market" for the shipbuilders, was also influenced by the effects of inflation. Raw material costs and wages, in particular, rose sharply. On the wages front the upward spiral was notably present in Japan, where wage rates rose by more than 20 per cent in the shipbuilding industry, while in Europe rates progressed by an average of between 12 and 16 per cent. On the raw materials front, the cost of bought-in materials such as engine room equipment and other machinery, which represents 60 per cent of the total cost of a large tanker or bulk carrier, rose steeply as a direct result of the sharp climb in steel prices.

Yet owners were prepared to pay the prices demanded with or without escalation clauses. Delivery was the important criteria. However, the vessels which were ordered in 1973 have to be funded. The shipping industry, which is highly capital intensive, is the largest mover of funds in the world. In March 1973 Wm. Brandts calculated that on the basis of the 197m tons of merchant tonnage on order at that time, all scheduled to enter service before 1977, and allowing for a scrap factor of 5 per cent annually, the world fleet would total around 517m tons by 1977. It was calculated that over the five years 1973-1978 the shipping industry internationally would require an estimated capital demand of $39,000m. The world fleet in service at that time was estimated at about 414m tons dwt (with an average value per ton of $100) producing a total capital investment in world shipping of $41,000m rising to $71,000m by 1977, assuming the same 5 per cent annual scrappage rate.

The scale of financing required for the shipping industry, therefore, can be seen to be vast, and at a conservative estimate the cost of financing new ships may be of the order of $30,000m to $50,000m at any one time, although it is virtually impossible to quantify the amount of money involved accurately. The financing of the shipping industry in recent years has attracted considerable attention from the banks because of the level of returns involved. Increasingly, pension funds and the large insurance companies may be attracted.

Throughout the world, through the offices of the Organisation of Economic Co-Operation and Development, attempts have been made to standardise the level of subsidies which all the major shipbuilding nations of the world offer their customers overtly or covertly. These have tended to distort the shipbuilding market, although the subsidies are less disruptive at a time when demand for tonnage is high, as it was in 1973. Governments have supported their respective shipbuilding industries in a variety of ways, such as credit schemes for domestic owners, demolition or modernisation subsidies, operating subsidies to shipping companies on particular routes, customs duty exemptions and tax exemptions and rebates. In 1970 the OECD estimated that the cost of government support to the shipbuilding industries of its members was running at a rate equivalent to between 12 and 15 per cent of the sales value of new ships. Since 1971 the members of the OECD with shipbuilding industries have been bound by regulations on the provision of export credit. Under this structure, countries are required to ensure that there was a minimum net interest rate on ship credit for export of 7.5 per cent with credit limited to a repayment period of eight years. The minimum rate, however, is only nominal, and in practical terms the level is considerably higher.

The sharp rise in new building costs and the somewhat protracted moves by OECD to eliminate the disruptive effect of the existing subsidies, have in fact contributed to a relative decline in the importance of shipyard credits, although they remain a useful tool at a time when world market conditions are not conducive to new construction. Historically, many owners have financed new tonnage out of retained earnings supplemented by mortgage loans. Although some countries do have ship mortgage banks, there tends to be a restriction of the amount they are able to lend.

Table 5/3: Subsidies and credit terms for eleven OECD ship-building countries in 1972

	Direct building subsidy	Home credit scheme	Export credit scheme	Comment
		(rates of interest shown are net of all charges)		
Japan	Nil	80% credit, 65% of which is publicly financed over 10 years at 6.5% with 3 years grace, 35% privately financed over 8 years at 6.5%	Joint public and private finance of 70% of ship's cost over 8 years at 7½% effective rate	Cheaper home credit is offered for liner and container ships. 7½% tariff on ships less than 10,000 grt
France	3% of contract price plus value of COFACE scheme	Interest rate 6½%. (Credit assumed to be 80% of price over 8 years. This is not specified in OECD paper)	80% credit over 8 years. 7½% interest rate specified includes charges, taken as 7.0% net of charges	
Italy	9% of contract price (proposed)	No preferential interest rates. Interest rebates exist, but their extent is not clear	80% credit over 8 years at 7½% interest rate	
USA	Maximum subsidy 43% reducing by 2% p.a. to 35%	Up to 87½% over 25 years at between 6 and 8%[1]	Not specified. Very little[1] export trade	Subsidy makes up the difference between US ship price and its price abroad
Spain	Nil	80% credit over 8 years at 5.85% interest	80% credit over 8 years at 7½% including charges, taken as 7% net of charges	14% tariff on any imported ships
UK	10% of contract value of work done[2]	80% credit over 8 years at 7% (net of charges)—7.8% gross	80% credit over 8 years at 7% (net of charges)—7.8% gross	
Norway	Nil	No special scheme for credit. Mortgage guarantees	Credit at 7%. Period not specified, but assumed to be 80% over 8 years	
West Germany	Nil	10% grant to ship-owners or 70% credit at 6% over 12 years with two years grace. The credit is more valuable	80% credit over 8 years at 7½%	The 6% home credit is limited and only applied to 10% of purchases in 1970
Sweden	Nil	Credit at 7%. Period not specified but assumed to be 80% over 8 years	No special scheme for credit. Mortgage guarantees	
Denmark	Nil	80% credit over 8 years at 7%	80% credit over 8 years at 7%	
Netherlands	Nil	80% credit over 8 years at 7½%	80% credit over 8 years at 7½%	

1 USA is not bound by OECD understandings
2 Current year 3%

Source: Department of Trade and Industry

Forms of ship finance

The shipping industry, and particularly the tanker operating business, faced with the sharp rise in the cost of new building has had to seek new forms of financing. The raising of equity has been a little-used practice in the past but may increase in the future, while leasing of ships, which has become a finely-tuned and highly-sophisticated exercise in the United States has, over the period 1970-73, been an area which has attracted considerable interest from more conservative European owners. The large capital costs involved in the construction of modern ships can lead to an unacceptably heavy burden being placed on the borrowing powers of companies and those engaged in the oil transportation business, and therefore leasing offers a useful alternative. But the lengthening financing terms now required—up to 20-25 years for specialised carriers and large oil tankers—pose their own problems since the major sources of long term dollars either cannot lend directly to the shipping industry, or are not prepared to do so. The two main areas for these funds are the United States domestic market and the Eurobank market. In recent years the American long term dollars have been the backbone of financing of the American shipping industry which, coupled with the sophisticated leasing schemes, have greatly offset the costs of building vessels in the United States and operating them under the American flag. On the European front, the Euro-dollar market has still to reconcile itself fully to the steady long term amortisation which is vital to the shipping industry.

Generally, the ship mortgage loan has continued to be the most common form of ship financing with repayments spread over a five to fifteen year period. The size of the loan has varied between 50 and 80 per cent of the cost, linked to the security of guarantees provided in addition to the ship mortgage. Such schemes can be modified to cater for multi-currency options and fixed or floating rates. With the huge increase in costs for specialised ships engaged in the transportation of energy cargoes, there has been an increase in the volume of loans arranged through a syndicate of banks, thus effectively spreading the risk. A deal signed in 1973 for the Algerian State shipping company, CNAM, for a twelve year $200m loan, involved no less than 43 different banks. There has been in some cases a tendency for banks to become even more closely involved in the operations of large

Chart 5/5: New building costs per ton

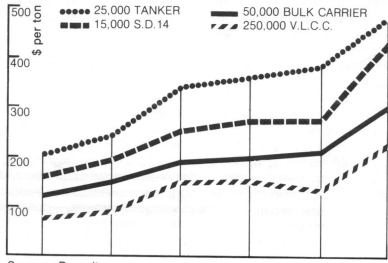

Source: Brandts

Chart 5/6: New building costs per vessel

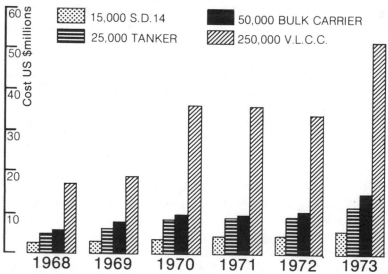

Source: Brandts

shipping groups or through an equity stake in a particular ship. The Hong Kong and Shanghai Bank has a substantial interest in the equity of the operations of the World Wide Shipping group of Hong Kong, controlled by Mr. Y. K. Pao.

Independent worries

The shipping industry has not only faced the problems of raising the necessary capital to finance the replacement of existing tonnage and the construction of new vessels, but in recent years has experienced a vicious increase in its overheads, particularly in insurance, manning, repairs and maintenance. There is no doubt that in the wake of the Arab oil price increases and production cutbacks of October 1973, these costs will continue to rise steadily and impose a further burden on the shipping industry.

The tanker industry will also face further additional cost increases in the future as a result of international measures being implemented to minimise the effects of sea pollution, both as a result of collisions and by direct discharge of oily waste into the sea during tank cleaning. The damage wrought by the collision or stranding of oil tankers was underlined by the strandings of the Torrey Canyon and the Pacific Glory off the south coast of Britain and close to the congested waters of the English Channel. The oil industry has defended the increase in size of tankers and the huge quantities of oil they carry—the existing fleet of 200,000 tonners each carry about ten times the amount of the oil carried by World War II tankers—by stressing that increased size in fact reduces the pollution risk. One 540,000 tonner is equivalent to five 108,000 ton dwt tankers and 35 of 16,000 tons. Most, if not all, of the very large crude carriers of more than 300,000 tons however are engaged on specific routes between loading and unloading terminals away from the major shipping routes.

In October 1973 a conference of the Inter-Governmental Maritime Consultative Organisation (IMCO) adopted two measures: the first, the International Convention for the Prevention of Pollution from Ships, 1973 and, second, a Protocol relating to Intervention on the High Seas in Cases of Marine Pollution by Substances other than Oil. Under the terms of the Convention, tankers of more than 70,000 tons dwt ordered after December 31, 1975 must be constructed with segregated ballast tanks. This is designed to eliminate the need for tankers to clean cargo tanks at sea and to discharge oily water from them. Existing discharge restrictions have been tightened while both new and existing tankers will have to incorporate discharge monitoring and control systems. The Convention also incorporated earlier amendments concerning the litimation of tank sizes which restricts the size of cargo tanks in tankers generally to 30,000 cubic metres and to a maximum of 40,000 cubic metres, in order to limit the level of outflow in the event of collision. The Convention will become effective twelve months after it has been ratified by fifteen states whose combined merchant fleets constitute at least 50 per cent of the world's merchant fleet. Following a series of explosions on board three very large crude carriers during tank cleaning, the oil companies and independent owners began to install inert gas systems on all their ships in an attempt to eliminate the possibility of further explosions. This was underlined by an IMCO recommendation.

The extent to which the charter arrangements can be upset with potentially devasting effects has been highlighted by the reaction of members of INTERTANKO, the International Association of Independent Tanker Owners, whose members control about 120m tons dwt of shipping representing about 70 per cent of the independently-owned tanker tonnage in service. Four days after the war in the Middle East broke out, the members of INTERTANKO revealed a scheme for combating the effect of currency fluctuations on long term charters of up to twenty years. Revenue for the shipowner on these charters has been massively eroded by the inflation over the past three years. Over the six years to the beginning of September 1973 INTERTANKO calculated that the reduction in the value of the US dollar and the pound sterling had been 22 per cent and 32 per cent respectively, while operating costs over the four years 1969-73 had risen by an estimated 70 per cent. Until a few years ago an annual operating cost increase of 5 per cent had been considered adequate. The tanker owners, fearful of bankruptcies amongst their members, suggested that the oil companies should agree to a scheme whereby the contract currency on the charter, generally the dollar, was related to nine other currencies in such a way that when these selected currencies moved by an average of 2 per cent against the dollar, the charter rate could be modified accordingly.

Chart 5/7: Insurance costs for tankers

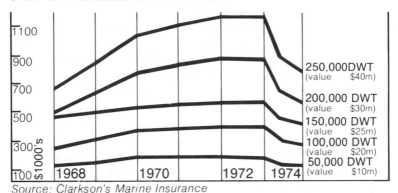

Source: Clarkson's Marine Insurance

Chart 5/8: Manning costs (UK able seamen)

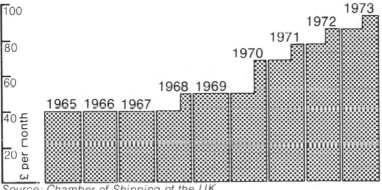

Source: Chamber of Shipping of the UK

Chart 5/9: Maintenance/repairs costs

Source: Salvage Association

Pipelines

In the context of total oil transportation, the role of pipelines will in the future become increasingly important to both the shipping industry and the financial institutions of the world. Attention was focussed on the tanker pipeline equation just before the 1973 Middle East conflict, due to the decision by the Egyptian Government to press ahead with construction of the 20 mile long SUMED pipeline, linking the Red Sea with the Mediterranean at a cost of $345.4m. The project had been under consideration since the 1967 war, and work on the scheme was scheduled to start early in 1974, with the first phase due to be completed by 1976. This would provide capacity for an annual throughput of 40m tons, with a second state, scheduled to be operational some time afterwards, to boost the pipelines total throughput to 80m tons annually. The 42 inch pipeline would connect Ain Sokhna on the Gulf of Suez, with Sidi Kreir, west of Alexandria. President Sadat's Government indicated that it would seek its contribution to the cost through a $200m Eurobond issue. Control of the pipeline would be in the hands of the Suez Gulf Mediterranean Oil Pipeline Company in which Egypt has a 50 per cent stake with other shares being held by Saudi Arabia, Kuwait, and Abu Dhabi (each 15 per cent) and Qatar, 5 per cent. Even allowing for Egypt's plans to re-open the Canal it was considered that the pipeline would still be an economic proposition.

Early in 1974, the first positive steps towards establishing the 750 mile long Trans-Alaskan pipeline, linking Prudhoe Bay on the North slope of Alaska through a 48 inch diameter line to Valdez on the south coast of America's most northerly state, were taken, following the dropping of legal manouevres by environmentalist bodies which have impeded the oil companies' plans for pressing ahead with the venture planned in 1969. There is little doubt that the effect of the embargoes imposed by the Arab producers led to a softening of the earlier determination to obstruct the project, in view of the urgent requirement to speed up the development of America's indigenous resources. The delays, however, have forced up the cost of the project which early in 1974 was estimated at $4000m, four times the original estimate.

Pipelines for both crude oil and oil products play an important role in the total energy transportation picture but in economic terms they have not been proved to be a substitute for the very large crude carrier over long distances. Because of their high fixed costs, capital charges and inflexible nature, pipelines are really only economic when they are operating at maximum throughput levels. They can, however, compete with seaborne transportation if the route followed by the pipeline is considerably shorter than the tankers route; if sea transport is subject to exceptional charges; and if the port closest to the centre of consumption can only accommodate vessels of uneconomic size. On the other hand, an overland pipeline can reduce demand for tankers if they bridge inter-oceanic areas. The utilisation of large diameter pipe in recent years has reduced the cost of transportation on a ton-mile basis, but this until recently has been more than matched by the economies of scale achieved through the ever increasing size of tankers. Equally, a pipeline can be complementary to a tanker route. So far as the Middle East is concerned, there must always be doubts about the possibility of pipeline supplies being severely disrupted by further conflicts.

In the United States product pipelines have been established for many years. The 65,000 miles of pipeline already in service is equivalent approximately to the total railroad mileage in the USA. The longest product pipeline in the world, some 3,110 miles long, is the Colonial Line which links Houston with New York. The length of pipeline mileage in the United States reflects the fact that approximately three-fifths of all bulk products produced by American refineries are moved onwards through pipelines. The development of pipelines in Europe has been less spectacular. The first truly commercial pipeline was the TRAPIL line which began operations in 1953 and connects refineries in the lower Seine region with depots in Paris. Studies have shown that multi-product pipelines generally require a minimum throughput of about 1m tons annually if they are to compete with other forms of transport. Because road and river distances tend to be longer than pipeline routes, and involve extra costs for loading and unloading, it is possible that pipelines might be able to operate at lower annual throughputs in the future.

In Japan there were a number of projects planned before the oil price-supply crisis. Two new product lines were scheduled to open by the end of 1974. These included a 110 kilometre line with a capacity of 7m kilolitres and a 290 kilometre line with a capacity

Table 5/4: Major World Pipelines

Crude Oil

Pipeline	Route	Diameter (In.)	Length (Miles)	Capacity (Thous.b/d)	Date of Commisioning
Interprovincial	Canada: Edmonton to Toronto and Buffalo (N.Y.)	16-48	3,553	1,300	1953
Comecon	USSR Hungary East Germany Poland Czechoslovakia	20-40	3,300	400	1964
Trans-Siberian	Tuymazy to Irkutsk Saudi Arabia (Abqaiq) to Lebanon (Sidon)	28 30/31	2,283 1,068	340 500	1964 1951
Trans-Mountain	Canada: Edmonton to Vancouver	24/30	718	400	1953
Capline	U.S.A.: St. James to Patoka	40	630	500	1968
IPC	Iraq (Kirkuk) to Syria (Banias)	12/32	556	1,100	1952
	Iraq (Kirkuk) to Lebanon (Tripoli)		531		1934
Tipline	Gulf of Aqaba-Ashkelon	42	160	460	1969
South European	France (Lavera) to FRG (Karlsruhe)	34/40	485	1,400	1963
TRAPSA	Algeria (Amenas) to Tunisia (La Skhirra)	24	482	240	1960
SOPEG	Algeria: Hassi Messaoud to Bougie	22/24	411	360	1959
	Libya: Sarir to Tobruk	34	317	600	
Transalpine	Italy (Trieste) to FRG (Ingolstadt)	40	290	700	1967
RRP	The Netherlands (Pernis) to FRG (Frankfurt)	24	285	700	1960
NWO	FRG: Wilhelmshaven to Cologne	28/40	223	900	1959
AWP	Austria: Wurmlach to Vienna	18	251	110	1970
RAPL	The Netherlands: Rotterdam to Antwerp	34	65	480	1971
	USSR: Aleksandrovskoye to Anzhero-Sudzhensk	48	500	1,000	1972

Source: OECD

Table 5/4: *continued*

Oil Products

Pipeline	Route	Diameter (In.)	Length (Miles)	Capacity (Thous.b/d)	Date of Commisioning
Colonial	USA: Houston to New York	30/36	3,110	1,200	1964
Plantation	USA: Louisiana to North Carolina	10/18	1,260	200	
RMR	The Netherlands (Rotterdam) to FRG (Frankfurt)	18/24	370	230	1966
UKOP	United Kingdom: Thames to Midlands and Mersey	6/14	245	200	1968
SPMR	France (Lavera, Dijon) to Switzerland (Geneva)	12/16	360	90	1969
TRAPIL	France: Le Havre to Paris	10/20	145	400	1953
	United Kingdom: Fawley to West London	10/12	64	140	1963
Explorer	USA: Houston to Chicago	12/28	1,300	263	1971

Natural Gas

Pipeline	Route	Diameter (in.)	Length (miles)	Capacity (10 xft.3/d)	Date of first commissioning
Trans-Canada	Canada: Burstal to Montreal	24-34	2,294	800	1959
Mid-America (LPG)	USA: Texas to Milwaukee/ Minneapolis	8/10	2,174	60,000b/d	1960
	USSR: Central Asia to Moscow	40.48	1,700	2,200	1967
Little Inch	USA: Baytown to Bayway	20	1,475		1942
Pacific Gas	Canada (Alberta) to USA (California)	30-36	1,366	415	1962
	USSR: Bukhara to Urals	40	1,360	1,700	1963
Big Inch	USA: Longview to Bayway	24	1,254		1942
	Argentina: Campo Duran to Buenos Aires	22/24	1,083	243	1960
	Argentina: Comodoro Rivadavia	30	1,045	350	1964
	United Kingdom: West Sole to Easington offshore	16	45	200	1967
	USSR: Ukhta to Torzhok	48	800	1,450	1970
	USSR to Czechoslovakia (Bratislava) and Austria (Vienna)	28-20	300	400	1967
	Iran (Agha Jari) to USSR (Ostara)	42/40	700	1,050	1970

of 13m kilolitres from refineries in the Chiba area to the Tokyo
area. Japanese refineries.have tended to be located on coastal
sites, and demand for oil and products further inland has been
insufficient to necessitate the demand for significant pipeline
networks while a further constraint has been the arcane legal
problems over landownership in Japan. Until the crisis, it was felt
that pipeline development in Japan would be influenced both by
the increased demand for oil and its products in the inland areas,
and also by the fact that the existing land based distribution
system by road and rail was fast becoming overloaded.

Chapter Six
Refineries–a Re-appraisal

During the 1960s and early 1970s, Europe, Japan and, to a very much lesser extent, the United States, embarked on a massive oil refinery building programme. The growth in demand for oil products meant that all but the smallest countries could support at least one, and possibly two, large refineries, and the increase in tanker size improved the economics of moving large quantities of crude oil from the producing countries to the consuming areas. The result of the building boom in refineries was the establishment of large refining complexes centred on deep-water harbours such as Milford Haven, in South Wales, and the Dutch port of Rotterdam. Refining technology kept pace with the acceleration in tanker size, and by the early years of this decade the average intake by units in Europe and Japan had almost doubled, to take full advantage of the economies of scale. However, in spite of the undoubted economic attractions, the whole pattern of location and construction of refineries may yet revert to the situation which prevailed a quarter of a century ago.

The transformation of the situation is being forced on the oil companies and the consuming nations by the newly-acquired market power of the members of the Organisation of Petroleum Exporting Countries, who want to construct refineries close to the oil fields and use them as the basis for the development of a western-style industrial infrastructure. If the OPEC countries are successful, there will inevitably be a significant impact on transportation patterns.

The first refineries were built close to the oil fields, and the products shipped to the main markets of the world because consumption in few countries was sufficient to warrant large scale domestic refinery capacity. The range of products required by itself the most sophisticated nations was limited, and demand for the highly-specialised by-products of crude oil, particularly chemical feedstocks, was exceedingly small by comparison with the present day. Refineries such as the Anglo-Iranian plant at Abadan in Iran were among the biggest in the world and capable of supplying a large proportion of market requirements for oil products in Britain and parts of Europe. During the early days of the oil industry, any refineries built in industrialised countries outside the United States tended to be small and geared to the requirements of individual companies.

The nationalisation of the Anglo-Iranian refinery at Abadan (see chapter three) highlighted the dangers of this policy and increased the growing concern, within the oil industry, on the wisdom of establishing the new and expensive refineries needed to meet the growing demand in politically unstable countries. Tanker sizes had been increasing dramatically (see chapter three) reducing crude oil freight costs *vis a vis* the transportation of refined products in considerably smaller ships.

From the oil companies' point of view the establishment of large refineries close to the market was an attractive one. The demand for conventional products was leaping ahead and new applications were being found for the by-products. This meant that practically none of the crude oil moved by sea went unused. In the early days of the industry many of these now valuable by-products were disposed of as waste. Another of the advantages in building refineries close to the market was the ability to import crude oils with varying characteristics from different parts of the world to help meet the increasingly more sophisticated requirements for new oil-based products. Refineries close to the oil fields tended to have only a limited range of crudes available.

From abroad to home

Governments also came to realise that domestically-based refineries provided important strategic advantages, as well as forming the basis for the development of petroleum-based chemicals industries and the ensuing benefits to their economies. This development was encouraged by the imposition of excise duties on imported refined products while crude oil imports entered duty free.

Table 6/1: World Refinery Capacities

	Nos.	Crude Capacity
Asia Pacific		
Australia	10	680,900
Japan	45	4,939,800
Singapore	4	699,600
Others	47	2,612,400
Total Asia/Pacific	106	8,932,700
Europe		
Belgium	3	816,700
France	23	3,140,000
W. Germany	33	2,825,700
Italy	34	3,882,000
Holland	7	1,825,500
Spain	9	1,163,000
Britain	20	2,762,100
Others	29	1,695,100
Total Europe	158	18,110,100
Middle East		
Iran	5	660,000
Kuwait	5	646,000
Others	21	1,576,200
Total Middle East	31	2,882,200
Africa		
South Africa	5	331,000
Others	34	761,200
Total Africa	39	1,092,200
Western Hemisphere		
Argentina	14	623,600
Bahamas	1	500,000
Brazil	10	791,800
Mexico	6	625,000
Dutch East Indies	2	945,000
Venezuela	12	1,531,600
United States	247	13,383,000
Canada	41	1,788,100
Others	47	2,248,700
Total Western Hemisphere	380	22,436,800
Total Non-Communist World	714	53,454,000

SOURCE: Oil and Gas Journal

Against the background of these changes in refinery locations and the growth in the size of individual crude oil tankers, with the phenomenal growth of the international oil tanker fleet, the role played by product carriers has tended to be overshadowed until recently. The multi-cargo product tankers, which began to emerge in the 1930s and in the post-war period to meet the particular transportation requirements of that era, are now on the verge of a rennaissance. For many years the products carrying fleet has been relegated to the role of supplying cargoes to those countries with insufficient refinery capacity of their own and to correcting imbalances in output in the major consuming areas.

Much of the products fleet, in shipping terms, is elderly, and a substantial replacement and new construction programme can now be expected. It is also apparent that the specialised product carrier will become even more sophisticated. To some extent this has already taken place, notably in the development of special tankers used by the chemical industry to carry cargoes such as sulphuric acid, ethylene, and anhydrous ammonia. Ships of this kind often have as many as 40 separate tanks capable of accommodating individual product cargoes of between 250 and 1,500 tonnes.

Transport of oil products in fact accounts for about 20 per cent of the total tonnage of oil moved by sea every year and will rise dramatically if OPEC plans for building their own refineries are realised. Product carriers play a vital part in the balancing of refinery outputs in the major consuming areas. Where demand for the large volume products cannot be met from domestic production, these are shipped in from other areas. The established refineries clustered round the oil fields in the Middle East and the Caribbean now provide the bulk of these "balancing" products. It is an important function, and refineries in these areas have continued to grow, although not on the scale of new units in the consuming countries. In the period between 1960 and 1970, refinery capacity in the Caribbean area increased by 120 per cent while that in the Middle East increased by 87 per cent. However, capacity in Europe over the same period increased by 200 per cent and in Japan by a colossal 450 per cent.

Refining—USA

Compared with Europe and Japan the United States has under-
gone a very modest increase in its refining capacity over the past
decade. There has been a tradition of small domestic refineries
based on local production, and according to the Organisation for
Economic Co-operation and Development in 1970 more
than 50 per cent of the refinery capacity in the United States was
concentrated in 12 per cent of the total number of refineries, each
with an average capacity of about 10m tons annually. Refinery
sizes are still substantially below those in Britain and Europe, and
expansion of existing facilities was made difficult during the late
1960s and early years of this decade by the tremendous influence
wielded by conservationist groups. New refinery sites were
almost impossible to find again because of pressure from the
environmental lobby.

The shortage of refining capacity accentuated the decline in
domestic crude oil production (see chapter four) and led to the
entry of the United States in to the world markets for both crude oil
and refined products. The United States had for many years

Table 6/2: Refinery Capacity in the Caribbean and the Middle
East 1960, 1965 and 1970

	million tons			
	1960	1965	1970	1973
Caribbean	88	133	194	216
Middle East	61	85	114	137

Source: BP Statistical Review of the World Oil Industry

suffered from an imbalance in its refinery product ranges on the
East coast and the deficits were made good mainly from Caribbean and Venezuelan sources. The Caribbean refineries had
originally refined crude from their own fields but as demand,
particularly for fuel oil, rose on the Eastern seaboard, large quantities of crude had to be imported from Africa and the Middle East
for processing. New regulations governing the sulphur content of
fuel oils added to the oil indussry's problems, since much of its
capacity was unable to use more plentiful supplies of crude, with

a high sulphur content, and cargoes of low sulphur crude had to
be imported.

Table 6/3: Average Intake Capacities of Refineries 1965 and
1970

	tons per day	
	1965	1970
OECD Europe	7,500	11,200
Canada	3,500	4,500
United States	5,300	7,000
Japan	6,600	12,500
Australia	6,000	8,500

Source: OECD

Unlike Japan and Europe, the United States refining industry has
not been under pressure to make large supplies of naptha available to the petro-chemical industry as a feedstock. The American
chemical industry has developed using natural gas as its principal raw material, although the growing shortage of gas combined
with rising prices has forced the chemical companies into a re-
appraisal of their feedstock situation. The chemical industry is
facing a sharp increase in transportation costs which are rising at
an annual rate of 5 to 7 per cent. In the United States, about 50 per
cent of chemicals by tonnage are transported by railway, with a
further 38 per cent by road and the balance by water transport and
pipelines. In 1973 it was estimated that transport of chemical
products in the United States on domestic waterways had
increased by 10 per cent over the previous year to about 120m
tons, and to cater for the anticipated demand it has been calculated that the capacity of the United States' inland waterways
system must be doubled by 1980 if it is to match the rate of
economic growth. But the pressures to which the inland waterways system is being subjected are growing. This is particularly
pronounced on the Great Lakes where important locks have been
made obsolete by the increasing size of ocean going ships. Apart
from the vital Great Lakes system, inland waterways in the United
States consist of more than 25,000 miles of canals and navigable
rivers.

Refining Europe

It is not only conservationist pressures that have held down the annual growth in refinery capacity in the United States to between 3.5 and 4 per cent a year. The relationship between oil, natural gas and coal in balancing the fuel economy of America remained almost unchanged during the 1960's while at the same time in Europe oil captured a major share of the expanding energy market at the expense of coal. Italy led the way in the expansion of refineries to meet the explosion in demand for oil products, as coal was quickly displaced. Discoveries of oil in Libya also hastened the construction of new plants in Italy which quickly became one of the largest exporters in Europe. Germany, France, the United Kingdom and the Netherlands also embarked on huge refinery building programmes, and these countries accounted for over 80 per cent of the total European capacity.

With the bulk of crude imports arriving by VLCCs, deepwater terminals were necessary and, when established, attracted three, or sometimes four, refineries around them. Oil companies have also been anxious to expand refineries on these sites, partly because of the difficulties in finding new sites close to deep water and also because of the economies that can be obtained from increasing the size of units. From these large refining complexes has sprung the network of pipelines that move the products into the distribution terminals in the main areas of consumption. But it is still cheaper to move crude oil than heavy fuel oil by pipeline,

Table 6/4: European Refinery Locations

	1959	1964	1966	1968	1970
			million tons		
Inland	29.2	107.0	139.3	184.5	209.7
Coastal	165.0	281.4	329.4	399.7	487.7
Total	194.2	388.4	468.7	584.2	697.4
			per cent of total		
Inland	15.0	27.5	29.7	31.6	30.1
Coastal	85.0	72.5	70.3	68.4	69.9

Source: OECD

and in inland Europe, new refineries, linked by large diameter pipeline to the coastal terminal, have been established to meet the heavy fuel oil demands.

The network of pipelines for both crude oil and products has meant that the refining and distribution network in Europe has grown up on a continental, rather than a national basis. According to the OECD, trade in oil products between its member countries in 1972 amounted to 112.5m tons, while exports to countries outside the OECD European area were only 16.7m tons. Rotterdam, with its five refineries and massive storage areas imported almost 140m tons of crude oil and products during 1972. Domestic consumption, including 11m tons for ships bunkers, only amounted to 36m tons and the remainder was exported, either as crude oil and product or crude oil in bond to its neighbours and to Denmark, Sweden and Switzerland which are dependent on product imports. Britain, France and Belgium are also net exporters and the Arab boycott on crude oil supplies to Holland, combined with tougher municipal restrictions on refinery expansion and limitations on the size of ships that can reach Rotterdam, could affect its future as the leading oil port in Europe. The port's position is not likely to be eroded in the short term, but the oil companies are giving serious consideration to the merit of the alternative terminals at Dunkirk and Le Havre in the north and Fos in the south of France for new developments. None of these centres is likely to grow to the eminence of Rotterdam, since the oil companies have learned the lesson of concentrating too much refining capacity in a single area.

In Europe the demands made on refineries for chemical feedstocks are heavy. Very little natural gas is used as a raw material, and the proportion of refinery output going into chemical works has increased from 2 per cent in 1960 to between 9 and 10 per cent. Meeting such a fast growth has been relatively easy, since the expansion of petrochemicals has coincided with the development of the oilfields of Algeria, Libya and Nigeria, all of which produce light crudes that have allowed refiners to increase the volume of light distillate feedstocks without installing new and expensive equipment.

The chemical industry is now facing a period when its rate of growth, which during the 1960s had generally been double the

Table 6/5: Netherlands: Petroleum Entrepôt Traffic

Jan-June
1973
Metric tons

Crude Oil
Moved into storage under bond from:

Norway	48 779
USSR	719
Albania	18 461
Algeria	652 059
Tunisia	116 098
Libya	3 116 755
Egypt	300 170
Nigeria	1 047 872
Venezuela	294 538
Syria	615 337
Iraq	179 381
Iran	3 218 662
Saudi Arabia	5 769 042
Kuwait	4 546 388
Qatar	561 369
Muscat	243 267
Total	20 720 897

Moved out of storage under bond to:

France	187 224
Belgium/Lux	6 422 584
W. Germany	10 683 326
Italy	78 455
UK	877 474
Ireland	377 118
Denmark	135 705
Norway	134 193
Sweden	152 454
Finland	80 744
Portugal	67 494
Spain	77 372
E. Germany	436 277
Netherlands	1 696 986
Total	21 407 406

Products

Moved into	3 423 799
Moved out of	3 736 790

Source: Maandstatistiek van de Buitenlandse Handel (CBS).

Table 6/6: Netherlands: Petroleum Imports and Exports

| | | January-June 1973 | |
		Metric tons	Thousand Fl.
Crude Oil			
Imports from:			
Norway		52 615	4 051
Algeria		241 250	20 593
Libya		1 662 056	127 520
Egypt		355 664	23 246
Nigeria		5 183 253	389 652
Gabon		436 840	31 549
Venezuela		157 984	10 213
Syria		373 883	26 212
Iraq		249 880	18 664
Iran		10 991 296	733 433
Saudi Arabia		16 722 236	1 098 515
Kuwait		9 439 612	620 915
Qatar		2 920 848	209 586
Dubai		16 279	1 156
Abu Dhabi		1 886 990	136 061
Muscat		123 662	9 427
	Total	50 814 348	3 460 793
Exports to:			
France		415 921	26 072
Belgium/Lux		4 302 382	279 636
W. Germany		3 053 972	200 129
Italy		61 523	3 569
UK		2 103 886	147 354
Ireland		119 020	8 252
Denmark		727 758	45 786
Sweden		493 795	29 548
Portugal		87 555	5 947
Spain		416 292	27 337
E. Germany		557 067	36 927
	Total	12 339 171	810 557

Products		
Imports of:		Thousand Fl.
(a) Light fuels (in kilolitres)	3 928 188	263 773
Heavy fuels and others		
(in metric tons)	2 254 750	217 455
Exports of:		Thousand Fl.
(b) Light fuels (in kilolitres)	7 541 001	657 225
Heavy fuels and others		
(in metric tons)	23 105 635	1 839 406

(a) Includes bunkers for Dutch aircraft and ships.
(b) Includes bunkers for foreign aircraft and ships.

Source: Maandstatistiek van de Buitenlandse Handel (CBS).

growth rate of manufacturing industry, is likely to slow down. This checking of chemical industry expansion has been particularly influenced by the uncertainties created by the effect of the oil embargoes implemented following the Arab-Israeli war of 1973. In 1971/72 the chemical industry demonstrably moved out of a period of recession which has dogged the industry since 1969/70, causing pressure on margins and on prices as a result of severe over-capacity. Investment was cut back through most of the OECD member countries, although growth rates showed signs of improvements. However, with inflation the major problem and reduced returns on capital invested, together with price restraints in some countries, investment continues to lag behind estimated capacity requirements for the end of this decade.

Consumption of ethylene, derived from the "cracking" of naphtha which in turn is obtained from crude oil, has been rising steadily and the size of ethylene plants has increased accordingly. But the reduction in supplies of oil has presented the chemical industry with serious problems. A survey last year by the United Nations (*Market Trends and Prospects for Chemical Products,* United Nations, Economic Commission for Europe) underlined the heavy dependence of the industry on both oil and natural gas as feed stocks. The ethylene obtained from gaseous or liquid hydrocarbons remains one of the most important basic raw materials products for organic chemicals, its derivatives including vinyl chloride, ethyl benzene, and polyetheylene. By 1980 it is estimated that ethylene demand in the United States will amount to some 20m tons—an indication of the requirement by the American chemical industry for oil based feedstocks, at a time when their normal natural gas feedstocks are being squeezed. Over the same period 1971-72 consumption of coal, coke and manufactured gas by the chemical industry continued to fall while both utilisation of both oil and natural gas increased.

Products trade has reflected this pattern and has been particularly pronounced in the case of Japan, where, despite the massive increase in refinery capacity, the oil companies have found it impossible to produce a balanced range of products. The demand for naphtha—a basic building block of the chemical industry—and for middle distillate fuel oil has been so great that there has been a substantial deficit in the lighter products such as petroleum and the very heavy products such as residual fuel oil.

Refining in Japan

The rate at which Japan has changed to an oil based energy economy accounts for the spectacular rate of new refinery building. But, compared with other industrialised nations, in the precautions taken against industrial pollution of all types Japan has a poor record. The result has been that the conservation groups that have emerged have been faced with a much more serious problem than their earlier counterparts in Europe and the United States. In the face of increasing pressure from these groups, it has become difficult to find new refinery sites, and even the reclamation of land from the sea is being criticised. Those new refineries that are being constructed are facing stringent regulations regarding atmospheric and cooling water emissions, which in some cases have added as much as 10 per cent to the cost of a project.

Before the 1973 supply crisis emerged there was a growing feeling amongst Japanese industrialists and oil companies that greater use should be made of new refinery projects in the Persian Gulf. Pressure was being brought on the Japanese Government to relax the import duties on imported products so that the purchase of refined suppliers from the Middle East would be an economic proposition. The development of Japan's trade in imported products would also have coincided with the producer countries' plans for increasing their own refinery capacity and enhanced Japan's standing in OPEC circles. But Japan's diplomatic overtures, particularly with the producers in the Persian Gulf, have been largely ineffective, and during the production cutbacks Japan, which had expected to be regarded as a "friendly nation", found herself excluded and suffered accordingly. Japan's business community as a result has become increasingly concerned about the desirability of relying too heavily on the importation of refined products from the Middle East.

OPEC—a change of mood

The OPEC countries of the Persian Gulf first mooted the idea of more refinery projects in the Gulf during their talks with the international oil groups on gaining particiapation in the companies' concessions. Even in 1972, when it appeared that the host Governments would be acquiring an initial 25 per cent stake in company operations, Saudi Arabia and Kuwait both made it clear that they would prefer to refine the crude they acquired under the participation rather than sell it direct. At this stage the host nations were prepared to make a substantial part of their "participation" crude available to the companies to satisfy their supply contracts. This type of participation agreement, that gives the host Governments only a 25 per cent holding rising to 51 per cent by 1982, however, was discredited by the Kuwaiti National Assembly's refusal to ratify such a pact. Instead, a new agreement giving Kuwait 60 per cent of the production formerly controlled by the companies was negotiated and seems likely to set the pattern for the re-negotiation of participation agreements in Saudi Arabia, Abu Dhabi and Qatar, as well.

The host Governments' efforts to dispose of their first parcels of "participation" crude were straight sales, and no mention was made of refinery construction. But, now that the national oil companies of the producing states have such vast reserves at their command, preliminary planning of refinery projects, together with related petro-chemical developments, is beginning. During the period up to early 1975 these countries, including Indonesia and Nigeria, are expected to begin seeking bids for refinery construction work and will make the first soundings for customers to take the product from the new plants

Iran has taken the lead in insisting that new refineries are built close to the oil fields. The country's five year development plan places great weight on the development of the petro-chemical industry in the industrialisation programme, and the Shah has emphasised the importance of new refinery projects to supply the feedstock for the embryonic Iranian chemicals industry. In the long term, the Iranian ruler is more concerned that his country's oil reserves are conserved so that the chemical industry will not run short of raw materials. During the supply crisis following the Arab-Israeli war of 1973, he warned the industrialised nations that they must develop alternative fuels, as oil was too "nobler" a commodity to burn. This policy has already brought Iran into conflict with Japan. The Japanese, during 1972, had agreed to make 1,000m dollars available to finance a major refinery in Iran and a further 500m dollars to building a petro-chemical complex and a cement works. The Japanese had understood that they would be able to export naphtha from the refinery to domestic chemical plants in Japan, but at the last minute the Iranians changed their mind and insisted that all feedstocks from the refinery went into the Iranian petro-chemical industry. The Germans have been more successful and have negotiated to build a 500,000 b/d refinery at Bushehr in Iran in partnership with the national oil company. Until the plant goes into production NIOC will make regular deliveries of crude oil to the Germans. Iran has also signed a protocol with five American companies for the establishment of a third 500,000 b/d export refinery. Companies involved are APCO, City Service, Clark Oil, Commonwealth Oil and Crown Central Petroleum.

By the end of the decade over 2 million additional barrels of refined products could be available in the Gulf. None of the industrialised countries who have suffered the trauma of Arab oil production cutbacks or complete embargoes will relish the prospect of a further decline in flexibility of supplies. But with the national oil companies in the host nations taking control of crude oil output there will be little that can be done to reverse this trend. One lesson that has been learned from the 1973 supply crisis is that refineries, even in embargoed countries can be kept running using alternative sources of crude oil. The amounts of refined products which will become available will however be only marginal, and in the even of another crisis there will be no alternative source of supply.

Products carriers

While this is unwelcome for the strategist trying to ensure the continuity of oil supplies it may not be such an unfavourable development for those interests involved in the supply of shipping tonnage. It is now clear that many of the oil producing nations of the world are gearing themselves for a rapid expansion of their domestic flag fleets in parallel with their policy of establishing a widely-based economy. Tonnage will be required for the export of basic products and for the import of finished goods and capita equipment from the major industrialised countries. In the interim period, however, shipowners of specialised tonnage may look forward to filling the tonnage gap. A key area will be refined product carriers and chemicals carriers where demand for both types of ships will be accelerated also by the consuming nations.

The future for the carriage of these cargoes would appear to be particularly sound since much of the existing products carrying fleet is nearing the end of its useful life. According to the OECD, the world's oil products fleet consists of about 1700 vessels of up to 30,000 tons dwt, and totalling more than 32m tons dwt. However, a more recent estimate has put the size of the fleet, up to 40,000 tons dwt, at almost 43m tons dwt with only some 29.3m tons actually engaged in product trading. In fact, some of the larger ships are still being used for carrying crude oil while others are switched from hauling crude oil to products according to the demand, but the cleaning involved between voyages is expensive.

In 1971 the major trading routes followed by the products carrier fleet were coastal shipments around the Japanese archepeligo, trade between the United States and the Caribbean, between the Gulf of Mexico and the US east coast, and in intra-European trade. By far the largest volume of trade was that engaged in the Japanese area. In a report (*The Product Tanker through the 1970s*, H. P. Drewry (Shipping Consultants) Ltd) published at the end of 1972, the Persian Gulf and Caribbean were classified as the principal loading areas accounting for just over 27 and 23 per cent respectively of total demand for product carriers in 1971. In terms of discharge areas, although Western Europe in 1965 took almost 33⅓ per cent of total product tanker capacity, its share for 1971, as a result of adequate refinery capability, had fallen to less than 20 per cent. But the continuing rise in demand, coupled with insufficient refinery capacity in both Japan and the US, increased the capacity utilisation to 25 per cent for each of these areas.

Future prospects

For the future, a number of factors will have an important influence on shaping the pattern of the products and chemical carriers trade. While there was a clear surplus of capacity at the beginning of this decade for products carriers, even before the crisis of 1973 it was anticipated that there would be a demand for 45m tons dwt, while estimated capacity was likely to be in the region of 22m tons. Deliveries of sophisticated, clean products carriers would remain abreast of demand, but the tonnage required to transport a limited number of major product grades between the main consuming areas is likely to fall short of demand since it is this type of ship which is not being replaced by new vessels.

This requirement stems from the continuing level of imports into the United States, coupled with the location of the new export refineries in the Middle East and Africa, which is likely to lead to the development of a fleet of products carriers much larger than the maximum 30,000-40,000 tonners currently in service. It is estimated that about 90 per cent of all existing products carriers are in the 20,000-30,000 ton dwt range, but already orders have been placed in Scandinavia and the United Kingdom for products carriers of between 50,000 and 55,000 tons. The oil industry has until very recently tended to concentrate its capital expenditure programmes in the transportation and on the construction of VLCCs to cope with the rising demand for oil and to minimise the problems caused by the continued closure of the Suez Canal. Policies are now being changed and, encouraged by the fact that freight rates for products carriers will almost certainly remain firmer than those of VLCCs, companies are seeking to make up for a considerable period of neglect.

Within the broad definition of products carriers is the increasing trend towards specialised tankers required to transport both primary and intermediate chemicals. The oil producing countries' policies of establishing export refineries and petro-chemical industries will give impetus to the growth of this class of ship. The activities of Japanese interests in the Middle East and Asia, for example, are an indication that increased seaborne trade in aromatics and olefins into Japan is likely to accelerate. The world's shipbuilding industries have huge backlogs of orders for VLCCs and, with a few notable exceptions, few yards have been keen to move into the construction of sophisticated chemicals carriers which are subject to rigorous standards and regulations laid down by international and governmental organisations.

Chemicals carriers fitted with stainless steel, rubber lined or specially coated tanks are used to carry a wide range of substances from ammonia to phosphoric acid and other petrochemicals including paraxylene, and propolyene. For ammonia, Venezuela is potentially a valuable source of supply for the United States and for the emergent industries of Brazil and Columbia, while other loading areas with new potential will be Kuwait, Iran and Qatar. Plans for the export of ethylene by a number of developing countries, could, if realised, produce a marked expansion for seaborne transportation of this product by the early part of the next decade. Regulations drawn up by the Inter-governmental Maritime Consultative Organisation (IMCO) for the safe carriage of chemical products could, however, prove to have a dampening effect on profitability expectations of shipowners engaged in this trade.

Chapter Seven
Natural Gas

On December 1, 1973 the keel was laid of the largest liquefied natural gas carrier yet ordered in the United States. The ceremony at the Quincey Shipbuilding division of the General Dynamics Corporation marked the entry of the American shipbuilding industry into the construction of these highly-sophisticated ships which are designed to carry large quantities of this pollution free fuel from often remote gas-producing areas to the major consuming nations, notably Japan and the United States.

Two days later in Jakarta, contracts for the largest LNG deal ever negotiated were signed for the shipment of 7.5m tons of LNG annually from Indonesia to Japan over a 20 year period. The $3,000m deal involved a group of five Japanese energy utilities and an industrial group, reflecting Japan's policy of securing its sources of energy for the 1980s and beyond—a policy given new importance by the catastrophic effects on the Japanese economy of the Arab oil producing nations' supply cut-backs.

The two events underline the vast amount of capital involved and are closely linked. The gas will be transported in four ships each with a capacity to carry 125,000m cubic metres of gas in liquefied form. Under construction by General Dynamics under contracts placed by Burmah Oil, valued at a total of £156m, these deals and the many others under consideration confirm the position of liquefied natural gas as an important constituent in meeting the world's total energy requirements.

The exploitation of the world's natural gas resources and its transportation will be an area of substantial growth over the next decade. Demand in Western Europe, Japan and the United States is already out-stripping supply, and by 1980 10,000m cubic feet of gas a day will be needed to supplement locally produced gas reserves. The oil producing nations of the world and particularly the Middle East have in fact been flaring off indigenous supplies of natural gas found in association with oil, for many years. It is only since the late 1950s the economically feasible methods have been developed for moving the gas in tankers in much the same way as crude oil is transported.

Natural gas can only be moved in bulk in liquid form at cryogenic temperatures of minus 160 degrees centigrade. In this form the liquid occupies one six hundredth of its original volume. The basic techniques of liquefaction have been known since the 19th century but the movement of this product by sea involves the use of complex and expensive ships in order to ensure acceptable safety standards. Leakage of gas either during loading or during the voyage would result in a fracture of the ship's hull. A number of factors have combined to give impetus to the development of global LNG transportation. These have included the growing shortage of natural gas in the United States, its increasing economic competitiveness in relation to other sources of energy, while its pollution free burning characteristics make it an attractive fuel at a time when energy producing industries are under strong pressure to observe more stringent controls on the amount of undesirable waste they discharge into the atmosphere. Certainly long term ecological considerations will become even more important.

Establishment of an LNG "chain" involves a liquefaction plant close to a port loading terminal. Gas is brought to the plant by pipeline sometimes from fields hundreds of miles away, liquefied, loaded on to tankers then shipped to its destination where the liquid is then regassified and in the United States used to boost local supplies at peak demand periods.

Reserves and production

Huge natural gas reserves in the major oil producing regions of the world remain untouched particularly in the Middle East and Africa because, in the past, pipelines have been the only economic method of moving gas and the fields have been isolated from their gas using markets by distance and seas. Early in 1974 total world reserves were estimated at 2,033 million million cubic feet compared with 721 million million cubic feet 12 years earlier. Reserves in fact doubled between 1965 and 1972. It is impossible to estimate the future size of resources as many areas have yet to be fully explored.

Typical of the areas which have yet to be properly evaluated are the discoveries of natural gas on the North Slope of Alaska and in the Canadian Arctic where there are plans to construct a 1550 mile long pipeline to transport the gas to the Canadian and American markets via the McKenzie Valley.

Chart 7/1: Location of existing and future potential natural gas reserves

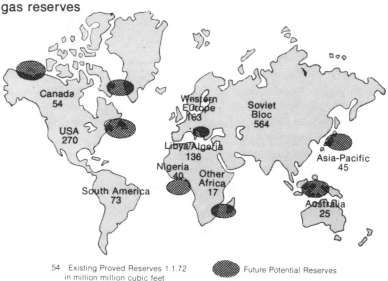

54 Existing Proved Reserves 1.1.72   ● Future Potential Reserves
in million million cubic feet

Source: H. P. Drewry (Shipping Consultants) Ltd

World production of natural gas has risen sharply reflecting growing demand. Output increased from 913,000m cubic feet in 1962 to 44,766m cubic feet nine years later. It is expected to rise from about 23,000,000 million in 1970 to around 48,000,000 million in 1985. In the United States natural gas is the second biggest source of energy after oil, and demand is continuing to rise from the 1970 level of 23 million million cubic feet. However demand has to be curbed because indigenous sources are only capable of increasing output to 23.5 million million cubic feet by 1985.

Supply and demand—USA

As it is so heavily committed to the consumption of natural gas, the United States has been forced to look to imports to allow a reasonable level of growth. The USA is also engaged on the perfection of techniques to produce synthetic natural gas from coal and crude oil—although with oil now in short supply, coal appears the most attractive feedstock. While millions of dollars are being ploughed into research on synthetic gas, in the short term, increased demand will have to be met from imports. Estimated seaborne imports will rise from 2,200 million million in 1980 to 3,600 million million cubic feet in 1985. Imports via pipeline from Canada are likely to increase from 1,600 million million cubic feet in 1980 to 2,700 million million cubic feet five years later.

Supply and demand—Japan

Japan, on the other hand, has not in the past used large amounts of natural gas. Coal and oil have provided the mainstays of the energy mix and the use of gas in any form has been extremely rare. Concern at the dangerous levels of pollution in Japan in recent years has reached almost hysterical proportions, and various Government agencies have made estimates of Japan's requirements and in some cases have estimated the potential, to be as high as 10 million million cubic feet between 1980-85—equivalent to more than one third of total energy in 1980 of 1.2 million million cubic feet in 1980 with seaborne imports accounting for 1 million million cubic feet in 1980. Total demand in 1985 is forecast to rise to 1.8 million million in cubic feet with imported LNG accounting for 1.3 million million cubic feet.

Supply and demand—Western Europe

In Western Europe LNG imported gas will play a less important role in meeting future energy demand than in the United States and Japan. Europe pioneered the import of LNG from Algeria, but before the trade could grow to sizeable proportions, gas was discovered in Holland and the North Sea, both more accessible and cheaper sources. Output of gas is expected to increase to 6.5

million million cubic feet in 1980 from 2.3 million million in 1970—the bulk of which will come from the North Sea. However these indigenous supplies will not be sufficient to meet the forecast demand of 7.5 million million cubic feet and the balance will have to be imported in equal quantities by pipeline from the Soviet Union and by sea from North Africa.

By 1985 domestic production of gas is expected to amount to 8.5 million million cubic feet with pipeline imports accounting for a 0.8 million million cubic feet and seaborne imports for a further 0.7 million million cubic feet.

LNG—the early years

Much of the pioneering work on the movement of natural gas was undertaken in the early 1950s by the American company Union Stockyards and Transit Co., which owned gas fields in Louisiana. The company at that time was experiencing difficulties in finding fuel for its stockyard operations in Chicago. A pipeline was ruled out for economic reasons but the company conceived the then revolutionary idea of moving the gas in liquid form by barge up the Mississippi.

The barge principle worked and opened up the possibility of moving natural gas over much longer distances. Union Stockyards was then joined by Continental Oil and together they formed the Constock Liquid Methane Corporation and in 1956 the prototype tank for incorporation on to an ocean going ship was completed. Constock linked with the British Gas Corporation to convert a 5,000 ton dry cargo vessel into a liquid methane gas carrier which was renamed Methane Pioneer in 1958. Trials took place on Lake Charles Louisiana and in the Gulf of Mexico and the vessel made her maiden Atlantic crossing to an LNG storage terminal on Canvey Island, Essex. Seven more transatlantic voyages confirmed that LNG could be moved safely by sea and in 1960 Shell bought an interest in Constock and the company's name was changed to Conch International Methane.

Soon after, negotiations opened between Conch and Algeria for the company to buy gas from the Hassi R'Mel field and to establish the world's first commercial liquefcation at Arzew, with the then British Gas Council (now British Gas Corporation) being the customer. Two LNG carriers were ordered and were launched in 1963 and in the summer of 1964 the first of the 100 million cubic feet a day of Algerian gas began to flow into the British gas network. The Algerian scheme however was overtaken by the discovery of natural gas in the North Sea. In 1965 the French established a smaller version of the British scheme between Arzew and Le Havre, but the proposed extension never took place.

The successful operation of the Algeria-UK/France schemes encouraged further small scale developments, and LNG chains were established to move Alaskan gas to Japan, and further supplies of North African gas to southern Europe. The real break-through came when Distrigas, an American company owned by the Cabot Corporation of Boston, and Gazocean of France, were given permission by the Federal Power Commission to import liquefied Algerian gas into the United States. A protracted dispute over whether imported gas should be subjected to the same rigid price controls had delayed the approval. There are now twelve projected schemes for importing LNG into the United States which, if implemented, would provide American utilities with between 2.8 million million and 3.4 million million cubic feet of gas a year.

Exploration

The search for sources of natural gas had taken executives from the utilities all over the world. In the Caribbean they have agreed on a scheme to import gas from Trinidad and they are also considering plans to import Venezuelan gas. On the Pacific coast of south America there are substantial reserves of gas off the coast of Ecuador, while in Australia they have looked at the feasibility of importing from fields discovered off the north west coast and from reserves in central Australia which would need a 650 mile long pipeline to transport the gas to a coastal terminal. Utilities on the west coast of the United States are also interested in Indonesian gas.

The value of natural gas has been demonstrated by the willingness of the Americans to consider shipping supplies from the

Persian Gulf—the longest sea route so far mentioned in any LNG project. But the greatest interest has been in the prospect of bringing Russian gas into the American system. The Soviet Union has the world's largest gas reserves, a large portion of which lie in the inaccessible parts of north west Siberia. It has been estimated that this region combined with the Yakutia fields in east central Siberia have total reserves of 1,060 million million cubic feet.

Outside the Caribbean, the most convenient source of exportable gas is located in Nigeria. The intensive exploration effort there has increased natural gas reserves from 1.7 million cubic feet in 1965 to 40 million million cubic feet in 1972. Shell/BP who pioneered the development of oil in Nigeria have been anxious to establish an LNG chain to the United States for several years but they have been prevented from doing so by Government delays. Shell/BP, in partnership with the Nigerian National Oil Company has a proposal to build an 800 million cubic feet a day liquefaction plant at Bonny using gas from the group's fields in eastern Nigeria. Gulf Oil also in partnership with the Nigerian state oil company is in the early stages of negotiating a scheme for an LNG chain to utilise gas from the American company's offshore fields.

Since 1971 a group of American oil and gas companies combined with shipping interests have been discussing the export of LNG from the north western Siberian fields to the east coast of the United States. In the north west, the Urengoi field is estimated to contain reserves of 100 million million cubic feet—the world's largest known reservoir. Export of gas will involve the construction of a 1,500 mile long pipeline from the field to the ice-free port of Murmansk in north west Russia. The Americans have talked of pumping 700 million cubit feet of gas a day through the pipeline. However the length of the pipeline and the difficult terrain over which it would have to be laid has cast some doubts over the economic viability of the venture.

The reserves in central east Siberia have attracted the attention of the El Paso Natural Gas Company and Occidental Petroleum who want to transport gas from two large fields in the Vilyuy basin to the Pacific coast for export. The Russians have estimated that total reserves in this inaccessible area are 425 million million cubic feet but at least $120 million would be needed for a further drilling programme to confirm these forecasts. The

Soviet Government has suggested two possible pipeline routes to move the gas to the Pacific. If all the reserves are destined for exports they would approve a 450 mile route, but there is a possibility that some of the gas would be required in the industrial centres being built up in the Soviet far east, and in this case 700 mile pipeline would be built to serve these areas as well as export terminals.

El Paso and Occidental plan to export 2 million million cubic feet of gas per day if the project is finally approved. Half of the exports would go to the west coast of the United States and the remainder to Japan. The USA and USSR, which together account for 75 per cent of existing consumption, also hold half of proven world reserves.

Japan already has two overseas sources of natural gas available. Since 1969, Phillips and Marathon have been exporting 50,000 million cubic feet of gas from Cook Inlet in southern Alaska to Tokyo Electric and Tokyo Gas, and, at the end of 1972, Shell began a 20 year contract to supply 260,000 million cubic feet of gas from Brunei to a group of Japanese utilities. The success of the Brunei scheme, which is the largest operational LNG chain in the world, has encouraged Shell to begin work on a second chain to export 250,000 million cubic feet of gas from nearby Sarawak to Japan. Apart from the LNG contract to ship Badak gas and Arun gas from Indonesia to Japan, Japanese utilities are interested in the potential of the Attaka field offshore, and other marine prospects in the South China Sea, the Gulf of Thailand and the Mekong Delta in South Vietnam. Japanese utilities have also been in competition with American west coast utilities for Australian gas supplies.

The Japanese consider that their geographical position makes them the most attractive customers for gas imported from the Persian Gulf. Work has begun on a liquefaction plant on Das Island to process gas from the Abu Dhabi marine areas, prior to export, to Tokyo Electric which has contracted to take 435 million cubic feet a day for a 20 year period starting in 1976. The most attractive LNG prospects however lie in Iran which has the largest gas reserves in the Middle East. Apart from supplies produced in association with oil. Iran has several large and undeveloped dry gas fields. US and Japanese and Norwegian companies in partnership with the National Iranian Gas Company have begun a 700 million US dollar project to build a 1,200 million cubic feet a day liquefaction plant to process gas from the Gachsaran and associated fields. Shipments are scheduled to start at an initial rate of 800 million cubic feet a day in 1976. Considerable interest has also been shown in the construction of an LNG plant on Qeshm Island which would be supplied from the large gas discovery made at Sarkhun in 1973.

LNG shipping

Ever since the development of the ocean going LNG tanker, as a result of the research work undertaken in America and in Europe, the carriage of LNG has aroused considerable interest. The ships are vital to the whole concept of the LNG chain. Although the pioneering work was undertaken in the United States, it is only in recent years that the American industry has re-established itself as an industry capable of building the large, costly sophisticated ships which are now required. France has also become a major force in the construction of LNG ships as have shipyards in Norway. By the end of 1973, liquefied gas carriers accounted for almost 4.1m tons out of the total world order book of 128.9m tons. Although in tonnage terms this would appear small the gas carrier tonnage in fact represents about 5.9m cubic metres of capacity. Out of this total 1.8m cubic metres is being built in France, 1.6m cubic metres in the United States, 1.2m cubic metres in Japan and 0.6m cubic metres in Norway.

Following the construction in Britain of the two gas carriers, Methane Princess and Methane Progress, each of 27,400 cubic metres capacity in the mid 1960s, a considerable number of new tank systems have been developed and the size of the ships has grown rapidly. In 1967, the Swedish yard of Kockums M.V. built two 71,500 cubic metre capacity vessels for the LNG chain between Alaska and Japan. Since then ship size has increased further.

Japan, which will rely extensively in the years ahead on liquefied natural gas as an energy source, had remained outside the field in terms of LNG construction because, while Japanese yards could compete effectively with other yards in the construction of large

Table 7/1: World LNG Shipbuilding Capability

Shipbuilder	Vessels per annum	
	Indicated capacity	Probable capacity
Europe		
Moss-Rosenberg	1	1
Kockums	1.5	1.5
Chantiers de l'Atlantique	2	2
La Seyne	2	2
La Ciotat	2	2
Dunkerque	1.5	1.5
Italcantieri	1.5	1.5
HDW	1.5	1.5
	13	13
USA		
Avondale	1	1
General Dynamics	2	2
Newport News	2	2
Todd	1	1
	6	6
Japan		
Mitsubishi	1	—
IHI	2	2
Kawasaki	2	2
Hitachi	2	2
Mitsui	2	—
Nippon Kokan	2	—
	11	6
Total	30	25

Source: H. P. Drewry (Shipping Consultants) Ltd. London

Table 7/2: LNG Ships on Order — Autumn 1973

M³	Delivery	Owner	Builder
75,000	End 1973	Shell Tankers (U.K.)	Ch. de l'Atlantique
75,000	1974	Shell Tankers (U.K.)	Ch. de l'Atlantique
120,000	1976	Zodiac Shipping N.V.	Ch. de l'Atlantique
120,000	1977	Odyssey Trading Co.	Ch. de l'Atlantique
40,000	Dec. 1973	Messageries Maritime	Ch. Naval de la ciotat
120,000	1974	Gazocean Armement	Ch. Naval de la Ciotat
120,000	1975	Transoceiangas Shipping S.A.	Ch. Naval de la Ciotat
75,000	1975	Shell Tankers (U.K.)	Ch. Naval de la Ciotat
125,000	1974	El Paso Natural Gas Co.	A&C de Dunkerque et Bordeaux
125,000	1975	El Paso Natural Gas Co.	A&C de Dunkerque et Bordeaux
125,000	1976	El Paso Natural Gas Co.	A&C de Dunkerque et Bordeaux
75,000	1973	Shell Tankers (U.K.)	C.N.I.M.
75,000	1975	Shell Tankers (U.K.)	C.N.I.M.
35,000	1974	Pancravette Ltd.	C.N.I.M.
35,000	1975	International Lofoten Maritime Enterprises	C.N.I.M.
29,000	Oct. 1973	Peder Smedvig	Moss Rosenberg
29,000	1974	Hilmar Reksten	Moss Rosenberg
87,600	Oct. 1973	Buries Markes/Lief Hoegh	Moss Rosenberg
87,600	1974	LNG Carriers Ltd. (P&O; A. P. Moller; F&E)	Moss Rosenberg
125,000	1975	Gotaas-Larsen	Moss Rosenberg
125,000	1976	Gotaas-Larsen	Moss Rosenberg
125,000	1976	Gottas-Larsen	Moss Rosenberg
5,000	1974	Nav. de Prod. Licuados S.A. (Naproli)	Ast. Tomas-Ruiz de Velasco, Bilbao
2,420	1974	Benard Schulte	Heinrich Brand K.G. Oldenburg
2,420	1974	Oil Carrier Co. (Danish)	Heinrich Brand K. G. Oldenburg
125,000	1975	Cryogenics Energy Transport Inc.	General Dynamics, Qunicy
125,000	1976	LNG Transport Inc.	General Dynamics, Quincy
125,000	1977	Liquegas Transport Inc.	General Dynamics, Quincy
125,000	1977	Gotass-Larsen	Howaldtswerke-D.W. A.G.
125,000	1977	Leif Hoegh	Howaldtswerke-D.W. A.G.
125,000	1976	El Paso Natural Gas Co.	Newport News
125,000	1976	El Paso Natural Gas Co.	Newport News
125,000	1977	El Paso Natural Gas Co.	Newport News
125,000	1976	El Paso Natural Gas Co.	Avondale Shipyards, New Orleans
125,000	1977	El Paso Natural Gas Co.	Avondale Shipyards, New Orleans
125,000	1977	El Paso Natural Gas Co.	Avondale Shipyards, New Orleans
128,600	1977	Gotaas-Larsen	Kawasaki
128,600	1977	Gotaas-Larsen	Kawasaki
125,000	1978	El Paso Natural Gas Co.	Avondale Shipyards, New Orleans
125,000	1978	El Paso Natural Gas Co.	Avondale Shipyards, New Orleans
125,000	1978	El Paso Natural Gas Co.	Avondale Shipyards, New Orleans
129,500	1977	Louis Dreyfus S.A.	At & CM de France, Dunkirk
129,000	—	"Methania" (Belgium)	Boelwarf, Tamise
130,000	1978	Leif Hoegh	Kawasaki
125,000	?1978	Sonatrach	La Ciotat
125,000	?1978	Sonatrach	La Ciotat
125,000	?1978	Sonatrach	C.N.I.M.
125,000	?1978	Sonatrach	C.N.I.M.
125,000	?1978	Sonatrach	Atlantique
130,000	1977	Pacific Lighting Corp. Subsid.	Sun SB & DD, Chester, Pa.
130,000	1978	Pacific Lighting Corp. Subsid.	Sun SB & DD, Chester, Pa.

Source: H. Clarkson & Co Ltd

Table 7/2 continued

Tank Design	Tank System	Employment/Remarks
Conch Ocean	Membrane, Stainless Steel	Brunei/Japan
Conch Ocean	Membrane, Stainless Steel	Brunei/Japan
Gaz Transport	Membrane, Invar	N/A
Gaz Transport	Membrane, Invar	N/A
Conch Ocean	Membrane, Stainless Steel	Algeria/France
Conch Ocean	Membrane, Stainless Steel	Algeria/U.S.A.
Conch Ocean	Membrane, Stainless Steel	N/A
Conch Ocean	Membrane, Stainless Steel	Brunei/Japan
Gaz Transport	Membrane, Invar	Algeria/U.S.A.
Gaz Transport	Membrane, Invar	Algeria/U.S.A.
Gaz Transport	Membrane, Invar	Algeria/U.S.A.
Gaz Transport	Membrane, Invar	Brunei/Japan
Gaz Transport	Membrane, Invar	Brunei/Japan
Gaz Transport	Membrane, Invar	N/A LNG/LPG
Gaz Transport	Membrane, Invar	N/A LNG/PLG
Kvaerner Moss	Free standing, spherical, aluminium	N/A LNG/Ethylene/LPG
Kvaerner Moss	Free standing, spherical, aluminium	N/A LNG/Ethylene/LPG
Kvaerner Moss	Free standing, spherical 9% nickel steel	Algeria/U.S.A./then Abu Dhabi/Japan
Kvaerner Moss	Free standing, spherical, 9% nickel steel	N/A
Kvaerner Moss	Free standing, spherical, aluminium	Abu Dhabi/Japan
Kvaerner Moss	Free standing, spherical, aluminium	Abu Dhabi/Japan
Kvaerner Moss	Free standing, spherical, aluminium	Abu Dhabi/Japan
Senor	Free standing, spherical, 9% nickel steel	N/A LNG/Ethylene/LPG
Sener		N/A LNG/Ethylene
		N/A LNG/Ethylene
Kvaerner Moss	Free standing, spherical, aluminium	Algeria/USEC
Kvaerner Moss	Free standing, spherical, aluminium	Algeria/USEC
Kvaerner Moss	Free standing, spherical, aluminium	Algeria/USEC
Kvaerner Moss	Free standing, spherical, aluminium	N/A
Kvaerner Moss	Free standing, spherical, aluminium	N/A
Technigaz	Membrane, stainless steel	Algeria/U.S.A.
Technigaz		Algeria/U.S.A.
Technigaz		Algeria/U.S.A.
Conch	Free standing, prismatic, aluminium	Algeria/U.S.A.
Conch	Free standing, prismatic aluminium	Algeria/U.S.A.
Conch	Free standing, prismatic aluminium	Algeria/U.S.A.
Kvaerner Moss	Free standing, spherical, aluminium	N/A
Kvaerner Moss	Free standing, spherical, aluminium	N/A
Conch	Free standing, prismatic, aluminium	?Algeria/U.S.A.
Conch	Free standing, prismatic, aluminium	?Algeria/U.S.A.
Conch	Free standing, prismatic, aluminium	?Algeria/U.S.A.
Gaz Transport	Membrane, Invar	Algeria/Europe (Sagape)
Gaz Transport	Membrane, Invar	Algeria/Europe (Sagape)
Kvaerner Moss	—	—
—	—	—
—	—	—
—	—	—
Conch	Free standing, prismatic aluminium	Alaska/Indonesia—California
Conch	Free standing, prismatic aluminium	Alaska/Indonesia—California

tankers and similar vessels, prices quoted for construction of LNG ships were considerably higher—some 10-15 per cent above European prices. But 1973 saw the emergence of Japan as a builder of these vessels with Kawasaki Heavy Industries gaining orders for three large ships including one for an LNG carrier of 130,000 cubic metres—the largest yet contracted. The two other ships ordered from Kawasaki were of 128,600 cubic metres capacity, illustrating the sharp increase in size which has taken place within a period of less than ten years.

Gas carriers are extremely complex ships to build requiring extensive and expensive outfitting. The tanks alone represent a high proportion of total construction costs. During 1973 prices for LNG carriers rose by about 25 per cent and the cost of a 125,000 cubic metre ship—which at present is the most popular size would cost between $90m and $100 million for delivery in 1978. But berths are at a premium since there are currently close to 40 LNG carriers on order and all scheduled for delivery in the period up to the end of 1978. Only a prolonged depression of the market would be likely to cause builders to revise their prices downwards.

In broad terms LNG carriers are about twice as expensive to build as a VLCC of equivalent size. The capital cost ratio between a gas carrier and a conventional carrier per unit weight is estimated at about 3:1 taking into account the 20 per cent higher calorific value of LNG. A compensating factor, for the present however, is the fact that insurance rates are considerably lower than those for the large oil tankers since an LNG carrier has yet to be involved in a major incident. There is a tendency towards building larger vessels in order to reduce the unit cost per deadweight carried, and the next generation of LNG carriers could well be vessels of 160,000 cubic metres carrying capacity and in the longer term, 200,000 cubic metres capacity vessels are likely to emerge.

In its liquefied form gas has a relatively poor heat density ratio. For example one barrel of LNG contains only about 60 per cent of the heat contained in an equivalent quantity of oil.

Distance therefore plays an important role in establishing an LNG chain since pressure for reducing costs is considerable. Recently there has been considerable interest in transporting methanol derived from natural gas—and although transportation costs are reduced this alternative suffers because of the substantial investment in processing.

Virtually all the technology of the tank systems involved has taken place in Europe notably in France, Norway and Britain. The various systems have been purchased by other shipyards on a licence basis. Although there are many variations the four main type of tank systems now available are the membrane, semi-membrane, prismatic and spherical free-standing tanks. The spherical tank design, developed in Norway by the Kvaerner Group has enjoyed the greatest success although other systems have been employed with great success on the earlier LNG carriers.

Future prospects

The Arab oil embargoes and supply cut backs have served to focus more attention on the role which natural gas is likely to play in the total world energy picture in future. 1973 saw a high rate of contracting for LNG ships. Apart from more orders placed in the United States and the breakthrough made by Japan, Germany also entered the field while Italy Spain and Poland are all potential LNG builders for the future. It is estimated that throughout the world there are some 15 yards with a combined output of 25 vessels annually which can be regarded as serious builders of LNG ships with eight of these yards having an aggregate output of 13 vessels per annum.

Certainly there is a strong trend in demand for the future but estimates vary on the overall requirement. It has been forecast that the number of ships which require to be ordered for delivery by the end of the present decade to meet transportation requirements would be 25 covering transportation chains serving the United States, Japan and western Europe. Between 1980 and 1985 there are indications that a further 39 LNG ships would have to be ordered. A feature of the LNG carrier building programme that has emerged is the number of ships which have been ordered without specific charters. At the end of 1973 there were more than a dozen of these high cost ships contracted without a charter party. However, with further growth in this sector of the shipping

industry most of these vessels should find employment without
difficulty. It is possible that a limited spot market could develop
for LNG carriers linked particularly to periods of peak demand
and also to the emergence of new natural gas exporting countries
anxious to take a share in the transportation of LNG.

Chart 7/2: Likely pattern of LNG trade by 1980s

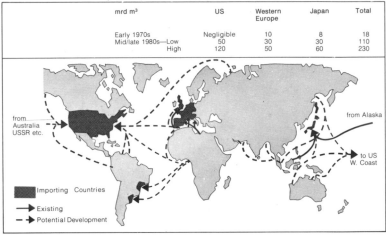

mrd m³		US	Western Europe	Japan	Total
Early 1970s		Negligible	10	8	18
Mid/late 1980s—Low		50	30	30	110
	High	120	50	60	230

from Australia USSR etc.

from Alaska

to US W. Coast

Importing Countries

Existing

Potential Development

Source: Shell

From the point of view of investors in LNG chains, Algeria's
decision not to include gas supplies to the United States in the
general embargo on oil following the 1973 Arab-Israeli war is
encouraging. But the Arab decision to cut off oil to the United
States has caused disquiet among the utilities in the consuming
countries. With sums ranging up to £1,200m involved in LNG
schemes, the producer nations will be asked to take a greater
share in the financing of the overall projects to ensure that they too
suffer proportionately if supplies of gas are cut off for political
reasons.

Chapter Eight
The Search for New Reserves

Oil exploration has acquired an unwarranted aura of glamour during the relatively short life of the oil industry. Gushers pushing crude oil hundreds of feet into the air were a rarity even in the early days of exploration, when technology had not been developed to control such wasteful spills, and, together with the hard and often ruthless activities in Texas that turned many explorers into millionaires, produced a fictional image of the explorer. In reality, modern exploration work is far from glamorous. Outside the United States, most of the prime prospective areas are either in desert, miles offshore, in previously unpenetrated jungle, or above the Arctic circle.

The explorers are continually moving into more inhospitable areas as it becomes important that new oil fields are discovered to keep pace with the expanding world consumption. Before the supply crisis of 1973, Mr. H. R. Warman, British Petroleum's Exploration Manager forecast that the oil industry would need to find a new North Sea every two years to satisfy the then current consumption trends—a tall order by any standards. But that was before the crisis. The sharp shock administered to the main consuming areas of the world by the Arab oil cut-backs and embargoes will stimulate the effort to perfect alternative sources of energy, but in the short term will not affect the massive exploration effort that is now in progress throughout the world.

The restrictions on production in the Middle East have triggered off new and much higher prices for crude oil. Disregarding the exceptional short term peaks in prices immediately after the Arab production cut-back and embargo on supplies to the United States and Holland, the average cost of crude oil will make the development of alternative sources of fuel an economic proposition. In the short term the quadrupling of crude oil prices between October 1973 and January 1, 1974 will present most of the major consuming countries with serious balance of payments problems and will impose even greater hardships on the emerging nations. The British attitude typified that of most countries groaning under the strain of paying the new prices for crude, but with the prospect of developing its own oil source by the end of the decade. Top priority has been given to exploration and development work, a trend that has been repeated in any country that has the opportunity to offset these additional costs by the early exploration of indigenous reserves.

But as the British are finding, exploration work is a long and painstaking business, and following up the discoveries and actually getting oil out of the ground can be an even longer process, especially if the find has been made offshore. Few countries now engaged in the hectic chase after new sources of crude oil, to enable their import bill to be reduced, realistically expect to find the kind of Middle East scale bonanzas, which would not only free them from the burden of expensive crude oil imports but elevate them into the exclusive exporters club. Major new reserves are undoubtedly still to be found in the established producing areas of the world but those discovered on the Arab side of the Persian Gulf are not likely to be exploited quickly. Only Sheikhdoms like Sharjah, which until recently had no oil and looked enviously at its rich neighbours, are likely to make a really concerted exploration effort in this part of the Arab world.

The record of the oil prospectors has been good since the end of World War II, but there are very real doubts whether they would be able in the next two decades to repeat their performance of the last 30 years even with the more sophisticated technology available to them. Since 1948, new reserves have been found in countries outside the Communist block at the average rate of 18,000m barrels a year, but in order to meet the pre-crisis demand trends the oil men would have had to improve on this record and find 20,000m barrels a year over the next ten years. The oil companies achieved this excellent average only because they were just beginning to tap the riches of the Middle East. In 1948, for instance, Aramco first drilled into the Ghawar field in Saudi Arabia which after 20 years of production still contains an estimated 70,000m barrels. In addition, Abu Dhabi and Qatar were

Chart 8/1: Free world annual oil discoveries

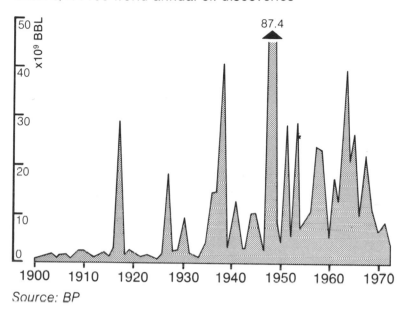

Source: BP

Chart 8/2: Estimated world future crude oil discoveries

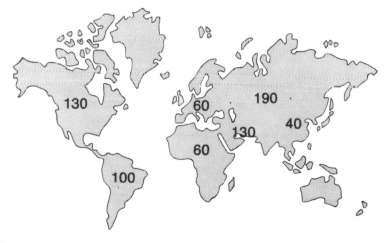

Source: BP

being opened up, and outside the Middle East major discoveries were made in Libya, Algeria and Nigeria. No matter how advanced the exploration technology becomes or the amount of money that is poured into the search, new oil bearing zones of similar sizes are extremely unlikely.

Oil men are still unable to explain why the Middle East is so prolific. Over 60 per cent of the world's proven oil reserves are to be found within a 400,000 square mile tract surrounding the Persian Gulf. Oil is normally found in sedimentary basins, but the Gulf area accounts for a very small proportion of the world's sedimentary basins. Other sedimentary basins throughout the world have been criss-crossed with exploration wells but only a few have emerged as large oil producing areas and none on the scale of the Middle East. Only part of southern United States, the Lake Maracaibo area of Venezuela, the North Slope of Alaska and Libya have come anywhere close to rivaling the Gulf, and individually they are not in the same league. Around 70 per cent of the world's proven reserves are to be found in about 125 large oilfields, and almost half of these are in the Middle East.

Are there any more of these really large fields to be found? It seems unlikely that any deposits similar to Ghawar or Burgan in Kuwait have remained undetected but as the North Sea has proven, there are still a number of medium sized fields yet to be uncovered that can make a significant contribution to the economy of the country in which they are found. Oil prospectors are the first to admit they are by no means infallible. Seismic surveys—charting subterranean geology by measuring the reflected sound waves bounced off underground rock formations—have often shown extremely favourable conditions for finding oil. Seasoned prospectors would have been prepared to stake money on the formation producing oil but, when the drilling bit has pierced the structure, nothing of value has been found. The North Sea is a classic example of an area ignored by the oil industry. It was not until gas was found onshore in Holland that the search was stimulated for further gas in the southern North Sea and from there oil exploration began in more northerly waters. The opposite also often happens. The discoveries on the North Slope of Alaska produced oil exploration fever in the Actic islands and far north of Canada. Drilling began, but no significant deposits of oil have been found and there are growing doubts among oil explorers whether anything ever will be.

During the mid-1970s the North Sea will probably continue to attract an above average share of the oil industry's new exploration budgets estimated at an annual £500m. Offshore exploration is also continuing off the East coast of Canada and the Gulf of Mexico, and there is both onshore and offshore exploration work in South America, West Africa, Indonesia, Malaysia and Australia. In all these areas the latest exploration equipment is being used which cuts down the possibility of failing to spot the smaller accumulations of oil that can be profitable on shore and even offshore if found close to much larger and economically viable fields.

New technology is not only making it possible to locate these much smaller fields, but is increasing the ability of the oil industry to recover more oil from the larger fields that are found. The most favourable geological structures will probably allow about 60 per cent of the oil present in a reservoir to be recovered. New methods of "secondary" recovery have been given a boost by the much higher prices that can now be obtained for crude oil. Pumping oil out of the reservoir, injecting steam or separating the oil when it has become contaminated with water, can make a small but noticeable difference to an established oil field approaching the end of its workable life. In the past these methods have been expensive and, except in special circumstances, the oil companies have found it more economic to look for fresh reserves rather than embark on secondary recovery. Iran, for instance, has criticised the international oil companies for not making better use of secondary recovery and is preparing to drain every available drop of oil from its fields.

Secondary recovery can, however, have only a marginal effect on the rate at which new reserves must be found. There is scepticism that the rate of 20,000 million barrels of new discoveries a year can be met and it is also doubtful whether the previous 25 years' average of 18,000m barrels a year can be equalled. Just how short of this target the prospectors will fall may depend on their success in overcoming the hazards posed by drilling for oil under the sea. As can be seen, considerable emphasis is placed on the offshore oil search, and by 1980 about one third of the world's total oil requirements could be flowing from submarine fields.

Offshore exploration is still in its infancy. The first fixed platforms were not installed in the shallower waters of the Gulf of Mexico until 1947, and there has been a slow progression through various types of drilling rigs and marine exploration is now the principal growth area for companies supplying equipment to the oil industry. Over 9m barrels of oil are being produced from under the sea each day—over 20 per cent of the world total. Much of the large scale offshore production is in the established oil bearing zones in the Middle East and the Gulf of Mexico.

Drilling in deep waters has to be done from a semi-submersible floating rig or a drilling ship. Offshore exploration technology has been developing rapidly and it is now possible to drill in over 600 ft of water. Specialised drillships that remain on station through fore-and-aft and sideways thrusting propellors controlled by computer can operate in depths of over 1,000 ft. Methods of actually getting any oil found in these depths to the shore are in a less advanced stage of development. BP and the Shell/Esso group are carrying out the pioneering work in developing North Sea fields that lie in over 400 ft of water. This involves the construction of steel or concrete platforms over 500 ft high, that have to be installed on the oilfield to process the oil before pumping it ashore by pipeline. Systems to carry out this work automatically on the seabed are also under development and are essential if oil from really deep water is to be produced.

The cost of drilling a well in deep water can reach £25,000 a day. The latest semi-submersible rigs to carry out the work cost over

---

Table 8/1: Offshore Drilling Rigs on Order

		Floaters		
Water depth capability Feet	Sea bed supported Jack ups	Semi- Sub- mersibles	Drill- ships	Total
Less than 200	0	0	0	0
200 to 350	16	0	0	16
350 to 700	0	33	5	38
700 to 1 000	0	12	2	14
More than 1 000	0	2	2	4
Total	16	47	9	72

Source: BP

£12m each, and shipyards throughout the world have orderbooks for drilling vessels worth over £650m. They will be used on world-wide exploration programmes, costing about £500m a year, looking for large offshore deposits. From the point of view of the oil companies it is essential that large fields are found offshore. Wells drilled offshore need to produce at least 5,000 barrels a day to make production a viable proposition. In terms of the 400,000 barrels a day from the Forties Field and 100,000 barrels a day from other North Sea finds, this may seem small. It must be remembered that onshore wells of 100 barrels a day can be profitable. In the United States the average output per well is only 180 barrels a day and for the state of Louisiana which contains some of the most modern facilities, the average is only 100 barrels a day. Against this must be balanced the low cost of onshore exploration—about one tenth of offshore costs—and the pro rata reduction in the installation of production facilities, compared with the £100m needed to build a permanent steel or concrete platform to produce oil in 400 ft of water.

Chart 8/3: World number of available offshore drilling rigs

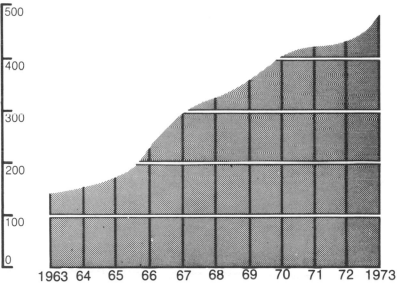

Source: BP

Working in the North Sea has tested offshore drilling techniques to their limit. Weather in the waters to the north-east of the Shetlands is as rough and inhospitable as anywhere in the world and the latest semi-submersible rigs have been designed to operate efficiently in these conditions. Efforts are now being made to ensure that these vessels can be supplied during bad weather so that drilling is not suspended because of lack of materials. Rigs certified to operate in the North Sea will certainly be able to undertake duties anywhere in the world except in certain areas of the Arctic.

No method has yet been found for drilling and producing oil in waters subject to thick ice coverage in winter. A land rig has been established on an artificial island in the Mackenzie River delta in the Beaufort Sea because no floating rig was available for these conditions. Oil has also been discovered in the Cook inlet in southern Alaska and is now in production through conventional platforms, but in this area the ice is relatively thin.

Table 8/2: World Oil Reserves and Production (Excluding USSR etc)

	Proved Reserves End 1972 Thousand million barrels	Production 1972 Million barrels per day
Offshore		
Middle East	75	3.0
Venezuela	10	2.4
United States	9	1.8
Others	33	1.7
	127	8.9
Onshore	340	35.2
Total	467	44.1

Source: BP

The North Sea

Considerable play has been made about the potential of the North Sea because it is in the unusual position of being close to a major consuming area. Five countries, Britain, Norway, Denmark, West

Germany and Holland have territory in the North Sea but the main exploration effort is going into the more northerly waters held by Britain and Norway. The search for oil began after sizeable quantities of gas had been discovered in the southern part of the North Sea off the East Anglian coast of Britain. The Ekofisk field was found in Norwegian waters and Forties field in the UK Sector which gave a tremendous stimulus to the exploration work.

Small finds have been made in Danish and Dutch waters but there has been little activity on West German territory. The more attractive terms for oil companies operating in British waters has diverted some equipment away from Norway where the Government is taking a tough line with exploration groups. The bulk of the UK exploration work is now being done in deep water about 150 miles off the Sheltands, where already there have been sizeable oil and gas finds. But there are still many excellent prospects to be drilled in Norwegian waters. The seas above the 72nd parallel have not yet been opened up for exploration, and some of the waters off the Actic Island of Spitzbergen are said to contain first class geological structures.

Apart from the Forties Field, major finds in British Waters have been made by Shell/Esso (Brent, Dunlin and Cormorant); Occidental (Piper); Conoco/Gulf, NCB (Hutton); Total (Alwyn); Mobil (Beryl); Phillips (Josephine and Maureen); Amoco (Montrose); Hamilton Brothers (Argyll); BP/Ranger and Burmah (Ninian). The increasing rate of discoveries makes the British Government's official estimates of 2m barrels a day of production by 1980 seem rather conservative. The most optimistic forecast has come from Dr Jack Birks of BP, who estimated total production from the North Sea at 4m barrels a day by 1980 with the UK sector contributing 3m of these. In Norway there are even more optimistic forecasts than Dr Birks' about the ability of the oil companies to get oil ashore. Mr Nils Gulnes, formerly deputy director-general of the Industry Ministry in Norway and now senior vice-president of Den Norske Credit Bank, expects production to top 2m barrels a day by 1980. Meeting all these forecasts will require an intensification of the exploration effort and a much greater involvement by local industries in the provision of the specialised equipment needed to land the oil. The northern North Sea search is also yielding considerable quantities of gas. Total and the Petronord Group have found the giant Frigg field, and commercial quantities of gas

are available in association with the oil in a number of discoveries.

There may be oil in other parts of North European waters. A Soviet
scientist has suggested that the Icelandic continental shelf may
contain large deposits of oil and gas. The optimistic view of
Iceland's prospects came after a research vessel had completed
a scientific investigation of the North Atlantic which had undertaken geophysical and geochemical work to the North of the
island and also collected numerous rock samples. French,
American and Danish companies have also formed a consortium
to apply for concessions on the continental shelf off Greenland's
west coast. Drilling is not expected to begin for two or three years
in this area although some geophysical surveys have already
been carried out.

Alaskan prospects

The North Sea took over the exploration limelight from Alaska
where environmentalist objections to the Trans-Alaska Pipeline
successfully delayed the start-up of production from proven fields
and also curbed new exploratory work. The go-ahead for the
pipeline in early 1974 has revived interest in exploration work,
since little work was done during the time when the future of the
line was in the balance and large tracts of territory have still not
been explored properly. Operating in Alaska presents logistical
problems comparable with the North Sea. The techniques of
drilling in sub-zero temperatures have been perfected and the
greatest difficulties arise from keeping the operations fully supplied. The companies have been forced to build their own refinery
at Prudhoe Bay to keep the drilling sites supplied with diesel and
heating oils but everything else has to be brought in from southern
Alaska.

Across the Canadian border, some 300 miles from BP's original
Prudhoe Bay discoveries, the Mackenzie River delta was at first
thought to be a similar excellent prospect. Exxon's Imperial Oil
associate has found gas in the area but reserves have not been
uncovered to justify the pipeline from the area that was first
mooted and doubts have now arisen about the potential of the
whole Canadian arctic area. Canada also has a more accessible

focal point for new exploration. Oil has been found off Sable Island off the east coast of Canada and the area is due for a more intensive drilling effort.

Action by environmentalists also held by for some time the distribution of new exploration leases in the Gulf of Mexico. A new bout of activity is underway in these more friendly waters, where the first serious offshore drilling took place after the Second World War. The Gulf is already a sizeable produced of oil and gas and the Americans are hoping that the latest allocation of licences will yield new and much needed finds. The moratorium on drilling off the coast of California is expected to be lifted. The huge spillage that blanketed the coastline following a drilling incident in the Santa Barbara Channel has resulted in an ultra-cautious approach to this geologically unstable area.

South American action

The United States southern neighbour, Mexico, has one of the oldest oil industries in the world but is no longer self-sufficient and has been forced to enter the market for supplies. Pemex, the state oil company that controls all products has raised a $50m loan from Japanese and European banks to finance further exploration and the expansion of existing reserves. Further south the established industries in Venezuela and Trinidad also suffering from the fall off in production from their more mature fields and are looking for new reserves. Venezuela is embarking on a further exploration programme in Lake Maracaibo and offshore. Other South American countries, including Brazil and Argentina have poured considerable resources into the search for new reserves without any conspicuous success. Operating in the interior has been hampered by the lack of roads but companies are learning to cope with the problems of working in inaccessible jungles and have been rewarded with a number of promising finds in Peru.

Across the South Atlantic, Nigeria commands most attention in the search for new reserves. Its offshore waters are far friendlier than Northern Europe and the issuing of new exploration licences, to American Japanese and European companies, all in partnership with the national oil company, are already beginning to yield impressive results. Further exploration work is in progress onshore but it is the marine concessions that are expected to produce the most spectacular results.

Nigeria tends to overshadow the work taking place on offshore concessions further south. The small Portuguese enclave of Cabinda is still considered highly prospective and Gulf Oil has hopes of increasing its output from the province while Gabon and Zaire are also encouraging offshore drilling. No other state in the southern part of the continent has been able to sustain a prolonged drilling programme.

North African programme

In North Africa, Libya can afford the luxury of a limited exploration programme while its neighbours search frantically for reserves that will provide new revenues. Even Algeria is looking for outside partners to uncover new fields although the tough terms have detered a number of operators. In Tunisia and Egypt every encouragement is given to outside companies to step up the prospecting programme. In the Mediterranean more enthusiasm is being shown. High-sulphur crude has been found off Spain and although there was a fruitless search in Maltese waters, more interest is being shown in concessions off the Italian mainland. The Aegean has also yielded a number of small but promising discoveries.

Iran and Iraq are the only countries in the Persian Gulf where exploration work is carried on with any sense of urgency. Large parts of Iran still remain to be explored properly and Iraq also has huge acreages that could yield new and exciting finds. As the increased costs of imports place an even greater strain on the currency reserves of India and Pakistan, moves to find more fields to supplement these countries indigenous reserves becomes a matter of urgency. Perhaps hardest hit by higher oil prices is Sri Lanka where a Russian oil survey has raised hopes of making discoveries off the north coast of the island.

Australia, like southern Africa, has been a source of disappointment to oil prospectors. Useful finds have been made in the Bass Strait and together with natural gas, oil has been found on numerous occasions on the mainland but always in relatively small quantities. The search goes on for bigger fields and has led to the discovery of sizeable natural fields off the north west coast.

In other parts of the Far East, it has been the offshore areas that have attracted most attention. Indonesia is expanding its established on-shore production by bringing in new offshore fields and with marine exploration activity at a high level, more significant finds are expected. In the neighbouring states of Sarawak and Sabah there has been intensive offshore activity by Shell which has resulted in a number of important oil finds as well as huge gas deposits. Output from the newly discovered fields is expected to push Malaysian production from about 100,000 barrels a day—roughly equal to the daily consumption—to around 500,000 barrels a day within two or three years. By the end of the decade the area may be a large exporter. Exploration is also taking place off the coast of West Malaysia and Conoco and Exxon have already made a number of finds.

South China Sea

Despite the uncertain political situation in Vietnam, eight groups have undertaken to explore local waters, although they are not required to operate from bases in south Vietnam. There are reported to be a number of very thick sedimentary structures south and east of the Mekong Delta. Exploratory drilling has also started in the Cambodian sector of the Gulf of Siam but a number of territorial disputes have arisen between Cambodia, South Vietnam and Thailand now that the prospects for finding oil in the area look promising. Thai waters have already produced both oil and gas finds. The seizure of the South Vietnamese Paracel islands in the South China Sea by the Chinese is thought to have been prompted by the possibility of large offshore oil reserves in the area. In the more northerly part of the South China Sea, interest in offshore oil and gas has been stimulated by the small oil and gas shows off the Philippine island of Palawan.

The extent of the exploration programme in mainland China is still shrouded in mystery but as output appears to have doubled during 1973, the state-owned oil industry has obviously been busy. Offshore exploration has started in Pohai Bay with the help of the Japanese.

Chart 8/4: Free world crude oil production

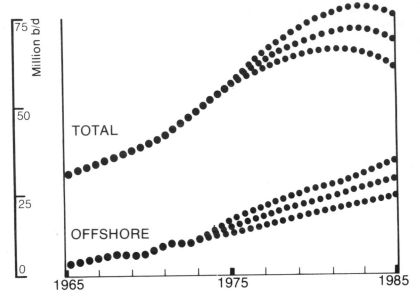

Source: BP

Chapter Nine
Alternative Power Sources

Alternatives to oil as the world's principal source of primary energy have been known for many years. The industrial nations developed and expanded by using coal and, with ample reserves available, could easily return to this source. Nuclear power has held out the promise of cheap electricity, but technical problems and severe competition from conventional power stations burning low-cost oil have produced a much slower growth in the spread of atomic power stations. Engineers also have the capability for tapping the energy of the sun, harnessing the power of the vast reserves of hot water that lie beneath the earth's surface and using the tides and the wind to produce energy. But cheap oil, coupled with the aggressive marketing policies of the oil companies have never really given any of these alternatives a fair chance of being tested on a large scale. In a world where the demand for cheap fuel has been paramount, the argument for oil over more expensive alternatives has been unanswerable.

Governments have been warned that oil resources are finite and could be exhausted before the end of the century. The warnings have, to some extent, been heeded, but there has been little sense of urgency or cash forthcoming for the research and development programmes needed to perfect nuclear power or extract synthetic natural gas from coal, or squeeze crude oil from the huge shale oil deposits of western America. Governments could perhaps be forgiven for looking sceptically at gloomy forecasts of exhausted oil reserves by the year 2000; after all, similar prognostications have been made in the past, they have always been proved grossly inaccurate and new reserves have been uncovered. A new and more potent reason now exists for pushing ahead with development of alternative sources at the fastest possible rate.

The price of oil quadrupled in the last three months of 1973 and rose from being the most economical to the most expensive fuel.

Revival of coal

How easily could the world turn its back on crude oil as an energy source? Millions of pounds have been spent on converting industry to burn oil products instead of coal but, provided the coal was available, the switch back could be accomplished without too much difficulty *if* part of a phased energy policy. Certainly, the use of oil for generating electricity has become uneconomic compared with coal. While the technology is available for making widespread and efficient use of coal in industry and power stations, the amount of additional coal supplies that could be made available in the short term is limited. Reserves of coal are vast and dwarf the combined reserves of crude oil and gas, but the opening up of new mines takes up to four years, while strip mining and open-cast operations cannot start up overnight. According to the World Energy Conference, world reserves are 6.7m million tons with a further 2.1m million tons of brown coal and lignite. In the terminology of the coal industry, about 460,000m tons have been "measured". This means reserves that have been properly surveyed to provide reliable geological data about the extent and thickness of the seams. However, in the days of cheap oil there was little incentive to look for new coal seams and carry out expensive and detailed surveys on their size. Soaring oil costs have brought a boom to coal prospectors. The National Coal Board in Britain has, for instance, been involved in a massive exploration programme in Yorkshire that has uncovered new and rich reserves in the Selby area. The Board has plans for a new drift mine producing 5m tons of coal a year and has revitalised its capital spending programme so that improvements can be made to other modern pits. Like most coal authorities and private coal companies, the NCB has for several years foreseen an upsurge in the demand for coal and has prepared to make more supplies available. Mr Derek Ezra, Chairman of the NCB, was, before the oil supply crisis and the quadrupling of prices in 1973, talking in terms of coal becoming more competitive than oil for power stations and industry around the end of 1975 or early 1976. The cross over point came sooner than he thought.

Coal reserves

The rapid transformation of the price structure of oil has brought the size and accessibility of coal reserves into sharp focus. Mr G. Armstrong, the former chief geologist of the National Coal Board, using the World Energy Conference figures and assuming a 50 per cent recovery rate, estimated that about 4.4m million tons of coal would be ultimately available. Assuming that world consumption would increase at five per cent a year until the end of the century, reversing the current stagnation, world output of coal would have risen to 12,000m tons by the year 2000. The total amount of coal extracted between 1974 and the end of the century would be 200,000m tons and sufficient reserves would still

Table 9/1: World Coal Reserves

Region	Bituminous Coal and Anthracite	% of World Total	Brown Coal and Lignite	% of World Total	All Coals	% of World Total
Within non-communist world–						
United Kingdom	7,325	0.11	—	—	7,325	0.08
Other European						
Countries	77,642	1.16	28,986	1.42	106,628	1.22
North America	1,164,467	17.37	430,104	21.47	1,594,571	18.23
Asia	132,900	1.98	6,335	0.31	139,235	1.59
South America	72,465	1.08	—	—	72,465	0.83
Australia	16,000	0.24	95,600	4.68	111,600	1.28
Others	40,108	0.60	10,414	0.51	50,522	0.58
Total	1,510,907	22.54	571,439	27.99	2,082,346	23.81
Communist bloc in Europe						
and Asia	5,192,418	77.46	1,469,962	72.01	6,662,380	76.19
World Total	6,703,325	100.00	2,041,401	100.00	8,744,726	100.00

Source: "World Power Conference of Energy Resources", 1968 (except United Kingdom). UK reserves from NCB revision of September 1970

Table 9/2: Position of Coal Reserves

Area	Approximate Percentage of World Coal Reserves
USSR	61½%
North America	17½%
Asia (mainly China)	17 %
Europe	2½%
Africa	1½%
South America	less than ½%
Australasia	less than ½%

remain to sustain output at the level of the year 2000 for over 300 years. He also took the more pessimistic case of only 10 per cent of total reserves being recoverable which would still allow the year 2000 output level to be maintained for 50 years. But as the table shows, coal reserves, like oil deposits, are not equally distributed and shortages could appear fairly quickly and make Europe, for instance, as dependent on coal imports as it is now reliant on foreign oil.

Britain is not the only country planning to step up its output of coal. The United States Interior Department estimated that coal production could rise from its 1972 level of 541m tons to 1,300m tons by the year 2000, about 700m tons of which would be earmarked for electricity generation and 100m tons for export. The Soviet Union, with its huge reserves, plans production of 1,000m tons by 2000 compared with 655m tons in 1972, and Poland wants to expand its output from 151m tons in 1972 to between 190m and 200m tons by 1985. Statistics about Chinese coal production are difficult to obtain but it seems there is no doubt that it is the third biggest producer in the world and could come close to equalling the output levels of the US and the Soviet Union. South Africa has ample reserves to meet its domestic requirements and is planning to become a major exporter by raising output from 58m tons in 1972 to 200m tons by 2000, while Australia will push production from the 1972 level of 54m tons to 70m tons by 1980, and Canada will increase its small output of 16m tons to a sizeable 70m tons a year by 1980. Developing countries have not always found it economic to exploit coal reserves but preferred to build their industries on cheap oil imports. With the cost of oil now placing an intolerable burden on less affluent nations, the rate at which coal reserves in these countries are opened up will certainly accelerate. India is typical. By the end of 1974 domestic output should be 93m tons an increase of 20m tons a year over the 1972 output.

Oilmen move in

The importance of coal as a major source of energy in the future has also been recognised by the international oil companies. As part of their efforts to diversitfy from oil producers and traders into comprehensive providers of energy, they have begun to take positions in the coal market. In the United States, over 32 per cent of the country's production is now controlled by the oil companies who have also taken options on huge tracts of land containing coal reserves, for future use. Research and development into the multiple uses of coal has also been stepped up. For years, the fuel suffered from lack of fundamental research into new applications and was simply used as a method of raising steam. But as the Germans proved during World War II, oil products can successfully be produced from coal, provided the cost is no object. The South Africans are currently working, with some success, on perfecting similar processes and making the products obtained, competitive with refined oil. Britain, until the advent of cheap naphtha and North Sea gas, manufactured most of its gas supplies from coal. Gas utilities in the United States, faced with growing shortages of natural gas, are using British technology for manufacturing a synthetic natural gas that is compatible with indigenously-produced supplies. The Nixon Administration is committed to huge sums on energy research as part of its Project Independence, and the more efficient utilisation of coal reserves is high on the list of priorities for further investigation. Under consideration are more advanced mining techniques, the manufacture of crude oil from coal and the production of synthetic natural gas from coal underground—a process that would elimate the costly mining element. Germany is also planning to make more money available for coal research. Over DM946m will be made available between 1974 and 1976 for coal gasification, hydrogenation and production technology.

The conversion problem

One of the problems that has bedevilled electricity utilities throughout the world has been the low rate of energy conversion when fossil fuels are burned in power stations. Between 60 and 65 per cent of the energy is lost in even the most efficient stations, and after transmission and distribution losses only about 30 per cent of the energy contained in the original generating fuel finds its way to the consumer in the form of electricity. One solution to the inherent inefficiency of conventionally constructed power stations is the magneto-hydrodynamic (MHD) open cycle power system. Linked with a steam cycle turbo generator the efficiency rate could be pushed up to 50 per cent. The Russians have a small pilot plant working on methane, and research is already in progress in the United States. This is one of the areas that will benefit from the injection of Government funds, and estimates that a new power station using MHD power is at least 10 years away, may have to be revised. Perhaps the most interesting idea to come from the coal producers in recent years is the Coalplex. This strange-sounding development would be the coal industry's equivalent to the oil refinery. The Coalplex would absorb all the production from one large mine or a whole series of mines. Supplies would be moved to a large central site where the coal would be processed to produce energy, in the form of electricity and synthetic natural gas and crude oil; coke for the steel industry; coal extract for conversion to carbon products; tars, creosotes and ammoniacal liquors suitable for further upgrading; sulphur and sulphur compounds, and a fine ash suitable as a building aggregate. Apart from abundant supplies of coal, hydrogen would be needed as it is necessary for producing crude oil. It would also require use of the fluid bed combustion techniques for burning the coal, an area that is undergoing considerable research both in Britain and America. By using the fluid bed burning method, sulphur and other noxious materials can be removed from coal (or oil) during the initial combustion stage, abolishing the need for expensive flue cleaning equipment to prevent harmful emissions.

Nuclear power

Of the proven or semi-proven technologies available to take-over part of the role played by oil in the world's use of energy, nuclear power is the one that must live up to the claims being made for it by the reactor builders. Ultimately, the industrialised nations will call on electricity to fill the energy gap, and sufficient supplies

---

Table 9/3: Indication of growth of generating capacity in the Western World

| | GW(E) | | | |
	1973	1975	1980	1985
Western Europe				
Total	239	273	375	509
Nuclear	14	25	79	165
% Nuclear	5.9	9.2	21.1	32.4
Japan				
Total	80	100	160	220
Nuclear	2.9	7.4	32	60
% Nuclear	3.6	7.4	20	27.2
USA				
Total	390	475	665	915
Nuclear	28.9	54	130	280
% Nuclear	7.4	11.4	19.5	30.6
Rest of Western World				
Total	108	135	200	300
Nuclear	3.5	5.0	11	41
% Nuclear	3.2	3.7	5.5	13.7
Western World				
Total	817	983	1400	1944
Nuclear	49.3	91.4	252	546
% Nuclear	6.0	9.3	18.0	28.1

Source: BNFL

---

can only be made available if nuclear power stations are built on a far wider scale than they are today. Estimates of what this will involve vary greatly. British Nuclear Fuels, the company that will play a major part in supplying the fuel to the new generation of atomic reactors, put demand for nuclear power in the western world at 546GW (Gegga watt) by 1985, just over 28 per cent of total demand. The OECD feels that even more nuclear capacity will be necessary and that by 1990 there will be 970GWE in service—500 in the United States, 370 in Europe and 100 in Japan. The industrial base to manufacture this volume of hardware has already been established in·the United States and Europe.

Reactor building on a commercial scale has developed over the past 25 years and because of the high capital costs involved and the complexity of the technology, there has been none of the proliferation of small companies that has surrounded the growth of other industries. Moreover, because nuclear power is basically an extension of the technology used for nuclear weapons and the propulsion of nuclear submarines, governments were anxious in the early stages to restrict the number of companies with access to potentially sensitive information. Government involvement, however, provided its share of benefits through research carried out in state funded laboratories and grants for programmes undertaken by the companies.

American domination

America dominates the industry and the world sales market. Westinghouse and General Electric developed the pressurized water reactor and boiling water reactor to complement their already established conventional turbo-generator equipment sales. These light water systems emerged from the US Navy submarine propulsion programme into which the Government ploughed $2,000m. Between them, Westinghouse and GE have licensed their systems all over the world including Europe where local nuclear reactor industries were growing up. With their huge resources and large home market, the two American companies have, with a few exceptions, excluded European technology from the world nuclear export markets. Pressure for more and more nuclear capacity in the United States has been restrained by the influential environmental groups who have questioned the safety of these types of reactors. And it has not just been uninformed criticisms. Leading figures in the industry have raised doubts, with the result that utilities have found it difficult to acquire site licences for new stations. The length of time between planning a station and bringing it into commission has widened from around four to five years to over eight years. More complex technology has contributed to the delays, but the most significant factor has been the hold-ups in licensing procedures. As part of Project Independence, President Nixon has promised a speeding up of nuclear power station licensing, but with such a potentially dangerous piece of plant, nothing should be allowed to interfere with the full and public consideration of any doubts about the safety of systems.

Gulf/Shell venture

While the two big American builders have been able to undercut outside competitors on capital construction costs and to adhere to a more stringent construction programme, the stations themselves have not always been so efficient. Many of the earlier reactors are working below their design capacity. Problems encountered in the early stations have been ironed out in more sophisticated upgradings of the systems. Westinghouse and GE are now being challenged, both on their home market and in the lucrative export fields, by a new and powerful competitor—the Gulf Oil/Royal Dutch Shell grouping. Gulf, in 1967, acquired the General Atomic Division of the General Dynamics Corporation, who had developed a gas cooled reactor working at very high temperatures. A 40 megawatt prototype had been constructed and a 330 megawatt leader station was under construction for a Colorado utility. The General Atomics design has been given a more favourable rating by environmentalists and safety experts and, before the leader station at Peach Bottom in Colorado was operational, Gulf had obtained orders from normally cautious utilities who like to see a design in operation before placing an order. Gulf cleverly tied up marketing agreements with French and German nuclear companies, and then pulled off a major coup by selling a 50 per cent stake in its nuclear operation to Royal Dutch Shell for $200m.

High temperature reactors look to be one of the systems that must prosper in the latter part of this century. As well as its more efficient heat production characteristics, the system produces "waste" gases at temperatures hot enough to be used in industries like steel making. North America also offers another and extremely attractive competitor to the established nuclear order. The Canadians developed a natural uranium reactor named Candu which, after a disastrous start with their Douglas Point prototype, was perfected for the first commercial station at Pickering, which will contain four 500 megawatt reactors. It is the only system that has been built on time, within budget, and has operated at its full design capacity with astonishingly high load factors within months of start-up. Candu has won an export order from Argentina.

The European record in nuclear energy has not been impressive. The French had to re-think their whole nuclear strategy after initial failures while the British industry had to be re-organised to improve efficiency. The first generation of Magnox reactors are, in some cases, working 25 per cent below design capacity because of corrosion problems, and the advanced gas cooled reactor programme has earned itself poor publicity through the technical difficulties that have delayed the Dungeness B station by six years and the Hinkley B station by two years. Germany has been more successful, working to basic American designs. The Swedish attempts to establish an independent industry have run into considerable technical difficulties that have resulted in one nuclear station being converted to oil burning before it had been commissioned. Vast technical problems posed by nuclear power have convinced everyone in the European industry, even the French, that no one country can pursue its own national policies and that a British style revamping of the industry may be necessary throughout the continent, eliminating duplication and concentrating all the available resources into a smaller number of projects. Britain has spent many months of heart-searching on deciding what type of reactor should power the next generation of nuclear power stations to succeed the discredited AGRs, but in the longer term there is little argument that the future belongs to the high temperature reactor and to the fast breeder reactor.

Fast breeder reactors

Britain, France, the United States and the Soviet Union are all building prototype breeder reactors that, like the thermal reactors of earlier days, are being hailed as the saviours of the future. Lessons have been learned from past experiences of being

Table 9/4: World Uranium Reserves
       (Data Available January 1973)

| Type of Resources | Price Range ($10/lb U3O8) | | | |
| | Reasonably Assured Resources (Reserves) | | Estimated Additional Resources | |
Country	10^3 tonnes uranium	10^3 short tons U_3O_8	10^3 tonnes uranium	10^3 short tons U_3O_8
Australia	71	92	78.5	102
Canada	185	241	190	247
France	36.6	47.5	24.3	31.5
Niger	40	52	20	26
South Africa	202	263	8	10.4
USA	259	337	538	700
Other (1)	72	93	57	74
TOTAL (rounded)	866	1,126	916	1,191

| Type of Resources | Price Range $10-15/lb U3O8 | | | |
| | Reasonably Assured Resources | | Estimated Additional Resources | |
Country	10^3 tonnes uranium	10^3 short tons U_3O_8	10^3 tonnes uranium	10^3 short tons U_3O_8
Australia	29.5	38.3	29	38
Canada	122	158	219	284
France	20	26	25	32.5
Niger	10	13	10	13
South Africa	62	80.6	26	33.8
USA	141	183	231	300
Other (1)	295	385	92	120
TOTAL (rounded)	680	884	632	821

(1) *Argentina, Brazil, Central African Republic, Denmark (Greenland),
Finland, Gabon, India, Italy, Japan, Mexico, Portugal (Eurpoe and Ango-
la), Spain, Sweden, Turkey, Yugoslavia, Zaire.*

Source: OECD.

over-optimistic, and the difficulties of building a system that as a by-product "breeds" nuclear fuel are not being under-estimated. In the long term it is vital that the system gains widespread acceptance. Uranium sources are finite and could run into short supply by the end of the century if the breeder fails and thermal reactors have to meet the burden of satisfying future electricity requirements. Even in the short term, demand for uranium is forecast to rise five-fold in the next ten years, and a report prepared jointly by the OECD's Nuclear Energy Agency and the International Atomic Energy Agency said urgent steps should be taken to increase the rate of exploration for uranium so that an "adequate forward reserve" can be maintained. The report stresses that the situation is becoming urgent because of the long lead time between discovery of new reserves, their evaluation, and the start of production.

The report adds that current prices for uranium do not provide incentives for further prospecting, especially in areas where it would be expensive to produce any new discoveries. Concern is also voiced about the growing demand for the enriched uranium needed for the American light water reactors and the British advanced gas cooled reactors. Britain and France both have their own limited enrichment facilities but the bulk of the western world's requirements are met by the United States Atomic Energy Commission. Beyond 1983, however, new capacity will have to be found, and the European countries would naturally prefer to be independent of the United States. Britain, Germany and Holland are partners in the centrifugal method of enrichment and are building large demonstration plants at Capenhurst in Britain and Almelo in Holland. The French are backing the diffusion method of enrichment. The capital cost of building a diffusion enrichment plant is considerably lower than that of building a centrifuge unit, but the diffusion method uses large amounts of electricity which could affect the future viability of the method. Capital charges represent 65 per cent of the cost of enrichment in the centrifuge process against only 40 per cent for diffusion, while electricity accounts for 50 per cent of the diffusion costs but only 10 per cent in the centrifuge. Dr D. D. Avery, Assessment and Planning Director of British Nuclear Fuels, estimated that an additional 30,000 tons of enrichment capacity, of either type, will be needed to make up the difference between the capacity of US plants and the 60.000 tons needed by 1980. He estimated that this would involve a total capital investment of around £1,800m, of which European demand would account for perhaps half.

Cost comparison

The possible scarcity of oil by the end of the century has provided an established argument for the long term future of the nuclear power station. However, the new prices being demanded for Middle East crude make the operation of nuclear reactors very much more favourable. At current prices it seems that the higher cost of oil as a power station fuel would more than offset the lower capital construction costs and greater reliability of a conventional fossil fueled power station, even if the huge amounts of residual crude oil could be guaranteed for the late 1970s when any new oil fired units would come into operation. Professor D. C. Leslie, Professor of Nuclear Engineering at Queen Mary College, London, produced valuable comparative costs for the operation of both oil and nuclear generation units. He said that nuclear power is very insensitive to the price of uranium ore. On calculations made before the quadrupling of oil prices in the final quarter of 1973, he stated that if uranium were to rise tenfold on the level of $0 a pound, the cost of electricity from the most efficient nuclear stations would rise by only 0.7p per unit sent out. He assumed that the centrifuge method of enrichment would be used to isolate processing from increasing energy costs. On the other hand, if oil prices went up tenfold on a cost of $3 per barrel, the electricity costs would rise by 2.0p per unit sent out. In the longer term, scientists are looking to the production of power from nuclear fusion, as opposed to a fission reaction as in existing atomic power stations. A fusion reaction produces power when fusile material is heated to over 100m degrees centigrade. All the major powers are experimenting and have produced fusion under controlled laboratory conditions but there are doubts as to whether the amount of power produced by the reaction will exceed the quantities needed to heat the materials to such high temperatures.

Tar sands

Exploitation of oil from shale rock and the mining of tar sands are more attractive, particularly in North America where there are abundant supplies of both. Tar sands, as their name implies, are merely sandstone impregnated with thick tarry oil. Reserves are available in large quantities in Canada and Venezuela, and it has been estimated that the tar sands in the Lake Athabasca area of Canada are roughly equivalent of half the total world proven crude oil reserves. There are three ways of extracting the oil from the sands and all of them are expensive. Hot water or steam can be injected into the formation, reducing the viscosity of the oil which can then be pumped out in the normal way. Diluents and emulsifiers can be injected into the sand to separate the oil, or it can be mined on the open cast principle and the oil extracted at a later stage. One American company has lost about $100m producing oil from the tar sands since it went into production in 1967. After these huge losses, Great Canadian Oil Sands, a subsidiary of Sun Oil, has only just started to break even, though the new crude oil prices should make their early pioneering effort worth while. Two other groups are planning to have production under way from Athabasca within the next four to five years. One is a consortium of the Canadian subsidiaries of Exxon, Gulf, Cities Services and Atlantic Richfield, and the other is Shell. Dr E. J. Walters of British petroleum's exploration and production department estimated that it would need ten plants, at a capital cost of $700m to $1,000m each, to enable production to rise to 1.25m barrels a day by 1985. To assure the viability of schemes on this scale the end-product would need to command a price of $8 to $10 a barrel, which is now possible. Extraction and processing also require large quantities of water, special materials, equipment and manpower. Sun Oil found it required about 1,500 men to staff the facilities to produce 50,000 barrels of oil a day. Similar quantities could be taken from a conventional oilfield with just a handful of men. Environmental issues are also raised by the large scale mining of tar sands. A 100,000 barrels a day plant needs a 100m tons of feedstock per year, much of which has to be disposed of without causing offence.

Shale oil

Extraction of oil from shale is the most promising of the unconventional methods of producing additional liquid fuels. The price of conventionally-produced oil has passed the $4 to $5 a barrel mark needed to make the extraction of oil from shale an economic

Chart 9/1: World conventional crude oil and synthetic crude recoverable reserves

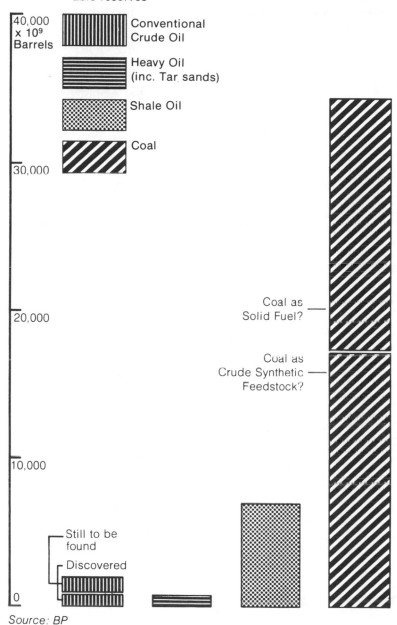

Source: BP

proposition. Huge deposits of shale are to be found in the United States and the US Government has commissioned a six volume study on the environmental impact of commercial extraction in three western states, Colorado, Wyoming and Utah. It has been established that shale could contain reserves of 600,000m barrels and that production could be pushed as his as 1m barrels a day. The great disadvantage of shale extraction is its impact on the environment. Two tons of shale have to be crushed and heated to produce about 1½ barrels of oil, posing massive waste disposal problems that the US Government freely admits could cause the destruction of vegetation, elimination of some wildlife, and a deterioration in air quality and in the beauty of the countryside.

Occidental Petroleum claims to have a method of extracting the oil for $1 a barrel without the waste disposal problems of extraction and crushing. Caverns are blasted in the shale oil to form an underground retort where natural gas is burned and circulates hot vapours through cracks in the shale, releasing the oil. Occidental says it has tested the method on its private shale oil reserves. Other oil companies are sceptical about the pricing claims, and 16 of them, led by Standard Oil of Ohio are taking part in a $7.5m programme to test a process for winning oil and gas from shale at facilities rented from the US Government in Colorado. The Colony Development Corporation is reported to have successfully completed the development of a retorting system, and in Brazil a prototype plant is under construction to produce 1,000 barrels of oil a day from 2,500 tons of shale rock at Sao Mateus do Sul. Large shale deposits also exist in China, the Soviet Union, Venezuela and Scotland, and the West German Government is considering the exploitation of sizeable deposits of shale in the Baden-Wurttemberg area. In March 1974 the British Government commissioned an economic feasibility study into Britain's shale reserves.

Solar Power

All conventional energy sources are finite and will one day be exhausted, but the world possesses one source of power that will never run out—the sun. Dr Peter Glaser, vice-president and head of engineering studies for Arthur D. Little Inc, has estimated that the earth receives from the sun 167,000 times more energy than is consumed. 300 square metres of land received sufficient energy when converted to meet the electricity power requirement of a single family, and a piece of land in the Arizona desert 150 miles square, covered with efficient energy conversion equipment could supply all the energy required by the United States. Houses with solar collectors mounted on the roof have been built and work efficiently. Arthur D. Little has designed an office building where 60 per cent of the energy requirements for heating and cooling will be from solar power. A report in America suggested that by 1985 10 per cent of all new buildings would use solar power for heating and cooling. Individual collection panels on property seem the most feasible way of introducing solar power; huge conversion units serving whole communities are much further away. Solar power has a number of obvious draw-backs. Storage or alternative energy sources are needed at night or during periods when cloud covers the sun.

The solar collector and convertor mounted on a roof, Dr Glaser has likened to a greenhouse. The absorbing surface is blackened or coated with selective radiation absorbing material. The flat-plate collector is covered by one or more panes of glass or plastic which are transparent to solar energy but opaque to the energy re-radiated by the absorber. Alternatively, the roof collector can concentrate energy on a tube similar to a fluorescent light tube where solar energy is converted to heat. The American space programme has stimulated research into solar batteries. These are available commercially and are widely used to power automated equipment in remote areas. Prices are still high but volume production over the next five years could reduce the cost by three-quarters, and bring the system into everyday use. Various types of solar cells are now available, and research has started into their use as a house and office heating and cooling agent. The potential of solar energy for heating and cooling homes and offices is tremendous, but it is not yet practical to suggest the system for large industrial users of power. Nevertheless, domestic and commercial consumption of power accounts for over half the electricity demand in most countries, and so the sun could make a considerable contribution to easing the future burden on conventional generating capacity.

Geothermal power

Tapping the heat that lies in vast underground reserves of hot water and steam is another previously obscure source of energy that is now demanding much closer examination. Certain areas of the world have for long been famous for their hot water springs, but this source of power does not always manifest itself, and exploration programmes similar to those undertaken for oil and gas would be necessary to prove their existence. Reykjavik, the capital of Iceland is heated by underground hot water and in California the Pacific Gas and Electric power utility wants to build more power stations using dry steam under pressure as a generating source; similar power projects based on this rather rare occurence have also been built in Italy. Dr Joseph Barnea, director of resources and transport at the United Nations Department of Economic and Social Affairs, says that the most common source of underground power is hot water between 200° and 370°C under high pressure. Drilling into such a field immediately transforms 20 per cent of the water into steam that can be transported to power stations, and the hot water can be used for a variety of purposes including desalination, house heating, refrigeration and crop drying. Hot water cannot be piped for more than 50 kilometres, so reserves must be close to the consumers. Exploration for geothermal power sources has not been undertaken on a large scale though geothermal sources have been found in Italy, Norway, Sweden, Denmark and Finland and are also available on a large scale on all the continents. Dr Barnea claims that geothermal power should be fully investigated in the more northerly parts of Europe and North America where a large part of the domestic energy consumption goes on home heating.

Tidal power

Two attempts have been made to harness the energy generated by the movement of the tides. The French have constructed a tidal barrage across the estuary of the River Rance in Brittany and the tide surge operates generators producing 240 megawatts of power. The Soviet Union has a similar scheme at Kislaya Bay. Capital costs are high and the number of estuaries where the tidal movement is high enough to warrant electricity schemes is very limited. An interesting variation of this basic theme has been drawn up by Dr T. L. Shaw of Bristol University for a power generating barrier across the Severn estuary. Behind the main barrage, a further dam divides the area into two separate basins. One is regularly replenished at high tide and the other is drained by each low tide. The turbines are set between the two giving the system the ability to generate power at any time or continuously. A barrage across the Severn estuary could generate 4,000 megawatts of electricity, more than twice the amount of any power station operating in Britain. However, the generating authority still has to be convinced that the capital cost could be offset by the cheap electricity production cost.

Wind power

Alternative sources of energy are also available for specialised applications. The power potential of the wind is enormous, and although it may appear that this is a remarkably unreliable source of power, statistics show that the frequency and speed of winds can be predicted with some accuracy. Studies have shown that wind power could generate 20 per cent of electricity requirements in the United States by the year 2000. Experimental wind power plants using light-weight aeroturbines have operated successfully in Denmark and the United States, and a remote communications mast in Norway that generated its own electricity from the wind recently blew down in a storm.

Other ideas

Apart from tidal power the sea contains another potential source of energy. The temperature difference between the upper layers of the sea heated by the sun and the deeped cold water of the oceans can be used to power very large heat engines. Dr Glaser said experimental plants were built in 1929 off the coast of Cuba and in 1956 off the coast of Africa but they failed because of design limitations and damage by a hurricane. But he estimated that if the system was developed, the Gulf Stream had the potential to generate 26m million kilowatt hours of electricity a year. Power is obtained by passing the warm surface waters through heat exchangers which boil a fluid such as propane to drive turbines coupled to generators. Cold water from the deep ocean is then circulated through the heat exchanger to condense the fluid. Scientists have never been short of ideas for producing energy but as long as there was cheap coal and then cheap oil, the funds for developing their ideas have not been freely available. The upsurge in oil prices in the fourth quarter of 1973 has now changed the position and ensured that funds will be available to investigate any promising new source of power.

Chapter Ten
Questions for the Future

The record of governments in ignoring warnings of an impeding Energy Armageddon is without parallel. Since 1970, numerous experts have produced prognostications which have cast doubt on the ability of crude oil reserves to match the relentless rise in demand for oil products. In September 1973 one of the most gloomy forecasts emerged—made all the more pessimistic as it came from a senior executive of one of the major oil companies, which traditionally have sought to allay fears of a world without adequate oil supplies. Mr H. R. Warman, British Petroleum's exploration manager, shocked a London audience with his prediction that demand would not be met fully after 1978 and that the next decade would see an actual decline in production. He added somewhat ominously that this would be the situation, "unless something quite unforeseen occurs."

His remarks were doubtless noted by the government agencies engaged in the formulation of long term energy strategy. But they clearly did not receive the degree of high level consideration which they deserved. Mr Warman, who emphasised that he was not a "doomsday" man, based his predictions on the discovery of new reserves at the optimistic rate of 20 000 million barrels a year and consumption continuing to rise at the rate of 5.5 to 6 per cent a year. Neither of these assumptions could be regarded as excessive. Governments could perhaps be forgiven for looking sceptically at depressing forecasts of exhausted oil reserves by the year 2000; after all, similar crystal-ball gazing in the past had proved notoriously inaccurate as the oil companies uncovered additional reserves. The Middle East war provided Mr Warman's unforeseen event. The supply crisis gave the consuming countries a taste of what life would be like in 1978 if his reading of the situation had been accurate. It is doubtful whether anything less than the Arabs' restricting of oil output and quadrupling of prices would have brought their attention to the gravity of the situation. The future of oil's rivals—coal and nuclear power—now looks assured. The extraction of crude oil from shale rock and tar sands is a viable proposition while even more futuristic sources of energy including solar and geothermal power and the harnessing of tides and winds will now command the research funds that were previously unavailable.

However, the development of alternative fuels will be influenced by the way in which the new structure of the world oil industry emerges from the upheavals of 1973. The producer nations have established themselves as firmly in control of the bulk of world production available for export. But for the international oil companies, the shipping industry, and governments there are still many basic questions to be answered regarding their relationship with the oil producing countries. Equally important issues confront the world: The question of how to pay the inflated prices for crude; the serious possibility of an over-supply situation both in tankers and in world shipbuilding capacity; ensuring that available fuel supplies are used more efficiently; and that the headlong rush to develop indigenous resources is not at the expense of hard won environmental improvements.

The participation question

Kuwait was selected in 1973 as the base for OPEC and OAPEC talks on price increases and production cutbacks during the crisis period. Overshadowed by these historic gatherings were a series of meetings between senior executives of Gulf and British Petroleum, the joint owners of the Kuwait National Oil Company, and the Kuwaiti Government. The two sides were attempting to re-negotiate the participation agreement that would have given Kuwait a 25 per cent initial stake in KOC, rising to 51 per cent by 1982. These conditions had been rejected by the Kuwait National Assembly, whose more militant members wanted outright nationalisation of the local oil industry. The deal which was worked out gave the Persian Gulf State an immediate 60 per cent controlling share in the company and the right to take full control within five years. The framework of the agreement was outlined at the end of January 1974, but is under revision following reluctance by the Kuwait National Assembly to accept all its provisions. The most crucial point is the amount of oil that the Kuwaitis will allow BP and Gulf to buy back from them under long term contracts. There have been suggestions that the international companies, in a desperate last ditch stand, have resisted demands to accept a price of more than $9 for these supplies.

Three other Gulf States, Saudi Arabia, Abu Dhabi and Qatar, had accepted the 25 per cent formula for participation. When the Kuwait Assembly failed to ratify this type of agreement for KOC, the three countries made it clear that they would require their own participation agreements to be re-negotiated in line with any more favourable terms secured by Kuwait. The effect of introducing Kuwaiti-style participation throughout the Gulf will be dramatic. Iraq which has stood back from the participation issue will want a similar stake in Basrah Petroleum. The Iranians have not intimated that they want a revision of the twenty year sales pact with the consortium of international oil companies that previously operated in the country. Iran has had considerable success in selling crude available to the National Iranian Oil Company and will find no difficulty in disposing of substantial new supplies. By the end of 1974, the national oil companies in the Gulf States will have more than 1.2m barrels of crude a day under their direct control. The consequences for world oil prices of this rapid transfer in the stewardship of the crude are uncertain. The crude oil price spiral began to gather momentum in May 1973 when Saudi Arabia placed a total of 69m barrels of oil on the free market at a price equivalent to 93 per cent of the posted price, which at that time was $2.742 a barrel.

The Saudi Arabian Government "take" from these sales was $2.550 a barrel compared with its revenue of $1.607 a barrel for the bulk of Aramco's production and $2.39 a barrel for the "bridging oil" acquired by the Government under the participation pact but sold back to the oil companies. The 69m barrels represented about 2.5 per cent of Aramco's total production but was sufficient to set world oil prices on a relentless upward movement. Abu Dhabi also put it's participation oil on the market and was able to command similar prices. Libya, which acquired a 51 per cent initial stake in the independent companies, set a buy-back price of $4.90 a barrel. Only a limited quantity of oil was required to trigger the price explosion. The amounts of oil offered for auction by Libya, Iran, Nigeria were also small but resulted in bids of up to $20 a barrel. Greatest concern of the international oil companies is that the auctioning system for the disposal of participation oil will become an established feature on the world oil market, although it seems that the producer nations are coming to the conclusion that now the market is settling down they cannot expect auction prices to exceed significantly the tax paid costs of oil being lifted by the major oil companies. A number of Japanese companies have not lifted oil bought at Nigerian auctions for over $20 a barrel. In February 1974 an auction of royalty crude in Kuwait failed to produce more than a handful of bids above the posted price which led to allegations by the Kuwaitis that the oil companies were conspiring to hold down prices.

Future price movements

The major companies have pointedly refrained from bidding against the independents in the oil auctions. The producing countries are, however, disenchanted with the auction system and are prepared to sell most of their participation oil to the concession holders at 93 per cent of posted prices. Thoughts that the open sale of crude oil could rebound on the producers if a world recession cut demand for crude and depressed prices are not well founded. The Arab producers have seen the ease with which they can reduce output and are unlikely to allow prices to fall because supply was in excess of demand. There is little prospect of sufficient supplies becoming available outside the Middle East that would negate production controls in the Gulf countries. The main hope must be that the more moderate voices in OPEC counsels will be heeded. The Saudi Arabian oil minister, Sheikh Yamani, felt that prices at the beginning of 1974 were too high, and that the additional burden on the balance of payments of the industrialised nations could precipitate a world recession that could hit the oil producers almost as hard as their customers. Price levels, however, are unlikely to show significant movement either way during 1974. The availability of alternative sources will not depress Middle East crude prices. New production, including the North Sea, coming on stream in other parts of the world will use Gulf levels as reference prices. Coal prices will tend to float upwards, a move that will assist in the provision of the finance needed to expand the industry.

As the producing countries begin to accumulate the increased revenues from higher prices, monetary agencies throughout the world have been coerced into studying the long term implications of such a radical change on the pattern of international currency flows. Ultimately, it will be the producing nations themselves who will determine how their customers for oil will solve their balance of payments problems. Basically, there are two courses open. The oil producers may decide to insist on some other form of payment other than dollars, or that they will continue to accept US currency. Initially, they will take their increased revenues in dollars, which have appreciated in terms of other currencies. The effect of this can be expected to be a reduction in the United States trade surplus as a direct result of increased European imports, and through a reduction in demand in Europe for more expensive American goods. Additionally, the revaluation of the dollar, *vis a vis* other currencies, is likely to give further impetus to substitution of oil by other fuels since every appreciation of the dollar represents, in effect, a rise in the price of oil.

Cash in hand

The broad objective of the producing countries is to convert their oil revenues into permanent assets that will enable their economies to flourish when oil reserves are exhausted. Long term restrictions on the level of output will delay this fatal day until well into the next century in some countries but eventually they will have to exist without the benefit of oil. Iran, Iraq, Venezuela and Indonesia, with their large populations and ambitious industrailaisation programmes, will require vast quantities of capital goods and services to carry through these schemes. But on the Saudi Arabian side of the Gulf the opportunities for industrialisation are more limited, and these countries will have to invest their funds abroad until the economy expands sufficiently to allow an increased rate of domestic spending.

The Arab nations are reticent about direct investment in the West. But the establishment of a "unit trust" managed by Western banks and guaranteed by the International Monetary Fund could conceivably provide the means of overcoming instinctive Arab distrust of retaliatory expropriations. Alternatively, Arab revenues could be fed into the World Bank, which is essentially multi-lateral in its outlook and is not open to allegations of bias in favour of particular nations. Ideally, the resolution of the balance of payments dilemma would be for 23 members of the OECD—excluding the Americans—to buy Middle East oil on a dollar base; the Arab nations investing the dollars in the developing nations; and the countries of the third world would purchase goods essential for their industrial advancement from Europe and Japan with the dollars. The third world was sent reeling by the effects of the quadrupled oil prices and appealed with no success for the introduction of a two tier pricing structure. Even with country-to-country oil deals, they have failed to gain preferential treatment and, in some cases, have paid more for oil than they would have done by purchasing through the international companies.

Companies in transition

The oil companies' policy of even-handed distribution of supplies has enhanced their reputation with many countries, especially with the smaller nations without much international bargaining power. The ability of the companies to maintain their policy of equalisation, despite considerable pressure, particularly from Britain and France, demonstrated the considerable hold they have on the world oil transport and marketing patterns. The fact that they will no longer have automatic access to cheap supplies of crude from the Middle East does not necessarily weaken the position of the major companies. Throughout 1973 the profitability of the majors improved even though their situation as crude owners was diminishing. In the United States a number of companies, including Exxon and Shell, felt obliged to take full page newspaper advertisements and make their executives freely available for television interviews to justify to the public the case for higher profits at a time of crisis. Most of the increased profitability of the American corporations came from their operations outside North America, where the margins on products had improved considerably as crude went into short supply. Fears, that the loss of control over crude, and the profits that could be earned through crude oil trading, would seriously undermine the financial position of the companies, have proved groundless. Crude oil is still available to them at much higher prices—which they have been able to pass on to the consumers and, in the process, improve their returns.

Table 10/1: Impact of High Crude Prices on Eight Developing
　　　　　Nations

COSTS
Million US dollars

		Oil (a) Estimated Cost	Foreign Exports	Trade (b) Imports	Balance	Foreign Exchange Reserves (c)
India	1972	—	2 372	2 598	(—226)	66
	1973	—	2 934	2 771	163	629
	1974	1 241	—	—	—	—
Pakistan	1972	—	784	644	140	101
	1973	—	983	928	55	254
	1974	266	—	—	—	—
Philippines	1972	—	1 009	1 354	(—345)	309
	1973	—	1 494	1 243	251	606
	1974	693	—	—	—	—
Thailand	1972	—	1 194	1 411	(—317)	838
	1973	—	1 382	1 662	(—280)	1 107
	1974	657	—	—	—	—
Tanzania	1972	—	307	390	(—83)	n a
	1973	—	399	363	36	n a
	1974	62	—	—	—	—
Sierra Leone	1972	—	152	125	27	35
	1973	—	145	125	20	36
	1974	29	—	—	—	—
Sudan	1972	—	355	356	(—1)	38
	1973	—	401	376	25	28
	1974	127	—	—	—	—
Ethiopia	1972	—	183	203	(—20)	53
	1973	—	285	180	105	114
	1974	51	—	—	—	—

(a) Assuming normal requirements and an average landed cost of $10 a barrel.
(b) Annual rates based on first quarter statistics.
(c) End of first quarter 1973.

Source: International Monetary Fund and Petroleum Economist

The new participation deal signed with Kuwait, and the prospect
that similar agreements will be concluded with most of the producer governments where the old concession system was in
operation, must speed up the companies' re-adjustment to their
new role in the oil industry. The national oil companies will have
gigantic amounts of crude oil at their disposal but their resources
in terms of trained manpower and expertise are far more limited.
The oil companies on the other hand have an unequalled reservoir of trained personnel in all aspects of the industry, and in the

transportation and distribution network, whose flexibility was proven during the early days of the crisis when countries, denied Arab oil, were supplied from other sources at very short notice. The acquisition of the crude oil production facilities in the producing nations will occupy the attention of the new national oil companies for some time, and it seems likely they will need the support of the oil companies, perhaps on a contract basis. Plans are also being drawn up for the establishment of refineries and petro-chemical industries through the state-owned companies and, with the possible exception of tanker owning, there is unlikely to be any serious competition between the two sides in the main consuming markets. Saudi Arabia has dropped its plans to invest in American refining and marketing outlets on a large scale, although the National Iranian Oil Ćompany, the oldest and certainly the most sophisticated of these state concerns, has acquired a 50 per cent stake in Ashland Oil's New York refining and marketing chain and has a share in a number of refineries throughout the world.

In this situation, the major oil companies are free to consolidate their position as refiners, marketeers and chemical producers. The movement towards a capability to provide all types of energy will also accelerate. The larger corporations including Shell, Gulf and Exxon, are already in the nuclear business and have positions in coal. They are also making funds available for research into other energy sources ranging from the semi-proven technologies for shale oil and tar sands extraction to more obscure ideas for energy production. Profits on the marketing of oil products have in the past been rather neglected by the majors and because of substantial return on internal crude oil transactions, they have been able to accept lower margins in the market place. Steps have already been taken to remedy this situation. Shell and British Petroleum have withdrawn from the Italian market because of the low level of returns and other loss making activities cannot expect to survive in future on the proceeds of crude oil profits.

The greatest threat to this new strategy could come from the consumer governments if attempts to prevent government-to-government oil deals on a large scale are unsuccessful. Any government acquiring a large quantity of oil needs a marketing outlet and there could be a temptation to form national oil companies to market, and possibly even refine this oil. A similar situation has already emerged in the African state of Zaire, where the Government nationalised the major oil company operations and established its own marketing company to use these facilities to distribute oil purchased by the Government. The loss of their supremacy in crude supply could reduce the number of allegations that the companies' influence over the entire industry outside the United States is unhealthy and tends towards a monopoly. The basis on which the majors acquire the bulk of their Middle Eastern crude will be much closer to that of the independent companies, which in the long term, could step up competition in the market place. Not least of the oil companies' worries is that of financing development of new crude oil sources which will be expensive, as will the diversification into other forms of energy. The companies make a convincing case for their higher margins as the financial world is hesitant about advancing funds for high risk activities like exploration. Funds are not likely to be available on a wide scale from the Arab countries, and the only alternative seems to be a higher debt ratio to supplement a reduced level of internal financing.

The changing role of the oil companies and their declining power in the Middle East has at last forced the consumer governments to take a more active interest in the future of their oil supplies. After years of leaving the business of oil production and transportation in the hands of the majors, the consumers were suddenly confronted with a situation where production had been cut back and the oil companies had been, at a stroke, deprived of the ability to negotiate and help form world export prices. There had been talk during 1972 and 1973 of some kind of consumer-producer relationships as prices continued to rise. The consumers feared that any collaboration on their part would be interpreted as a hostile action by the Arabs and provoke a confrontation that would lead to production restrictions.

The Organisation of Petroleum Exporting Countries (OPEC) is no longer apprehensive about conferring with the consuming nations. In fact, they have been quite anxious to discuss the problems of inflation caused by high oil prices. The new attitude stems from a greater confidence within the inner circles of OPEC that they have the ability to control world prices, and that there is little that the major world powers can do to thwart their policies. The main apostle of a joint approach to the oil producers has been

American Secretary of State Dr Henry Kissinger. It was his efforts that brought twelve of the largest oil consuming nations outside the communist bloc to a special energy conference in Washington in February 1974. France, already involved in a number of bilateral deals with Middle Eastern Governments, maintained a steady opposition, but the conference agreed to the establishment of a high level group that could work closely with international institutions—the OECD, the World Bank and the International Monetary Fund—in tackling the energy problems confronting the world.

Matters that the group will look into include methods of persuading Governments to co-operate in methods of reducing the wastage of fuel and the allocation of oil supplies in an emergency—a feature of OECD oil policy that was a singular failure during the October 1973 crisis. The group will also look at alternative energy resources and the need to step up the amount of research and development in these fields.

But the most important point was the requirement of the twelve nations to build up a multilateral relationship with the producing countries and also other smaller consumers, particularly in the developing nations.

Throughout the crisis France maintained an independent stance, and with her high standing in the Arab world, put the case for Governments making their own deals for oil. Bilateral deals certainly do nothing to help hold down prices—one of the main aims of consumer nations—and depend very much on the continuation of good relations between the two countries since there is no longer a group of oil companies to act as a buffer between the two sides. France went into the government-to-government oil deals at a time when crude oil prices were reaching their peak at the beginning of 1974. Even in France some doubts were being expressed about the wisdom of these bilateral contracts once prices began to fall, leading to fears that the country might have to pay above the market rate for her "secure" supplies. French action in pushing ahead with bilateral deals in the face of opposition from her European partners undoubtedly stems from her long history of being frustrated in the Middle East by the actions of British, American and Dutch oil companies. Without the prospect of any large finds of indigenous oil, French policy has been aimed at securing deliveries, even at the expense of her neighbours.

First of the French deals was with Saudi Arabia. In exchange for a guaranteed supply of 800m tons of crude over 20 years, the French are to provide the Saudis with equipment, services and technical expertise to help with the country's programme of industrialisation. This was followed by a massive goods-for-oil agreement with the Iranians. The amounts of oil involved in the deal have not been mentioned, but in return the French are to provide five 1000 megawatt nuclear power stations and to assist the Iranians in a domestic exploration programme, and also to act jointly in exploration projects in third countries. In addition, French companies will co-operate in the development of petrochemicals and the natural gas industry in Iran. France has offered to build a pipeline to take Iranian gas to Europe and to provide a liquefaction plant and LNG tankers so that gas could also be exported.

Britain's own government-to-government deal with Iran was a much less grandiose affair. Goods including steel are to be sold to the Iranians and in return the British Government with BP acting as its agent will buy over 5m tons of oil. Price per barrel has not been officially disclosed but it is believed to be about $7 a barrel around the tax paid costs of crude bought by the oil companies under their 20 year contract with the Iranians. In a modern industrial society even the most efficient countries find it difficult to deliver goods on time and delays could trigger disputes between the two sides. The French offer of nuclear power stations, not the easiest item to construct to a tight schedule, could provide more problems than most other items. But the future of bilateral deals will not rest entirely with the success or failure of one or two contracts between governments. Working arrangements covering all aspects of supply and financing could make headlong rushes by countries to grab all the supplies they could afford unnecessary in the future.

Tanker orders orgy

Much of the orgy in tanker ordering which occurred throughout 1973 was directly attributable to the huge demands being made for increased crude imports, principally from the Middle East to the United States of America. This would involve a projected level of American imports of about 7m barrels a day in 1975 rising to some 11m b/d five years later. The events of October, and President Nixon's Project Independence Programme, must inevitably raise serious question marks over the future of much of the tanker tonnage on order at the end of last year. Even before the crisis it had been forecast that by 1975, at the latest, the tanker industry would for the first time in its history, be faced with a prolonged period of adequate tonnage supply, continuing possibly for several decades with a corresponding effect on ship values. Yet, at the end of 1973 there were 1,096 tankers totalling nearly 187m tons dwt on order with the world's shipyards with by far the largest bulk of the orders concentrated on ships of more than 100,000 tons dwt. On the basis of the end 1973 order book, deliveries were expected to total 41.6m tons dwt in 1974, rising to 49.5m tons in 1975, to a peak in 1976 of 54.8m tons, and a drop in 1977 to 41m tons, boosting the world's tanker fleet to around 346m tons dwt by the start of 1977 *(Review, 1973, Fearnley & Egers Chartering)*. It

---

Table 10/2: World Order Book December 1973

Figures in '000 DWT

Year of Delivery	Tankers	Combined Carriers	Bulk Carriers	Others	Total
1974	41600	4700	8800	5500	60600
1975	49500	2400	6200	2500	60600
1976	54800	2200	4500	800	62300
1977	41000	500	2900	500	44900

Notes: The table is based on scheduled deliveries with estimated postponements. Additional deliveries for 1975–of bulk carriers and "Others" are expected.

Table 10/3: Estimated World Fleet 1974-1977

Figures in million DWT

	Tankers	Combined Carriers	Bulk Carriers	Others	Total
1/1 1974	212.4	36.6	87.6	103.3	439.9
1/1 1975	251.0	41.1	95.9	104.8	492.8
1/1 1976	296.0	43.1	101.6	106.0	546.7
1/1 1977	346.0	45.2	105.6	107.0	603.8

Notes: Estimated scrapping and losses are deducted. Expected new orders with early delivery are added.

Source: Fearnley & Egers Chartering

would seem, therefore, that there is a considerable threat of serious over-tonnaging of the tanker fleet in the years ahead, particularly if, as seems likely, the cost of energy which the industrialised nations are obliged to pay leads to a reduction in the growth of world trade. Oil companies and the independent owners who have indulged in this mammoth buying spree must be re-appraising the efficacy of such high levels of spending in the light of the changed circumstances.

Oil tankers account for slightly more than 75 per cent of the world order book (expressed in gross tons) and, although many of the contracts have charters already arranged, substantial quantities of tonnage have been ordered on a speculative basis. The future of these orders must be open to question, and most certainly the banking community, which has been attracted to the shipping industry on a lemming-like scale in recent years, has already begun to review its attitudes towards the very large crude carrier in the longer term. Banks, and others, will tend to shy away from lending owners large sums of money for the construction of ships on which an owner is unable to provide adequate security in the form of a long term charter agreement which is sufficiently flexible in the bankers' eye in its allowance for the effects of changes in currency parities and for inflation. In future, both shipowners and banks can be expected to take an increasing interest in the search for alternative energy resources and particularly in the provision of finance for the production of oil from offshore areas. Norwegian shipowners already have substantial interests in exploration rigs and the construction of steel and concrete production platforms. British owners are also turning their attention towards this area. Undoubtedly, the financing of these ventures will see increasing use made of funds available on the Euromarkets, while the dismantling of capital controls in the United States will provide another huge source of finance for shipping and associated interests.

The oil crisis has also raised doubts about the wisdom of unfettered expansion of the world's shipbuilding industry. Output of the industry world-wide has been expanding at an annual rate of about 10 per cent with a huge expansion of capacity particularly in Japan, and to a lesser extent in Europe. Apart from the major plans by Japanese shipbuilders for a further increase in capacity, South Korea has plans for a huge development of its

Table 10/4: Order Book of the Leading Shipbuilding Nations—end 1973

Figures in Thousand Tons Gross

Country	Tankers	Bulk/Oil Carriers	Ore & Bulk Carriers	General Cargo	Specialized Carriers	Fishing	Total Order Book
Japan	49,032	1,371	6,439	1,457	836	95	59,599
Sweden	9,298	1,207	130	8	27	1	10,677
Great Britain & Northern Ireland	5,008	358	1,280	586	134	22	7,519
Germany, Federal Republic of,	5,580	86	829	461	210	5	7,359
Spain	5,379	314	777	397	9	197	7,221
France	3,594	76	—	196	1,215	16	5,163
Norway	4,028	72	246	115	485	17	5,021
U.S.A.	2,294	43	130	317	1,170	8	4,067
Italy	2,769	725	264	119	33	20	3,969
Denmark	2,472	—	358	89	—	3	3,058
Netherlands	2,120	—	—	3	31	14	2,316
Yugoslavia	403	1,224	244	60	—	—	1,960
Poland	—	168	287	673	267	130	1,541
Brazil	261	655	169	248	—	3	1,341
South Korea	1,277	—	12	—	—	5	1,300
China (Taiwan)	1,124	—	54	—	—	—	1,178
Finland	692	—	—	139	2	—	1,046
World Total	97,556	6,300	12,146	5,753	4,551	682	128,900

1 Figures shown for general cargo ships are for 2000 tons gross and over.
2 Specialized carriers includes liquefied gas and chemical tankers.

Source: Lloyds Register of Shipping

shipbuilding industry which would enable it to construct 6m tons gross of merchant shipping by 1980. Other developing countries have similar plans, as, have certain East European countries. Since the new fields discovered in recent years, principally the Alaskan North Slope and the North Sea will require tankers for extremely short haul, the advisability of adding substantial chunks of new capacity for the construction of VLCCs and ULCCs almost certainly will tend to depress prices to the disadvantage of shipbuilding internationally. The wisdom of such policies must be doubted.

Suez versus Cape

The possibility of the Suez Canal being re-opened has placed the shipping industry in a further quandary. Its closure prompted the sharp increase in tanker size. The fact that tankers carrying Middle East crude had to pass south of the Cape of Good Hope has added £250m a year to Britain's import costs. The shipowning industry has exercised a degree of prudence, however, for despite the increase in tanker size, with some ships on order of more than 500,000 tons, the largest single concentration of orders is for vessels of between 260,000 and 280,000 tons dwt. Certainly ships at the lower end of this scale could use the canal on the outward ballast journey and therefore take advantage of the shortening of routes, assuming that the Egyptian plans are realised. Oil companies have welcomed the decision to re-open the waterway, but clearly a critical factor will be the charges levied by the canal authority. In a study in early 1973, the United Nations Conference on Trade and Development (UNCTAD) suggested that the rapid rise in costs of construction and operation of VLCCs had substantially altered the economics of oil transport via the Cape. Based on estimated costs for the SUMED pipeline and a re-opening of the waterway, UNCTAD calculated that the cheapest method of transporting crude oil from the Gulf to Rotterdam would be for a 200,000 ton dwt tanker to travel to the loading terminals through the canal and return via the Cape at a cost of US $5.92 per ton. For a 250,000 tonner using the Cape route in both directions, on the basis of estimates of tariffs for the canal and the pipeline, the cost would be $5.95. Interestingly, the United Nations Organisation concluded that the most expensive way would be the use of even bigger tankers and a trans-shipment port, where the rate for a

300,000 ton tanker using the Bantry Bay trans-shipment terminal would cost $6.81 per ton. Major tanker operators responded to the report's estimates with scepticism, pointing out that the cost of building smaller ships was proportionately greater than for a VLCC. While the canal would enable smaller quantities to be carried rather more cheaply, the advantage of transporting much larger quantities via the Cape would still exist. However, further studies will certainly be given to the equation in the light of the canal being re-opened, while important political and strategic questions are also raised, particularly in relation to the position of the Russian naval presence in both the Mediterranean and the Indian Ocean.

The million ton tanker

There has been a growing emphasis on the growth in size of tankers to continue to derive economies of scale from these large ships. Japanese shipping and shipbuilding companies have been keen to extend still further the level of technological progress with the construction of ships between 650,000 and 700,000 tons dwt, and, as recently as November 1973, the Japanese Ministry of Transport indicated that some Japanese shipbuilders would be authorised to build a one million ton tanker. This pressure to build the large ships had been accelerated by the regulations to limit the size of cargo tanks and to insist on a segregated ballast tank system to minimise oil pollution in the event of collision. The implication was that both construction and operating costs of big tankers would be driven upwards. These large ships would require to operate on specialised routes between specially-constructed deep water terminals and in view of the supply constraints, particularly on Japan, the impetus for such a technological breakthrough would seem to have been weakened. Other schemes, notably the Delta design developed by the Onassis group which involved the construction of four 250,000 tons caissons could, however, be more attractive. Its main attraction is its flexibility in that, although it has a 100 foot draught which would restrict severely the number of ports it was able to enter, the individual caissons could be detached from the "mother" ship at various discharge points in North West Europe, or elsewhere in the world.

Chart 10/1: Privately owned VLCC tonnage league

(in service and on order June 1973)

		Total Tonnage DWT
1	Pao Y.K.	9,149,012
2	Sanko Kisen	6,648,201
3	Moller A.P.	5,329,500
4	Bergesen, Sig.	5,293,673
5	Onassis Group	4,204,550
6	Japan Line	4,133,320
7	Ludwig D.K.	4,072,280
8	N.Y.K. Group	3,630,650
9	Tung C.Y.	3,460,583
10	Salen, Sven	3,132,274
11	Reksten H.	3,090,330
12	Goulandris B.P.	3,090,330

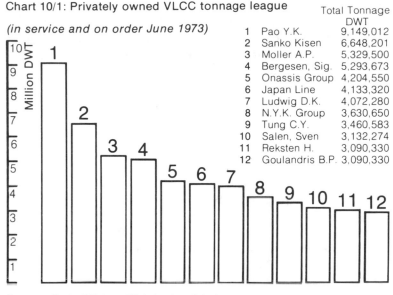

Source: E. A. Gibson (Shipbrokers) Ltd

Chart 10/2: International majors owned VLCC tonnage

(in service and on order, June 1973)

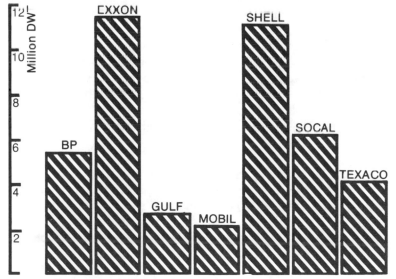

Source: E. A. Gibson (Shipbrokers) Ltd

More immediate possibilities prompted by the fuel crisis are being explored by the shipping industry. New plastic-based hull coating materials which, it is claimed, could reduce the operating costs of a VLCC by up to US $20,000 a month have been the subject of investigations by Scandinavian shipowners and by scientists at Newcastle University. The material reduces resistance as a ship passes through the water, providing the owner with additional speed for every ton of bunker fuel consumed, together with a marked reduction in the number of dry dockings required.

Nuclear ship prospects

The prospect of much intensified research into nuclear propulsion has also been promoted by the soaring cost of bunker fuel. Three prototype nuclear powered merchant ships have been built by the United States, West Germany and Japan in recent years. Nuclear propulsion had been pushed into the background in the early 1960s with the introduction of high-powered diesel engines which are able to operate economically and reliably on low grade fuel oil. But talks between British and German nuclear energy authorities began in the final quarter of 1973, directed towards a joint programme for the construction of a series of large container ships for the European-Far Eastern trade. The basis for the venture was the fact that while such vessels would demand high initial capital costs, with each ship costing between £40m and £53m, these would be balanced by lower operating costs. Britain's Department of Trade and Industry, in a report published in 1971, had concluded that nuclear propelled merchant ships would only be competitive if the price of fuel oil rose between 70 and 200 per cent in real terms, or if there were a dramatic reduction in the cost of nuclear plants.

One West German shipyard, early in 1974 produced a design for a nuclear powered catamaran ship, able to carry up to 2,200 containers at speeds of up to 45 knots. France, in a sharp policy *volte face*, has also said that it would investigate the viability of nuclear powered container ships for the North Atlantic route. In the United States the Ceres Shipping Group has advanced proposals for the construction of three 600,000 dwt nuclear powered tankers, while the Energy Corporation of America has submitted plans for a series of twelve 414,911 ton dwt nuclear tankers. The promoters claimed that, by 1980, a 600,000 ton dwt VLCC would involve annual costs of $2.5m against $4.2m for a conventionally-powered tanker of the same size, based on fuel costs of $42 per ton. Operating between the Persian Gulf and the United States the nuclear tanker could make seven round trips, compared with five for an oil powered tanker, lifting the comparable efficiency by about 30 per cent. The oil crisis has also increased interest in the possibility of using nuclear powered submarine oil tankers, initially for moving crude oil from North Alaska under the ice round the North West passage of Canada, and conceivably for transporting oil from offshore fields. The use of a submarine cargo ship in the Arctic would effectively reduce the distance between many parts of Europe and the North Pacific. Considerable interest has also been shown in plans for the construction of 17,000 ton merchant sailing ships with designs developed both in the United States and in West Germany. However, the long distance transportation of crude oil will for the time being rest with conventional VLCCs.

State owned fleets

The established shipping nations and the tanker industry in the future will have to take account of the policies being implemented by the oil producers, who are keen to develop their own merchant fleets. In line with the policy of most other developing countries, these nations will insist that a considerable proportion of their seaborne trade must be carried in ships controlled and registered with them. Libya, Kuwait, Algeria, Indonesia and Venezuela all have programmes for developing national fleets and, it seems likely that much of the tonnage involved, will be sophisticated vessels such as chemical carriers, LNG ships and products tankers. The high cost of LNG ships and the associated liquefaction and re-gasification plants has led to detailed investigations into the conversion of natural gas to methanol, the simplest of the alcohols, which has been seen as a cheaper alternative to the transportation of energy to distant markets. Methanol could be shipped in conventional oil tankers and would eliminate the need for the cyrogenic processes required for LNG. In the main markets, methanol could be reformed into gas or burned directly as a pollution free fuel.

High manufacturing costs for methanol *vis a vis* LNG have been shown to be more outweighted by the transportation factor, particularly where the shipping leg is in excess of 3,500 to 5,000 miles. However, the critical element, as with LNG, is the delivered price. Possible routes could be from the Persian Gulf to Japan and the United States, or from Australia and Russia to the United States. The demand for additional gas supplies to compensate for shortage of oil in the consuming nations could well be complemented by a sharp increased demand for tonnage to transport coal. Bulk carriers which at the beginning of 1974 throughout the world totalled 87.6m tons dwt could well increase as owners direct their attention to the possibilities that the bulk trades offer. Indeed, there was evidence in late 1973 and early 1974 that some shipbuilders who have devoted virtually all their production to the construction of large oil tankers were preparing to enter the field for specialised coal carrying ships.

The need for efficiency

At a time when energy is in short supply the inefficient way in which society uses its available resources is at last beginning to attract the attention of governments. Inefficiency in converting

Table 10/5: Oil Savings Capacity Compared with Fuel Self Sufficiency

	"Oil saving capacity"	Degree of self sufficiency in:	
		oil	total energy
		per cent	
Japan	0.6	—	11
Italy	0.7	6	15
Belgium	0.8	1	18
France	0.8	5	22
United Kingdom	0.9	2	53
Germany	1.0	7	51
Netherlands	1.1	7	64
Canada	1.1	98	110
United States	1.4	74	89

Source: OECD

primary fuels into electricity, plus losses in transmission means that 70 per cent of the energy value of the original fuel is lost by the time it reaches the consumer who then proceeds to waste it even further. Principal causes of waste are the poor energy conversion characteristics of electricity generating equipment and of the internal combustion engine (combined with the large number of private vehicles that carry only one person); heat losses in industrial processes; and lack of insulation in houses where the wrong type of heating is often installed. The greater the affluence of a country the more scope there is for savings, a US Government sponsored study early in 1973 showed that a concerted conservation effort could produce savings of 7.3m b/d of oil equivalent in 1980 rising to 11.7m b/d by 1985 and 16.4m b/d by 1990.

The message is clear. Massive savings can be achieved if the right policies are fixed by central governments and serious attempts are made to educate consumers in the prudent use of resources. At government level, policy directives should stipulate that new fossil fuel power stations should use coal rather than oil and that gas turbine stations should only be used for meeting peak loads. In the long term, oil should not be encouraged to compete for industrial business that could be satisfied by coal, and instead should be reserved for specialised applications like chemicals and, until there is a viable alternative, road and air transport. Greater thought must be given to the use of waste heat from power generation. The trend towards building large generation units away from population centres makes it difficult to utilise waste heat for district heating systems and expensive cooling towers have to be built to dissipate valuable heat.

Homes in the past have not been properly insulated because the cost of the work far outweighed any savings in fuel because it was so cheap. Electricity also gained a sizeable share of the heating market—a sector that judged purely on an efficiency basis should be dominated by other fuels. Great potential also exists for producing gas from agricultural manure of domestic cess pits. The method has proved to be safe and efficient but will need promotion by an efficiency-conscious body. Local authorities are also beginning to grasp the potential of producing electricity by burning domestic refuse and of district heating schemes for large housing developments.

Few attempts are made to compensate for the inherently inefficient operations of the internal combustion engine by improving
the overall efficiency of the transportation networks. Two car
families are becoming less rare outside the United States,
mileages travelled are growing and the combination of these two
factors contributes to more traffic congestion, another source of
fuel waste. In America there is a realisation that cars will have to
become smaller and more freight will have to be taken from the
roads and moved by rail. Air services have suffered from the fuel
allocations but the introduction of the widebodied jets has enabled more passenger miles to be covered per litre of fuel. Super-
sonic transport reverses this improvement. Concorde has a fuel
capacity of 90 tons and in airline terms has a consumption of only
7 passenger kilometres per litre while a Boeing 747 will do 31
passenger kilometres per litre.

The final analysis

Conservation of energy supplies should, however, not take place
at the expense of improvements in the environment which have
occurred over the period 1963-1973. Ominously, one of the first
actions of European Governments when faced with the supply
crisis was to suspend the programme for reducing the lead content in petrol. American oil and car companies have been surprised that the programme for reducing lead and cleaning up car
exhausts has not suffered. Introduction of both these measures
would increase petrol consumption by between 15 and 20 per
cent. Large industries including oil refineries and electricity generation utilities have said that savings of 8 per cent of the fuel bills
could be made if regulations governing the emission of sulphur
from chimneys were relaxed. Similarly, planning authorities
throughout the western world are under pressure to give preferential treatment to developments involving alternative energy
sources or those assisting in the search for other sources of oil. In
Britain, the Government proposed to speed up the development
of North Sea oil by relaxation of some of the planning procedures
for essential on-shore projects. President Nixon promised that the
nuclear licensing programme in the United States would be
expedited. Conservationists were among the first to emphasise
that the world's energy and mineral resources were finite and
were being used in the most inefficient and wasteful fashion. It
would be unfortunate if their other warnings on the danger of

pollution were forgotten at a time when the validity of their arguments on the use of resources had gained wide-scale acceptance.

In the next five years fundamental changes in the total energy and transportation picture must emerge. It is of vital importance that the lessons of the supply crisis of 1973-1974 are learned. Failure to implement a planned development of all energy resources will expose the world to far greater consequences in the next decade.

Appendix One
Conversion Tables and Glossary

1 barrel	35 imperial gallons (approx)
	42 Us gallons
	159 litres (approx)
	0.159 cubic metres (approx)
1 barrel crude oil a day	50-55 metric tons per annum according to the specific gravity of the crude oil
1 metric ton	2204.6 lb
	1000 kg
	7.3 barrels (approx) of crude oil

1 million barrels oil per day (b/d)
equals 50 million metric tons oil per annum (approx)
   or 77 million metric tons coal equivalent per annum (approx)
   or 5000 million ft^3 natural gas per day (approx)
   or 50 milliard (1 mrd = 10^9) m^3 natural gas per
     annum (approx)

1 million metric tons oil per annum
equals 1.6 million metric tons coal equivalent per
     annum (approx)
   or 20 thousand barrels per day oil (approx)
   or 100 million ft^3 natural gas per day (approx)
   or 1 milliard m^3 natural gas per annum (approx)

1 million metric tons coal equivalent per annum equals 13 thousand barrels per day oil equivalent (approx)

Gross Tonnage: is the measure of the cubic capacity of a vessel's enclosed spaces both under and above deck including holds and deck houses.

Deadweight Tonnage: is a measure of the ship's total carrying capacity in tons weight avoirdupois including fuel, cargo, passengers and crew when fully loaded down to her permitted load line.

Worldscale: code name for the freight scale used in the world tanker market. It is designed to provide a yardstick which reflects accurately the relationship between one voyage and another on all voyages which tankers ply.

Average Freight Rate Assessment: a method of assessment for charging freight. Published on the first of every month, although the AFRA relates to vessels on charter and in service during the month terminating on the fifteenth day of the previous month.

Appendix Two
Bibliography

Steamships and Their Story, E. Keble Chatterton, 1910, Cassell & Co.

Ocean Transportation, Carl E. McDowell and Helen M. Gibbs, 1954, McGraw Hill Book Co. Inc.

Tanker Performance and Cost, Measurement, Analysis and Management, Ernest Garnett, 1969, Cornell Maritime Press Inc.

Tanker Shipping, J. Bes, 1963, Barker & Howard.

The World's Tankers, Laurence Dunn, 1956, Geo. Harrap & Co.

Tanker Handbook for Officers, Capt. C. Baptist, 1954, Brown, Son & Ferguson.

Oil Tanker Cargoes, John Lamb, 1954, Charles Griffin & Co.

Onassis, Willi Frischauer, 1968, The Bodley Head.

The Geography of Sea Transport, A. D. Couper, 1972, Hutchinson.

Oil: The Biggest Business, Christopher Tugendhat, Eyre & Spottiswoode.

The World Petroleum Market, M. A. Adelmann, John Hopkins University Press.

Oil: The Present Situation and Future Prospects, A Report by the OECD Oil Committee, (1973, OECD).

The Demand for Chemical Carriers, H. P. Drewry (Shipping Consultants) Ltd, Feb 1973.

World Trade in Liquefied Natural Gas, H. P. Drewry (Shipping Consultants) Ltd, July 1973.

Pantaraxia, Nubar Gulbenkian, Hutchinson.

History of the Standard Oil Corporation, Ida M. Tarbell, McClure Phillips & Co.

Middle East Oil, George W. Stocking, Allen Lane, The Penguin Press.